INTERNATIONAL HARVESTER
Photographic History

Lee Klancher

Motorbooks International
Publishers & Wholesalers ®

Dedication
For my late grandfather, Paul C. Klancher

First published in 1996 by Motorbooks International Publishers & Wholesalers, 729 Prospect Avenue, PO Box 1, Osceola, WI 54020-0001 USA

Motorbooks International books are also available at discounts in bulk quantity for industrial or sales-promotional use. For details write to Special Sales Manager at the Publisher's address

Library of Congress Cataloging-in-Publication Data Available

ISBN 0-7603-0130-1

On the front cover: The cover of a sales brochure advertising International tractors to be sold under the Deering brand name in Holland. International used a variety of different names on their tractors for promotional purposes, and export models were typically badged as either International or Deering models. Domestically, International tractors were known as Internationals, McCormick-Deerings, and Farmalls. Early IH tractors were badged as Titans, Moguls, Reliances, and a few others. *McCormick-International Harvester Company Collection*

On the back cover: Top: The T-20 TracTracTor, one of the first International Harvester crawlers. *McCormick-International Harvester Company Collection, State Historical Society of Wisconsin*. Bottom: The Cub brought the farm tractor to thousands of farms and homesteads too small to efficiently use the larger Letter Series machine. *McCormick-International Harvester Company Collection, State Historical Society of Wisconsin*

Unless otherwise credited, all photographs and illustrations are part of the McCormick-International Harvester Collection, property of The State Historical Society of Wisconsin, and are reproduced with their permission.

Printed in the United States of America

Contents

	Acknowledgments	4
	Introduction	5
Prologue	From the Reaper to the Merger	7
One	The First International Gas Tractors	15
Two	Early Standard Tread Tractors	41
Three	The Birth of the Farmall	75
Four	Unstyled TracTracTors	95
Five	The F Series	105
Six	Farmall Model A, B, and C	131
Seven	Farmall Model H and M	149
Eight	Styled Standard Tread Tractors	163
Nine	Styled TracTracTors	175
Ten	Cub and Cub Cadet	183
Eleven	Hundred Series	197
Twelve	The 1960s and Beyond	209
	Appendix	222
	Recommended Sources	
	Clubs and Magazines	
	Tractors on the Internet	
	Index	223

Acknowledgments

Thanks to all the folks at the International-McCormick Archives at the University of Wisconsin in Madison, Wisconsin. First and foremost, Cindy Knight, a rare gem of an archivist who is doing a wonderful job of turning a pile of boxes into an accessible treasure-trove of historical nuggets; Nicollette Bromberg, for making this project possible; Harry Miller and rest of the staff at the archive desk, for dragging box after box of documents, photographs, and company literature out for me; Andy Kraushaar, who lent some valuable tips on photography.

Thanks to Guy Fay, who was more than generous with his expertise and knowledge of the archives and International tractors. Serious International enthusiasts should remember his name, for he and Cindy Knight are turning the archives upside-down for new tractor information, and have found some incredible data. Some of Guy's finds made their way into this book, but he is reserving a marvelous chunk for his upcoming book on International experimental tractors.

Thanks to Jim Becker, whose input and information on the Cub and Model A were invaluable; Scott Satterlund of Binder Books, who kept sending package after package of International literature (if you need to find some original literature for your International, give Binder Books a call); Steve Offiler, who provided a lot of valuable copy editing and style input, and prompted me to rewrite several sections; and Matt Laubach, who put in a lot of time and effort and convinced me to include more information on modern tractors. Also, thanks to Daryl Miller of *Red Power* magazine for his review and insight; LeRoy A. Baumgardner, Jr. for a thorough review and crucial input on the Titans and Moguls (LeRoy also loaned the incredible photographs of the IH 8-16); and to Mike Androvich for his review and great information on the W-tractors. The book would be much less than it is without these people, and I wouldn't have found any of them if Spencer Yost didn't maintain the Antique Tractor Mailing List on the Internet. If you are a tractor enthusiast, this discussion list is reason enough to get on the Internet. It is one of the few discussion lists with both great information from some of the more knowledgeable folks in the hobby and a friendly, helpful discussion with more signal than noise. (More information on the AT List can be found in the appendices.)

The engineers who took the time to share their knowledge about the tractors they built also offered great input: Harold Schram, Robert Oliver, and Gordon Hershman.

A special thanks to the people at Motorbooks International who helped put this book together; editor Zack Miller, who got me into the book business; editor Michael Dapper, the man brave enough to contract me for the book and unlucky enough to end up freelance editing the book after running off to a juicy job in the industry; editor Anne McKenna, who endured the duress of an endless stream of additions and changes, and anal retentiveness from the author; publishing director Jack Savage, who was brave enough to read through a very rough draft, gave me some valuable input, and saw the project through to the end; Katie Finney, the fastest designer in the world, and a good one to boot; Jana Solberg and Carol Weiss, who assembled the cover, (I owe them both a beer for scanning 300 photos); Jenny Branum, the Queen of All Knowledge; and to those in the company who are decent enough to let me do this.

Thanks to my friends and family who accepted the fact that I would be trapped at my computer for a long while, and kept me sane by pulling me away from the damn thing once and a while.

Last, but far from least, thanks to Renee Latterell, who has given so much for so long that there's a little of Renee in everything I do.

Introduction

When the International Harvester Company (IHC) formed in 1902, some of the best and brightest engineers of the time were brought together, eventually under one roof. That group quickly took a leadership role in the rapidly forming tractor industry, an IHC tradition that continued until International tractors were no more.

The early IHC tractors were remarkable in both their quality and sheer crudity of construction. Using total-loss lubrication and hit-and-miss ignitions, the early Titans and Moguls harnessed internal combustion in the form of a heavy, difficult-to-operate, and low-horsepower machine. The fact that they worked at all is just as amazing as the thought that farmers could actually get anything done with these crude pieces of equipment.

The first machine to showcase the talents of the IHC engineers was the International 8-16, a machine that was truly ahead of its time. It was the first mass-produced tractor to be equipped with a power take-off, and only supply and manufacture difficulties kept it from being a runaway success.

The next machines of note were the McCormick-Deerings, the 10-20 and 15-30: designed by committee, ruggedly constructed, well-built, and economical to produce in quantity. The quality of construction was such that they were leading sellers in their time, and carried the ball well against the Fordson until the revolutionary Farmall appeared a few years later.

The Farmall may be IHC's crown jewel. It changed the way farmers viewed the tractor, and became the standard tractor design for the following 30 years. The industry had known for some time that the tractor that replaced the horse and could do it all—turn a belt, pull a plow, and cultivate—would be a big winner. The Farmall was that and more. Its gangly looks and questionable pedigree made it a hard sell to management, but its performance won over farmers and—eventually—International executives.

The next great leap was the Letter Series tractors, which incorporated lots of small improvements that added up to a timelessly graceful and useful line of tractors. The ultimate compliment to these machines is the multitude of battered, mud- and manure-splattered Letter Series machines still working the farm today. Very few 50-year-old machines have worked as hard and long as Letter Series tractors.

After the Letter Series, the company continued its tradition of innovative products, although the great strokes had been painted. The tractor was thereafter refined rather than revolutionized, with advances like shifting on the fly, independent power take-off, more powerful and versatile hydraulic systems, more horsepower, and four-wheel-drive finding their way to the farm.

Flashes of brilliance kept coming, though. The Cub and Cub Cadet put IHC tractors onto the home and hobby farm. The Model 706 and 806 tractors of the 1960s were high-quality examples of how good a high-horsepower tractor could be, and the 2+2 four-wheel-drive tractors brought maneuverability and unified production to articulated machines.

Tragically, high technology wasn't enough to combat changing times. Tractors were so good that farmers didn't need to replace them every 2 or 5 or even 10 years. When hard times hit, the 10- or 20-year-old tractor was overhauled rather than replaced, and manufacturers were crushed by a sagging market.

The times forced every manufacturer but one into mergers. John Deere, not IHC, was the only company left standing when the smoke of the 1980s cleared. In October of 1984, the announcement was made that IHC's agricultural division was to be merged with the Case tractor division to form Case-IH. (The actual sale took place early in 1985).

However, the enthusiasm, tradition, and innovation of the International Harvester Company tractors live on, in the hearts and minds of thousands of former employees who made IHC their lives and in millions of farmers who benefited from the company ingenuity. And thanks to restorers and enthusiasts across the globe, today you can still see the tractors as they appeared in showrooms and fields 50 or more years ago.

MY CHILDREN, ON THIS GLOBE YOU SEE THE HARVEST FIELDS OF THE EARTH WHERE THE McCORMICK IS EVER KING!!

TEACHING OBJECT LESSON

From the Reaper to the Merger

"Power farming really began to appear in 1831 with the invention of the reaper. Its story is perhaps not yet finished, even with the twentieth century and the invention of the tractor."–Cyrus McCormick III, from *Century of the Reaper*

The story of the International Harvester Company most often begins with Cyrus McCormick I, the man who started the McCormick Reaping Company, and the man who is credited with inventing the reaper. While this hangs the story on a very capable pair of shoulders, it is a simplified version of the story. For one, it is unclear who actually invented the reaper. The closer one looks, the more blurry the lines become.

Despite Cyrus and his grandson, Cyrus McCormick III's best efforts to tell the world that Cyrus I invented the reaper, it may have been Obed Hussey who built the first workable reaper. Although Patrick Bell was said to have been using such a device in 1828 . . .

It will probably never be completely clear who invented the reaper. Too many people with vested interests loudly proclaimed that they were the genius behind the reaper. Even if one person did invent the reaper, that person was helped along by the efforts of previous attempts. Inventions are always collaborations of a sort, with the person who first puts the pieces together and becomes famous for it being tagged as a genius, while the other men and women who have

McCORMICK'S TRACTION OR SELF-PROPELLING FARM ENGINES. Pat. Feb. 13, 1875.

toiled, created, and dreamed are left to die in ignominy. The invention of the reaper is an especially tawdry tale, with several men loudly proclaiming in books, magazines, and on street corners that they invented the reaper and, by the way, have a model for sale.

The story begins with McCormick's father, Robert, who experimented with a grain harvester as early as 1816. Cyrus would have been 7 years old when his father field tested the machine. By age 21, young Cyrus had built and patented a self-sharpening plow. The story goes that young Cyrus took charge of the reaper's development in 1831 and made the machine workable. He was said to have demonstrated a working model of the reaper in the same year, 1831, but he did not file a patent at that time. Certainly, Cyrus was a bright young star with the smarts and determination to pull such a feat off.

McCormick continued to improve upon the machine until 1834, when McCormick found a photo of Hussey's reaper patent in *Mechanic's Machine* magazine. When he saw that there was competition in the field, McCormick immediately filed a patent on June 21, 1834.

Left

The International Harvester story cannot be told without touching upon Cyrus McCormick the first, the man who became known as the inventor of the reaper. The McCormick family played a huge role in the International Harvester Company (IHC), with the company's first president a McCormick, and the family held crucial positions in the company right until the end. Cyrus I was a fiery, driven man who forged through difficult times to build one of the most powerful industrial companies of the twentieth century.

Above

McCormick also sold steam engines (although they weren't manufactured by McCormick). This model is shown in a brochure from 1878. The brochure lists five different steam engines ranging from 8 to 16 horsepower. These early steam engines were favored for farm power at the time, although they were heavy (from 2 to 4 tons), clumsy to move, and required quite a large volume of fuel (wood, coal, etc.).

The famous scene above portrays the first public test of Cyrus McCormick's reaper, said to have taken place in July 1831. McCormick didn't actually market a reaper until after Obed Hussey found some success with his design in the 1840s, and the test at Steele's Tavern may or may not have truly taken place. Whether or not McCormick actually invented the reaper is debateable. What is known is that McCormick produced the first *successful* reaper and was able to continue doing profitable business throughout the mid- and late-1800s.

McCormick would show that he was not one to back out of a challenge, a characteristic that would endure in the family and become a defining part of the International Harvester culture. McCormick wrote a letter to *Mechanic's Machine* challenging Hussey to a public competition between the two reapers. Hussey did not have a machine available, and the challenge went unanswered. In 1843, however, the two met on the field to settle the business, reaper-to-reaper. The McCormick machine was declared the better of the two because of its superior performance in wet grain. Thus, the Reaper Wars had begun.

Early on, the war was fought mainly in court. McCormick would sue anyone who produced a machine anything like his own. He didn't always win, but he did cause the buyer to consider the fact that if the offending manufacturer lost, the farmer's piece of equipment could be dispossessed by the court.

By the 1850s, reaper sales began to climb enough to attract more and more competitors, and McCormick took his battles back to the fields. These "competitions" truly characterized the savagery of the day, as competitors sabotaged each other's machines, cussed each other roundly on the fields, and occasionally dropped all pre-

The reaper was first experimented with by McCormick and Hussey in the 1830s, but it was not really widely used (and sold) until the 1850s. When use of and sales of the reaper took off by the mid-1850s, dozens of competitors joined in and the resultant competition was fierce. The unit in the picture is a later machine, a grain binder.

As the reaper business became more prosperous, the battle over who actually invented the device heated up, with an assortment of folks loudly proclaiming to have been the first to build a working reaper. The invention has been credited to Cyrus McCormick in most scholarly works, but Obed Hussey and Robert McCormick (Cyrus' father), also claimed to have invented the reaper. Robert went so far as to say that Cyrus stole the invention, and joined with Cyrus' brother Leander McCormick in a lawsuit filed against Cyrus. The court ruled in Cyrus' favor.

tense and broke into a good old-fashioned brawl. None of the machinery was especially reliable, so failures were common, leaving the fields covered with broken reapers and foul-tempered (and often bloodied) salesmen.

J. W. Wisehart worked as a salesman for Osborne, Deering, and others before joining the International Harvester sales staff in 1902. He recalled the field trials as all show, and no trial: "During the early years of my harvester experience, the field trial was an important part of the sales argument to the farmer. We never entered a trial unless we had it fixed and won beforehand. That was the idea of them all."

The farmers of the day apparently accepted this mayhem as standard business, and bought reapers like crazy. Of course, the farmers didn't pay cash. For the most part, they couldn't. Farmers of the day made their money when their crops came in, so machinery (and most everything else) was bought on credit. They relied on what was basically one paycheck a year. If the weather was bad (and any good farmer will tell you it's always bad), the paycheck was less than hoped. If the weather was truly awful, there was no paycheck. And if the farmer didn't get paid, the reaper salesman was left holding the bag.

Getting farmers to pay their notes on machinery was a big issue with the companies of the day. Selling machinery in a buyer's market was only half the battle; extracting the money from poor and famously independent farmers was just as important. One company representative recalled the difficulty of tracking down salesmen who didn't collect on their sales:

"One interesting phase of my work was the straightening out of accounts of general agents who were behind with their collections and lax in their business methods. . . . This work was difficult and at times dangerous because agents behind in their accounts were frequently hostile to my activities and many of them refused to cooperate at all. I remember on one occasion the agent happened to be a U.S. Marshal. I called at his office and told him that I wanted to check up his collection lists with him and take with me his cash received by him from the McCormick notes. When he refused to discuss the matter and indicated he was not prepared to make a settlement I told him that I had an officer downstairs ready to serve a warrant for his arrest if he tried to depart before reaching an understanding with me. However, he left the room anyway and waved aside the man who was supposed to stop him. The latter, one of his deputies, was afraid to serve the warrant. I followed the agent across the street and into a building. Finally he drew a gun, which he carried in his capacity as a Marshal, and stuck it against my ribs and I stepped aside and away he went. We finally located him in Canada."

Two of the companies that prospered in these hard times were the McCormick Harvesting Machinery Company and the Deering Harvester Company. Deering fared better at getting farmers to pay their notes, but both companies were highly successful and were fierce competitors.

The Deering company was managed by the Deering family, Charles, William, and James. They were fair and reasonable men who ran a tight ship. One of the driving

9

forces behind the Deering Company was John F. Steward, a controversial man who was something of a thorn in the McCormicks' side. Steward was heavily involved in the grain harvesting industry, and became the major detractor to the claim that Cyrus McCormick invented the reaper.

A Deering employee described Steward as follows: "In appearance and manner he was uncouth and very difficult to get along with. He seemed to make an enemy of almost everyone with whom he came in contact."

Rodney B. Swift, a long-time McCormick employee, vividly described the times: "In the period between 1879 and 1902, much rivalry existed between McCormick and other companies. Competition was particularly keen with the Deering Company. The latter vigorously pushed its machines into every place grain and grass was harvested and fought for sales, challenging the other makers to trials and took every opportunity to attack the McCormick machines in its catalogues, circulars, and other advertising matter. John F. Steward, who was a prolific inventor of trivial devices and who was head of the Patent and Experimental Division at the Deering Company, wrote and published numerous articles in the Deering Farm Paper and friendly trade

As more and more competition arose in the grain harvester business, head-to-head competitions became quite common. Those at the big expositions held periodically were especially critical, and winning awards at one was worth some sales back home.

papers. Steward had induced the Deerings to bring suit against the McCormick Company in the U.S. courts on some of his inventions and we defeated them. In his zeal to belittle McCormick, he gave the honor to Hussey, Bell, Ogle, and anyone else for whom he could put up a shadow of an argument."

The competition between Deering and McCormick was fierce at the turn of the century, but greater still was their shared fear of a changing market. The leaders of both companies recognized that they were at risk as independent entities, while as one dominant company they could survive and prosper. According to Cyrus McCormick, Jr., in *The Century of the Reaper*, the Deerings and the McCormicks met several times to discuss the possibility of merging, but could not come to terms.

From the glimpse at the nature of these men afforded by the dusty yellow paper trails they left, it is easy to see that the leaders of these companies were confident people accustomed to tremendous power and to having things go their way. Packing such colossal egos around one bargaining table must surely have made sparks fly, and one doubts the gentlemanly accounts of these early meetings found in Cyrus McCormick III's tainted but

Besides competitions held at huge expositions, the harvester manufacturers would hold field trials at a farmer's field, hoping to attract sales in the immediate area. According to J. W. Wisehart, a harvester salesman whose interview was recorded in company documents, the results were fixed. "We never entered a trial unless we had it fixed and won beforehand. That was the idea of them all," he said.

During the 1880s, local field trials became fairly common. This period became known as the Harvester Wars, and salesmen were urged to challenge their competitors to a field trial. Afterward, huge posters were printed and used as sales tools. One Champion poster showed a McCormick mower smashed and broken, and read, "The custom of the McCormick Company is to claim in print a victory when badly defeated in the field... Therefore, we hereby offer to donate to... any charity that the McCormick Company may designate, $1,000 if they can bring proof that the statements of the circular signed above are not true."

fascinating book, *The Century of the Reaper*. It is impossible to discern what kept these two powerful companies from completing the merger themselves, but it is easy to speculate that the meetings were wrestling matches between some of the most powerful, stubborn, and shrewd business leaders of the day.

Yet the prize of ruling the market—even if this power were shared with former competitors—was too great even for the proud, independent people that drove International Harvester to pass up. A combination of a slowing market and the allure of controlling the industry resulted in consummation of "the deal" and the creation of the International Harvester Company. The deal involved a dozen or more of several company's leaders, and would have put people like the previously mentioned J. F. Steward—who openly challenged most everything the McCormicks had to say—in business with several McCormicks and a pile of Deerings as well as miscellaneous executives from the Milwaukee, Champion, and Plano companies. Not to mention Nettie Fowler

McCormick, the formidable widow of Cyrus, Sr. Nettie took a very active role in company business, more so than was expected of a woman of her time; more, in fact, than most people even dreamed possible. Only the foolish or the ignorant made major company decisions without consulting—in some manner—with the Harvester matriarch.

The deal was made with sweat and sleepless nights. The McCormicks reportedly didn't sleep for a week straight. When all was said and done, the Harvester companies had forged a dynasty that would rule the agricultural industry for nearly half a century.

The Formation of a Giant

Imagine that Ford, General Motors (GM), and Chrysler combined to form one company called, say, the International Automobile Company (IAC). Imagine that on that very same day, Toyota, Honda, and Nissan were bought out by an anonymous company that turned out to be the newly formed IAC. Then imagine that immediately afterward, this monstrous company began buying

By the turn of the century, the farm was nearly saturated with harvesters. The tight competition and heavy demand force-fed grain harvesting machinery to the farmer. As sales began to drop, the grain harvesting companies realized that not all of them would survive into the twentieth century. In 1902, a group of companies that included McCormick, Deering, Plano, Milwaukee, and Champion banded together to form the International Harvester Company. Those five companies controlled 85 percent of the grain harvesting market.

Nettie Fowler McCormick was a very powerful woman, especially in the early days of the International Harvester Company. When her husband, Cyrus McCormick, became ill, Nettie oversaw the business matters. Cyrus died before the formation of the International Harvester Company, and Nettie was the principle shareholder of the McCormick Harvester Company when IHC formed in 1902.

up steel mills, carburetor manufacturers, battery companies, and tire manufacturers. Despite the fact that the IAC would still have some competition—Saab, Porsche, BMW, Yugo, and so on—such a merger would be considered a monopoly.

The formation of the International Harvester Company was just such a merger. Literally overnight, about 85 percent of the domestic harvesting machinery manufacturers joined forces under one roof. Some of the companies claimed to be unaware of who bought them, and those that knew kept the deal close to the vest. The prestigious law firm of J. P. Morgan swung the deal and walked off with an exorbitant sum of money—rumored to be as much as $5 million—for the firm's efforts.

The principle parties in the merger were McCormick, Deering, Champion, Milwaukee, and Plano. They, along with a few smaller companies, became the International Harvester Company (IHC). The company was valued at $120 million, and controlled the market overnight.

The Deering Company was McCormick's main competitor, and was actually starting to take a lead when the merger took place. But both companies knew that the market was changing and the only way to guarantee survival was to merge. Corn harvesting was one area that was not completely saturated, and corn pickers like this Deering model became popular just early in the 20th century.

The company did not initially become a single entity, nor could it have. As the upper echelons of power consolidated, the extremities—the dealerships—remained completely autonomous. In some towns, IHC owned as many as five separate dealerships. In most towns, there was both a McCormick and a Deering dealership. Whether the customer bought from McCormick, Deering, or a host of others, the money went into IHC coffers. This behavior got the company evicted from several states, but the money came pouring in nonetheless.

In 1912, the Sherman Anti-Trust Act was created, and IHC was at the top of the wrong list. A tremendous five-year court battle ensued, but the company managed to escape mostly intact. International had to sell off several smaller companies and consolidate dealer-ships, but the settlement could have been much worse for IHC. One of the key points in the defense of International was that the company wielded its tremendous power with a relatively gentle touch. Competitors were spared no quarter, but the farmer undoubtedly bene-fited from fair pricing and good products. Tremendous resources were devoted to research and development, making IHC one of the most innovative companies of the early part of this century. That tradition of innova-tion and commitment to quality allowed IHC to take control of the tractor market and hold it for nearly 50 years. Even in the waning days of the 1980s, IHC con-tinued to be a powerful, creative force in the industry. But the dark days of the mid-1980s are many pages away, and the beginning of a long, proud tradition begins with the first International tractor.

Chapter One

The First International Gas Tractors

"The beauty of the tractor business is that, once started,
it usually comes fast."
Early IHC tractor advertisement

The power on the farm at the turn of the century was the horse. The horse was versatile, economical, and performed a host of farm tasks. Working with a horse was often as back-breaking as doing it by hand, but it was the most efficient way to farm.

Mechanized power was relegated to a few specialized tasks. Lumbering steam tractors were useful for turning the belt on the threshing machine or perhaps pulling some otherwise immovable object, but not much more. Besides, they were expensive and blew up often enough to keep them out of the hands of the average farmer.

Gas-powered machines of the day were crude, foul-tempered machines, but they had their advantages over steam. To get steam up and running took from 40 minutes to an hour and a half, and required large quantities of combustibles. In the wooded north or areas near a adequate source of coal, this wasn't as much of a problem. The Great Plains were another matter, and powering threshing machines to harvest grain required hauling tons of wood or coal from far away, which made steam engines expensive to run in such regions.

So, while it might require a few minutes of fiddling to get a gas-powered machine up and running, such a machine was ready to go to work once it was started.

Fuel was often easier to transport, if not simpler to find, than bulkier combustibles, not to mention that the fuel—gasoline, kerosene, or distillate—was relatively cheap when compared to fueling a steamer all day.

The wise, the well-read, and the gambling business folk of the time recognized that gas-powered tractors were going to change the farm, and were doing what they could to capitalize on the trend. Most also realized that gas tractors were the future, and it didn't take a fortune teller to see that useful, powered farm machinery had almost unlimited potential. With IHC buying companies as frequently as traveling salesmen buy lunch, it was only natural that they would put a few dollars into a not-so-long-shot—tractors. The company's initial tractor efforts were created by going to an outside company for a chassis and fitting an IHC engine on board.

The company turned some of its best minds—which were some of the elite agricultural engineers of their time—loose on designing and building International Harvester tractors. But research and development takes time, and International needed to get its feet wet with some product.

The company already had a successful line of stationary gasoline engines. All they needed was a chassis to

Left

International Harvester's early tractors were state-of-the-art at the time, although they were extremely crude by today's standards. Such early machines were difficult to use and intimidating to farmers who had limited experience with internal combustion, but with machines like this Mogul 8-16, International began a tradition of quality that carried into the modern day.

Above

This Morton tractor was built by S. S. Morton of York, Pennsylvania, in 1899. He patented several features of the design in 1902 and again in 1903. In 1904, Morton consolidated with the Ohio Manufacturing Company. In 1905, Morton and the Ohio Manufacturing Company supplied the chassis design to IHC, and the first International gas tractor resulted.

The first Friction-Drive Tractor was constructed in 1905 by mating the Morton tractor chassis built by the Ohio Manufacturing Company to an IHC Famous stationary engine. The tractor used friction drive, which meant that the engine was mounted on rollers and was moved to engage the drive wheels. Between 14 and 25 of these tractors were built and sold during 1906. The date on the photo is incorrect, although this is one of the friction-drive machines. The earliest Friction-Drive Tractors had an exhaust pipe that ended below the canopy, unlike this later model.

This 1907 Friction-Drive Tractor on display allows a good look at the friction drive. Note the small pulley on the end of the crankshaft and the large, smooth drive pulley behind and below. Only about 1,000 Friction-Drive machines were produced. The engine ran at about 250 rpm, and top speed was about 2 miles per hour. Considering that a 20-horsepower tractor weighed more than 10,000 pounds, that's not too bad.

be in the tractor business. They found one, the Morton tractor, and began building tractors in 1906.

The company originally had its tractors built under contract, although IHC soon sold more than the Ohio Manufacturing Company's Morton plant could build, and began production in two IHC factories. Things moved rapidly from that point, with the original design—the Friction-Drive Tractor—refined and shaped into the Type A and B. The tractors were crude and difficult to use, but the experience convinced IHC that there was a future in tractors.

The ensuing few years saw a rush of development yet a low volume of sales. Sales of a few hundred units a year was considered successful, and selling less than a hundred units during a season was not uncommon.

The first decade of International Harvester tractor production was a confusing time, as development was continuous and chaotic. The company's factories were ill-equipped to build such machines, with space hard to find. In fact, some of the early 45-horsepower machines had to be built in crude shacks due to the lack of space!

A plethora of machines which appeared quite similar but used distinctly different designs were built. To further confuse things, separate departments were formed to build independent tractor lines. The original IH tractor line—the Friction-Drive Tractor, Type A, and Type B—were built in Ohio with engines from the Milwaukee, Wisconsin plant. The more popular Titan and Mogul lines were built in the Milwaukee and Chicago, Illinois plants.

The diversity of product lines and model names may have been a deliberate attempt to have separate machines for different dealerships. In *The Century of the Reaper*, C. H. McCormick states that the company intention was that the Mogul line would be sold in McCormick dealerships and the Titan line would appear in Deering dealerships. McCormick also wrote that the plan didn't work, insinuating that all lines were sold in either of the dealerships.

Perhaps more likely is that the people brought together by the merger and subsequent flurry of acquisitions were a large, diverse group of people, even if they were part of the same organization. These people didn't necessarily share the same ideas, and were often located many hundreds of miles apart. In some cases, they had been sworn enemies one day, and engineering department bedfellows the next. Perhaps it is surprising that so few lines developed, considering the company infrastructure.

Despite all of this, IHC found that it could produce reliable, well-made examples of the crude tractor of the 1910s and make a profit. As tractors rolled out, money rolled in, and the company saw fit to invest in into research and development. By 1910, with only five years of experience building tractors, IHC was doing what it would do throughout its history: building quality machines for sale and experimenting wildly behind the scenes.

Friction-Drive Tractor

Before the company could experiment, it needed to put a tractor on the market. It did so by making a deal with the Ohio Manufacturing Company, a company that owned the rights to the Morton tractor. So the first

This Type A or Type B tractor used the distinctive triangular cooling tower used on the Type A, B, C, and very early Type D tractors. The cooling system used a plunger circulating pump to move the water through the tower. As the hot water trickled down the tower, it evaporated and cooled. Early IHC advertising literature claimed the system would keep the engine "cool at all times and there is no bother in either winter or summer with a large cumbersome water tank." Winter starting was especially bothersome, requiring the water to be drained after use and replaced with hot water the next time the tractor was used.

This Type A or B Gear-Drive Tractor is shown in a German advertisement from about 1910. International tractors were first exported in 1908, when several tractors were shipped to France and Australia. In 1909, an early International took part in a plowing contest in Amiens, France, and won the company the Diploma of Honor and a price of 2,000 francs for plowing two days without stopping.

gas tractor to bear IHC markings, the Friction-Drive Tractor, was an International engine installed in a chassis produced by the Ohio Manufacturing Company.

The chassis was based on the Morton tractor, which was developed by S. S. Morton of York, Pennsylvania. Morton developed his tractor around the turn of the century, and patented several of its designs. Morton soon joined forces with the Ohio Manufacturing Company. In 1906, IHC contracted the Chio Manufacturing Company to combine IHC's Famous engines with the Morton tractor frame. The first Friction-Drive Tractors were produced in 1906 in very limited numbers (14 or 25, depending on whom you believe).

The first IHC tractor was a friction-drive machine powered by a one-cylinder engine. The crankcase was not sealed, and used total-loss oiling. "Total-loss" is a bit deceptive. Grease or oil cups steadily released lubricant on the bearing surfaces, keeping them more or less lubricated. Once the cups warmed, they emptied quickly. If it was really cold outside, they wouldn't empty at all, with predictable results.

The engine was engaged by moving it back and forth on rollers. By moving the engine, a 12-inch pulley mounted on the end of the crankshaft was brought into contact with a 50-inch wheel. When the larger wheel turned, it drove the rear wheels through bull gears and pinions.

Keep in mind that the 20-horsepower Friction-Drive Tractor weighed in at about 10,500 pounds. Friction-drive is questionably effective on lawn mowers (some cheap ones use such a system); one can only imagine the problems of trying to move more than five tons of tractor through adverse conditions with friction-drive.

The Famous engine was from International's stationary engine line. Several ignition systems were avail-

Early International tractors ran at about 240 rpm, which allowed them to move forward at about 2 miles per hour. The belt pulley ran at about the same speed, 240 rpm. Collector LeRoy Baumgardner has several of these early Internationals, and says that driving the tractors is a two-person job, as visibility is negligible from the driver's platform.

A fascinating shot of a 15-horsepower Type A tractor operating an asphalt mixer in Grant Park in Chicago, Ilinois. This photograph appeared in a 1914 International Harvester catalog. Early IH tractors were especially useful on the belt, where their lack of maneuverability wasn't a hindrance.

able on early IHC engines, all of which were a bit cantankerous unless properly maintained. Early ignitions were problematic, at best, and needed to be kept in tip-top condition to actually work. For the few who took the time to master the new technology, the tractors could work. For those baffled or uninterested in learning to use the machines, the tractors became a liability.

Spray or open tank cooling kept the engine cool but used a lot of water due to evaporation. Spray tank cooling uses a pipe with holes, a screened tank, and a catch basin at the bottom of the tank. Water is pumped through the engine's jacket and up into the pipe and out the holes,

This is a 20-horsepower Type B two-speed tractor pulling double disk harrows and a three-section peg tooth harrow. The tractor is equipped with the optional front and rear wheel extension rims. Farmers of the day had to be impressed; a team of horses could only manage to pull a single disk. Note the text on the rear of the canopy, which reads, "Mfd for International Harvester Company of America;" early IHC tractors were built at plants in Ohio.

where it runs down the screen and cools. Most of it is captured and flows back into the engine, where it is pumped through the water jacket and back up the pipe. As you can imagine, water loss due to evaporation was a problem, and cold-weather operation a pain, because the water had to be drained out every night. In the morning, you had to fill the cooling system with hot water. The hot water helped warm the engine, but starting was still quite difficult.

The Morton frame was constructed of heavy channel iron, with several main beams connected by cross-members. This frame style was known as a channel frame, and was the most popular type of frame used on early tractors. A few used an integral frame, which meant that the engine, transmission, and/or final drive housing were stressed members of the frame. The channel frame was relatively simple to construct, but twisted under load. The low horsepower and loose tolerances of early tractors kept a bit of chassis twisting from being much of a problem, but later machines would struggle with channel frames.

The first few Friction-Drive Tractors to roll off the line had tops made of slats with painted canvas and exhaust pipes that ended short of the top. R. W. Henderson, manager of the road engineers with the company, reported that these early machines blew so much exhaust gas, sand, and grit about that they were nearly impossible to operate. The roofs were quickly changed to corrugated tin, with elongated exhaust pipes that extended beyond the roof, which improved operation of the tractor.

Type A

The next International tractor was still a collaborative effort, with the Ohio Manufacturing Company designing a gear drive to replace the friction-drive on the original chassis. The design was an exercise in manufacturing techniques, as the specifications from Ohio had such loose tolerances that the gears simply would not mesh. IHC engineers adapted the design and constructed the Type A gear-drive machine. The tractor used a gear-driven forward and gear-driven reverse. Note that a 12-horsepower Type A was built with a two-speed transmission and a gear-drive forward and friction-drive reverse. The 15- and 20-horsepower machines used gear forward and gear reverse drives.

The Type A design arrived from the Ohio Manufacturing Company in crude form, probably as a hand-built sample. C. N. Hostetter, the Superintendent of the Experimental Department, recalls that the sample did not come with drawings or specifications, and that the gears did not use a standard pitch. The first try to duplicate the gear-drive design resulted in a machine with gears that either could not be driven into place or simply did not touch at all. According to Hostetter, the IHC engineers conferred and decided to make an appropriate engineering drawing and simply discard the samples. Despite the fact that IHC bought the Type A design, enough of the engineering was performed in-house for the Type A to earn the IHC name!

With the friction-drive replaced, a new system had to be used to engage the engine. The Type A used two friction clutches, one for forward and another for reverse. The larger one moved the tractor forward, while a smaller one engaged an intermediate gear that put the tractor in reverse.

In 1909, the 12-horsepower, two-speed Type A was introduced. The tractor featured a gear-driven two-speed forward drive and friction-drive reverse, a Famous engine, and stub (independent) rear axles. The friction-drive reverse was an interesting choice. International said it reduced the possibility of stripping the gears by putting it in reverse while still moving forward. Whether this was actually a problem or the friction-drive reverse was cheaper and simpler to build is unknown, but many of the early tractors used a gear-drive forward and friction-drive reverse (see chart for specific models).

Two forward speeds had obvious advantages over one, and International describes the tractor as meeting the need for a "fast-moving tractor." Considering the early tractor engines ran at about 240 rpm and propelled the tractors forward at a couple of miles per hour, "fast-moving" was only relative.

Type B

The next new model was the Type B tractor, which was similar to the Type A. It used the gear reverse and forward, larger 64-inch rear drive wheels, and was available only with a 20-horsepower engine. Like the Type A, the Type B was built initially with a single-speed gear forward and reverse; a Type B Two-Speed model with a gear forward and gear-drive reverse was built later.

This Type C tractor uses the gear-drive forward and friction-drive reverse. Note the bull gears on the rear drive wheel and the intermediate pulley. The initial gear-drive tractors built at Ohio used a gear-drive forward and reverse, but later versions switched to friction reverse and gear forward drive. The Titan and Reliance tractors, in comparison, used gear forward and gear reverse drive throughout their production.

This unlabeled gem shows a early International Type C tractor with an early IHC car, most likely an Auto Wagon. These vehicles were the forerunners of International's successful line of trucks. Tractor designer extraordinaire E. A. Johnston played a key role in the development of the Auto Buggy and Auto Wagon before moving to the tractor division. International trucks are still being produced, more or less. The International truck division became known as Navistar when Tenneco absorbed the International tractor division in 1984.

This photo captured a Type D Titan tractor at work near Manhattan, Kansas. The Titan was in its 11th year of service when this and the following photos were taken. The most easily identifiable indicator of the Type D is the square cooling tower. The Type D used a gear-drive forward and gear-drive reverse, like the Type C. Note that the Type C and Type D tractors were built at similar time periods by different groups of engineers. The Type D was a much heavier, more ruggedly built machine.

Both versions of the Type B were produced in low quantities, and only a few are known to exist (five as of May 1996). According to LeRoy Baumgardner, one of the few collectors who actually own such early Internationals, the Friction-Drive, Type A, and Type B tractors use a different part numbering system than other International tractors. Also, the IHC trademark is not to be found on any of the castings used to construct the Friction-Drive, Type A, and Type B tractors that are still known to exist, with the exception of engine castings and replacement parts. The engines were the same as those used in the Type C and Type D tractors.

Type C

The next new model for International was the Type C. The Type C debuted with the friction-drive reverse and gear-drive forward different from the friction-clutch system found on the Type B tractors. The Type C used a single-cylinder engine and a spring-loaded clutch; earlier models used only a spring-loaded drawbar to ease the shock of engine engagement. The Type C also had the spring-loaded drawbar.

The Type C was the first early International tractor to sell more than 1,000 units in a year, selling 1,787 in

Despite the snappy dress of the operator of the Type C, working with these beasts was a dirty, difficult affair. An employee who test drove the early Friction-Drive Tractors at the IHC factory described them as follows: "The gas coming from the crankcase together with the sand and grit rising from the ground made it practically impossible for a person to work."

1910. This tractor was one of the first to be designed by the International team of engineers, and was quite different from the Type A and B (although the appearances are similar). The tractor was developed in the fall of 1909, and was built at Akron Works for a short time, with production transferred to Milwaukee Works in 1910. About the same time, the name became the Mogul Type C, making it one of the few early tractors built at Milwaukee Works to bear the Mogul name. These tractors were available in 20- or 25-horsepower versions.

Type D Titans (Reliance)

The Type D Titans began life as the Type D Reliance line. Experiments began on the big 45-horsepower machine in 1908 and on the smaller 20- and 25-horsepower models in 1909.

The 45-horsepower model was the first International tractors to use an engine designed specifically for a tractor. The engine used replaceable cylinder sleeves and a throttling governor. The governor was replaced with a hit-and-miss unit before production began, as management felt the throttling governor was too complex for the average farmer.

The smaller Type Ds were heavy-duty units, despite their low horsepower ratings. They weighed in at about

This Titan Type D Road Roller is one of several variants that IHC built. This one is based on an early Titan chassis with the square cooling tower, and the roller front end bolted onto the stock chassis. The tractors were convertible, and a regular tractor front end could be bolted on for field work. According to C. H. Wendel, fewer than 100 of these machines were built from 1912 to 1914.

The first production 45-horsepower Titan (or Reliance) tractors appeared in 1910, powered by a twin-cylinder tank-cooled engine that was hit-and-miss governed and equipped to run only on gasoline. These early models were known as Type D Reliances; the name was changed to Type D Titans in 1911. The tractor shown above is blowing silage into the silo and was built between 1911 and 1912. The giveaway to the tractor's vintage is the preheater pipe running from the top of the carburetor over to the exhaust pipe, which indicates this model is equipped with hit-and-miss governing and is outfitted to burn kerosene.

14,000 pounds, and differed from the Type Cs in their use of a live axle and larger 70-inch rear drive wheels. The tractors were sold as "Reliance" tractors for a time, and became known as Titans in 1911.

Official production for the new 45 was authorized in May 1910, and the tractor was to be built as the 45-horsepower Reliance. It used a heavy channel frame with the new two-cylinder engine. The tractor was to be manufactured at Milwaukee Works in Milwaukee, Wisconsin.

The Type D 45-horsepower was significantly larger than previous Internationals, weighing in at 20,600 pounds and standing about 16 feet long and 9 feet wide. The tractor

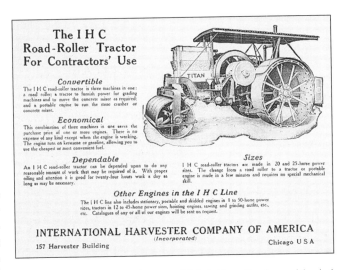

The Road Rollers were targeted at contractors of all kinds. The steel bands around the wheel lugs and the roller front end could be removed, and the tractor could function normally.

was a radical design for its time. It used removable cylinder sleeves, crankcase compression, automobile steering, and a rear differential. The rear wheels had flat spokes and were riveted together as a solid assembly.

The tractor's biggest problem was reportedly hard starting. The big twins had a 9x14-inch bore and stroke, and ran at 335 rpm. To get the charge fired in the huge combustion chambers, the engine needed a strong spark. Early engines used dry-cell batteries and low-tension coils, which didn't provide much of a spark when working perfectly. Early tractors were typically stored outside and maintained poorly, making starting a chore. The Titan 10-20 partially solved this problem with a high-tension mag-

This Titan 30-60 and Sanders plow are shown plowing heavy growth that had been left unplowed for 50 years. Note the exposed valve train inside the cab. The Titan 30-60 was the next generation of the Titan 45. It featured a larger bore that brought displacement and horsepower up.

In 1915, the cooling tower on the 30-60 was abandoned for a more efficient sealed radiator cooling system. Note the exposed starting motor just in front of the flywheel. Less than 200 of the Titan 30-60s were built from 1915 to 1917.

neto and an impulse couplings, but the Titans were stuck being hard to start.

In 1911 and 1912, IHC conducted experiments in an effort to get the 45 to run on kerosene. One attempt involved installing a throttle plate into a hit-and-miss carburetor and removing the pushrod lockout mechanism from the governor. The change made higher operating temperatures possible. At least two tractors equipped with this setup exist today.

International provided a solution to the starting problem in 1912 by inroducing a throttle-governed engine for the Titan 45 equipped with an air starter. The air starter was an opposed twin in which one cylinder was an engine and the other was a compressor. Air was pumped into a tank until the pressure reached 200 psi. The air was released into the right-hand cylinder head, firing the left-hand cylinder. Along with the engine changes to the Titan 45, a locomotive-style cab replaced the canopy.

Late in 1914, the Titan 45 was redesigned. The engine was designed with mechanically operated intake and exhaust valves. A fan and radiator cooling system replaced the tank cooling, and a starting engine from the Mogul replaced the compressed-air starting system. The

frame was strengthened with truss rods. The tractor was released for production early in 1915. Several of these models still exist in Montana.

Mogul 45

Experiments on the tractor that would become the Mogul 45 began in 1908. In 1910, the company authorized construction of 25 Mogul 45s. Regular production began in 1911. The Mogul and Titan line began life at nearly the same time and the Mogul's specifications—horsepower, size, and weight—were nearly identical to the Titan 45s, yet the design was almost completely different. It is easy to see that the Titan 45 and Mogul 45 were built by two separate departments, with different ideas about what would work on a big tractor. Some advances crossed over, as the starting engine used on the Mogul was later used on the big Titan.

The Moguls used distinctly different designs than the Titan line. In fact, the Moguls were actually developed by a separate group of engineers, giving International two completely different lines. This is one of the smaller Moguls, the Mogul 15-30.

This Mogul Jr. was shown at the 1915 Paris Exposition. Note the distinctive cooling tower and exposed gear drive. The Exposition was an important place for farm equipment manufacturers to court international customers and, apparently, to garner press coverage. In 1900, Cyrus McCormick threw an absolute snit because a report on the 1900 Paris Exposition gave more space to Deering and the other manufacturers than to McCormick. Of course, the fact that McCormick only had 17 exhibits compared to hundreds by the other companies didn't slow Cyrus down a bit. An absolute gem of a letter from Chas. Richard Dodge, described his exasperation with the matter. "For heaven's sake, have these people gone daft? What in Hades name is the use of talking about such a claim six months after the close of the Paris Exposition and almost three after the report has been sent to the press!"

The Mogul 45s built in 1911 used an opposed-twin-cylinder motor with a bore that was slightly larger (9 1/2 inches) and a stroke that was slightly smaller (12 inches) than the Titan 45 engine; horsepower, however, was the same, at 45. The Mogul engine was hit-and-miss governed, like the Titan, and ran at 330 rpm. The early Mogul 45s also had a large belt-driven cooling fan on the cooling tower and were designed to burn gasoline only.

Sometime late in 1911, a major design change took place. The engine was switched to throttle governing, a new cooling tower replaced the belt-driven fan, and the carburetors were setup to burn kerosene. A throttle was also added, to vary the rpms from 330 to 370. A one-horsepower air-cooled starting engine was also added at this time.

Building the new engine caused all kinds of problems at the factory. The factory was set up to produce smaller parts associated with auto buggies and reapers, so the casting of larger items had to be contracted out. The wheels alone were so large and heavy that a shed had to be outfitted with a large roll, drill press, and a chain hoist. The roof of the shed had to be strengthened to handle the load of hoisting those massive wheels! The spokes and rivets were riveted by hand or with a pneumatic rivet hammer, a time-consuming method for even that early period. The first sheet metal tractor cab was also constructed in this shed.

In 1912, the Mogul 45's bore was increased to 10 inches and the rating was upped to 60 horsepower. The tractor was designated the Mogul 30-60, and was built until 1917.

The big 45s—the Mogul and the Titan—reflected the common belief of the time that tractors would be

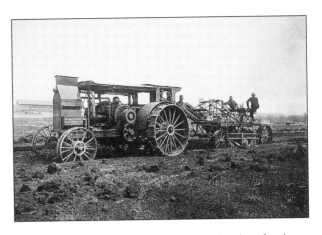

The Mogul 30-60 used an opposed twin-cylinder engine, quite a change from the parallel twin of the Titan 45. The Mogul 30-60 began life as the Mogul 45-horsepower, and evolved into the 30-60. An air-cooled starting engine was introduced on the Mogul 45, and carried over to the big Titans.

The Titan 18-35 was put into production in 1912. The engine was a twin-cylinder, cooled by a cooling tower with an air starting system. Less than 300 of these machines were built between 1912 and 1915, and only two are known to exist today.

The Titan 12-25 evolved into the Titan 15-30. According to IHC records, the Titan 15-30 was renamed the International 15-30 on Nov. 21, 1917. This change would have been made as a direct result from the anti-trust suit filed against IHC. The biggest change that came from the suit was that all IHC products had to be marketed under the name "International" rather than under different names in different dealerships. The International 15-30 was one of the first machines in which this change was recorded. Note the fan-cooled thermosyphon cooling system and fully enclosed drive to the rear wheels.

Early International Tractor Production

The production of the early International tractors can be quite confusing. This chart shows data for the earliest International tractors, none of which were produced in great quantities. Note that the drives gradually switched from gear forward and friction reverse to gear drive in both directions. Also note that the factory in which the tractor was built represents three separate design tracks. The earliest were built at the Ohio Manufacturing Plant in Upper Sandusky, Ohio. International soon shifted production to its own plant at Akron, Ohio. Then, two separate development teams designed tractors, one of which built tractors at the Milwaukee, Wisconsin plant, while another group's designs—mostly Moguls—were built at Tractor Works in Chicago, Illinois.

Model Name	Horsepower*	Drive**	Years	Factory***	Production
Friction-Drive Tractor	10, 12, 15, 20	F/F	1906–09	Upper Sandusky	376
Friction-Drive Tractor	12, 15, 20	F/F	1908–10	Akron	446
Friction-Drive Tractor	NA	F/F	1908–09	Milwaukee	236
Type A Gear-Drive	12, 15, 20	G/G	1907–11	Upper Sandusky	248
Type A Gear-Drive	15, 20	G/G	1909–11	Akron	359
Type A Two-Speed	12	G/F	1909–12	Upper Sandusky	65
Type A Two-Speed	12, 15	G/F	1910–17	Akron	203
Type B Gear-Drive	20	G/G	1908–12	Upper Sandusky	255
Type B Gear-Drive	20	G/G	1910	Akron	46
Type B Two-Speed Gear-Drive	20	G/G	1910–18	Upper Sandusky	383
Mogul Type C Gear-Drive	20	G/F	1909–14	Milwaukee	2,441
Mogul Type C 25-hp	25	G/F	1911–14	Milwaukee	862
Titan Type D 20-hp	20	G/G	1910–14	Milwaukee	274
Titan Type D 25-hp	25	G/G	1910–14	Milwaukee	1,757
Titan Type D 45-hp	45, 60	G/G	1910–15	Milwaukee	1,319
Titan 30-60	60	G/G	1914–17	Milwaukee	176
Mogul 45-hp	45	G/F	1911–17	Tractor	2,437
Mogul Junior 25-hp	25	G/F	1911–13	Tractor	812
Mogul 10-20	10	G/F	1912–13	Tractor	85
Titan Convertible Road Roller 20-hp	20	G/G	1912–14	Milwaukee	39
Titan Convertible Road Roller 25-hp	25	G/G	1912–14	Milwaukee	51
Type D 18-35	35	G/G	1912–15	Milwaukee	259
Mogul 15-30	30	G/F	1913–15	Tractor	527
Mogul 12-25	25	G/G	1913–18	Tractor	1,543

*Horsepower is rated by IHC; roughly equivalent to belt horsepower
**Drive refers to gear or friction-drive, with forward listed first and reverse listed second. "G/F" refers to gear forward, friction reverse.
***Note that separate factory production is noted as a separate listing.

Source: McCormick/IHC Archives, "Tractor Production Schedule"

The 15-30 was quite a useful tool compared to earlier tractors, but it was still quite crude. Fuel systems on early tractors were a bit cantankerous, but ignition systems were these early machines' Achilles heel. The 15-30 used magneto ignition and dual fuel mixers. The International 15-30 shown is at work in Lafayette, Indiana, in July 1921.

most useful for heavy plowing and other work requiring more muscle than a few horses. But big tractors were useful only to a limited fraction of farmers. The machines were expensive to own and operate and they were effective mainly for plowing large tracts of land and turning a belt all day long. Horses were still much more effective for most tasks, and the big machines were built and sold in very limited numbers. Although International was completely committed to building tractors by the mid-1910s, its doubtful the profits

Another 15-30, working hard on the belt. The fully enclosed rear drive chain was a needed innovation that was not used on later, more popular models like the Titan 10-20, perhaps due to cost. Fewer than 400 15-30s were sold in 1917, compared to over 900 Titan 10-20s.

The Anti-Trust Suit
International's Skeleton in the Closet

In August of 1902, several of the largest agricultural companies in the United States joined to become a powerful, unsettled giant capable of dominating the farm machinery marketplace. The biggest companies were McCormick Harvesting Company and the Deering Harvesting Company. Both were huge, essentially family run businesses, and the two were savage competitors in a tough, increasingly crowded market. The merger also swallowed up a number of lesser (but still large) harvesting companies, including the Plano Harvester Company, the Warder, Bushnell, & Glessner Company (who produced Champion harvesters), D. M. Osborne & Company, and the Milwaukee Harvester Company. Approximately 85 percent of the harvesting business instantly joined forces under one corporate roof. The end result was a monopoly.

The architect for the deal was the J. P. Morgan law firm. George W. Perkins would take the fall when the firm and IHC ended up in court over the matter, but one would suspect Morgan to have taken a more active role than reported considering the fact that the Morgan family came away from the deal with $20 million worth of IHC stock.

The deal was arranged so all of the companies sold out to one George W. Lane, who in turn sold them to the New Jersey-based International Harvester Company. Each participating company received stock in the new company, a $120 million company that would be controlled for 10 years by a voting trust made up of the top three shareholders: Cyrus H. McCormick, Charles Deering, and George W. Perkins.

The Morgan firm is credited with coming up with the name International Harvester Company, perhaps to create the illusion that the company was formed to dominate internationally rather than domestically. But domestic control was something in which IHC excelled, and the company swallowed dozens of competitors and suppliers over the next few years.

One of the issues to debate is whether the company *actually* formed at all. At least in the early days, an IHC logo was stamped next to each company's product logos and dealers remained independent. For 10 years, the "company" controlled several different product lines sold in different dealerships in towns across the country. In 1912, most of the lesser lines were dropped and McCormick and Deering were pretty much the only remaining dealerships. Still, there was a McCormick and a Deering dealership in almost every town, according to Cyrus McCormick, each with identical product lines but different marketing.

Several states, including Texas and Missouri, forbade IHC from doing business within state lines. The governments of these states felt that IHC was a trust, or monopoly, and competed unfairly. Why there was not more public outcry or legal action taken by the government is a mystery. IHC would later be accused of bribing legislators, dodging taxes, receiving kickbacks from steel manufacturers, and purchasing competitors solely for the purpose of dismantling them, but none of these charges surfaced until 1910, eight years after the company was formed. The reason for the eight-year reprieve is not totally clear, although newspaper accounts of the day (a dubious source, at best) say that President Roosevelt restrained the justice department from prosecuting due to threats from Morgan and the trust that they would fight Roosevelt and his policies. The fact that the press would even consider such an insinuation is indicative of IHC's power and standing.

When the International Harvester Company formed in 1902, it was the result of a giant merger that combined 85 percent of the harvester market. International Harvester neglected to consolidate dealerships, or even to add logos to dealerships until 1905 or later. Equipment was built as late as 1906 with no IHC logo. Such practices were questionably legal at that time, and would be illegal today. International Harvester's formation caused several state governments, including those of Texas and Missouri, to ban IHC from doing business and, in 1912, the federal government filed a lawsuit against IHC for violating the anti-trust act.

Whatever the reason, the Sherman Anti-Trust Act of 1912 incriminated Harvester, and a lawsuit was almost immediately filed. The result was a trial drawn out by IHC promises to correct its errors, and then by IHC proposals that were rejected time and again by government officials. A protracted, sordid lawsuit took place, amid which IHC fought bitterly to keep both McCormick and Deering under the same roof. The company prevailed, and the end result was that IHC had to sell off the Champion, Osborne, and Milwaukee lines and unify its product line. International was also forced to market all products under the name "International."

So, in 1917, the Titan 15-30 became the International 15-30, as did a handful of other IHC tractors. Renaming the tractors was not really the issue of importance, as all that was required was essentially a new set of decals. Besides, the International name didn't really stick, and the company continued to market its tractors under a variety of names—Titan, Mogul, McCormick-Deering, and Farmall.

The real issue that affected IHC was the requirement to consolidate its dealerships. As mentioned above, there were often several IHC dealerships operating in the same town under a different name; a McCormick and a Deering dealership, for example. In some cases, there were as many as five dealerships in a single town. As a result of the order, IHC had to close hundreds of dealerships and consolidate these into one per town. This didn't cost IHC quite half of its dealerships, but it was close. According to Cyrus McCormick in *The Century of the Reaper*, IHC had 21,800 dealers in 1917, and cut back to 13,860 by 1919.

While McCormick stated that the court's decree cost IHC some business volume, he pointed out there were advantages. The company combined the harvesters, creating the McCormick-Deering line. The new machines combined the best features of both lines. McCormick stated that salesmen were pleased to be selling a better product, that customer service improved, and that the resultant joint experimental department had increased resources and improved focus.

During the trial, IHC was able to flex enough might to cool President Taft's public declarations of war against the company and diffuse the anti-trust suit. The company called the result a "moral victory," because the government could not prove that IHC had abused its market dominance. The decision was more than that. While perhaps not a total victory, as the company was forced to sell several subsidiaries, IHC went on to control the tractor market for 40 years and become one of the dominant tractor manufacturers of the twentieth century.

Despite the lawsuit, Cyrus McCormick was optimistic when he spoke at the seventh annual Harvester Club Dinner in February of 1917. He said, "Whatever the decision, we know there is a large future ahead for this organization, because an organization like this cannot be turned aside from doing a great deal of good in the world."

The company survived the lawsuit, but there is really little question that the formation IHC created a monopoly. Most of the competition was absorbed, independent dealers competed for the customers' dollar under the umbrella of one organization, and the sales to Charles Lane and huge payment to the J. P. Morgan law firm was a convoluted (and mostly successful) attempt to dodge the law.

The supreme irony of the deal was that IHC didn't blatantly abuse the power it possessed. Certainly, money was made in great quantities and much of the market was swallowed up by the conglomerate, but the ultimate consumer, the farmer, did not suffer as a result. That was probably one of the most compelling reasons for the government to leave IHC nearly intact. The competition suffered, but the consumer did not. And by the time the trial was complete, competition was appearing.

As time went on, the company continued to prosper, but the shadow of the anti-trust suit lurked in the wings. A long-time IHC employee who was hired in the 1940s once remarked that the lawsuit was a topic that was simply not discussed, even through the 1960s and 1970s.

The fact that the formation of the company was illegal is supremely ironic, because throughout the 80-plus years of IHC, the company was one of the most innovative in the industry. Perhaps, just perhaps, some of that commitment to innovation and experimentation stemmed from a ghost of a feeling in the back of the collective corporate mind that IHC owed someone something.

The company repaid any real or imagined debt with a long history of advances that made the farmer's life easier and more efficient. Whatever the Harvester trust cost American business of the early 1900s, IHC repaid—plus interest and dividends—several times over in the ensuing eight decades.

The anti-trust lawsuit was a long and drawn-out affair, taking more than five years to be settled. The settlement required International to sell some subsidiaries, unify the product line, and combine dealerships. Although the effect on the company was substantial, the result was a victory in the sense that IHC emerged mainly intact. The anti-trust suit was considered a taboo subject in company corridors, even in modern times.

This Titan 12-25 was one of IHC's earliest small tractors. It was probably developed about 1914, and the engine that powered it was a four-cylinder unit. The tractor market's future was with small tractors, but the Titan 12-25 didn't give IHC many clues, with poor sales resulting in very limited production.

The 15-30's four-cylinder engine was somewhat of an innovation in the mid-1910s. Despite it being a multi-cylinder unit, it still ran at an amazingly low 575 rpm. Modern tractor engines are still relatively low-rpm engines, but peak power is developed in the 2,500 rpm range. Most passenger cars idle faster than a 15-30 at work!

from the sales of the 45s was significant enough to attract much attention in a $120 million company.

Moguls and More

There were a host of smaller models built during the early and mid-1910s, none of which enjoyed the success of later small International tractors. These included the smaller Moguls, as well as an assortment of Titans. These tractors were built in such limited production numbers that they could almost be considered experimentals. The experience gained in designing and building the machines was certainly more valuable than the revenue they generated.

The Mogul Junior 25-horsepower was a smaller Mogul. It used a single-cylinder engine that was basically one-half of a Mogul 45 engine. The Mogul Junior weighed 16,300 pounds.

The Mogul Junior 10-20 was also built at Tractor Works in Chicago. A total of 85 units were built in 1912 and 1913. It used a single-cylinder engine, and was the forerunner to the Mogul 15-30. Both of these models were reasonably successful. The 15-30 was discontinued in 1916, and 527 were built. The Mogul 12-25 was an opposed twin and was produced until 1918, with a total of 1,543 built.

The Titan 18-35 was a smaller twin-cylinder with two forward speeds and automobile-type steering. Less than 300 examples were built from 1912 to 1914.

The early small International tractors were extremely crude, heavy, and underpowered machines. On most of them, the cooling and oiling systems were completely exposed, as were most of the engine's moving parts, so the tractors were poorly suited for work in dust or dirt. The machines required constant maintenance and attention if used on a field or around the farm. Visionaries could see that the future of farming lay with powered equipment, but the average Joe undoubtedly had a chuckle or two at the expense of these unreliable, awkward machines as they sat wheezing, steaming, and smoking in the yard of some farmer rich or gullible enough to purchase the thing. The farm tractor's beginnings were not pretty.

The First Small Tractors

One of the trends that characterized the flurry of tractor development of the mid- to late-1910s was the attempt to build a successful small tractor. Dozens of tractor manufacturers sprang up overnight to attempt to satisfy this perceived need. And most of the agricultural world knew that the company that built a tractor small enough to be used for everyday tasks and powerful and reliable enough to perform them with ease would make a bundle. The only question was who and when (a simplistic answer to that being Henry Ford in 1917, but that story is reserved for a bit later).

Although International had produced several machines with less than 20 horsepower, all of the early

The Mogul 8-16 was the machine that convinced IHC of the viability of the small tractor. It sold briskly, quickly outpacing the larger machines that had received the lion's share of the company's efforts.

models had been nearly as large and heavy as the more powerful machines. Despite this, International had been plugging away at light tractors from day one, with strange little machines crabbing around the yard since as early as 1905.

With the Titan 15-30, the Mogul 8-16, and the Titan 10-20, International found success with smaller tractors. These machines were relatively light at less than five tons, and reasonably priced. The tractors were fairly reliable, and well-built by the standards of the day. They reflected the beginning of the tractor's transition from a heavy, limited accessory to a vital farm tool.

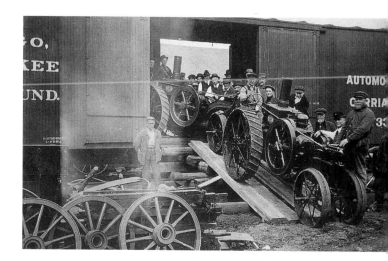

These Mogul 8-16s being unloaded from a rail car demonstrate the tight turning radius and narrow profile that made the tractors so popular. Only 56 inches wide and 5 feet high, the machines fit easily into a box car. Also, the 20-foot turning radius made it possible for them to make the sharp turn out of the rail car and onto the ramp.

This Mogul 8-16 is at work on the belt, where the little machines performed ably, producing 16 horsepower (hence the "8-16" moniker). The belt drive was activated by a friction drive activated by pushing in on the small wheel on the belt pulley, a mechanism that was used for many year on IHC tractors.

This photo of an Mogul 8-16 and plow was marked "do not use because of 3-bottom plow." Most likely, advertising types didn't want to insinuate that the Mogul would pull a three-bottom plow when the tractor didn't have the power and weight necessary to pull one. Perhaps this was part of the reason that the tractor was redesigned with greater cylinder bore and a two-speed transmission to become the Mogul 10-20.

Another 8-16 at work in the fields, picking corn. Note the worm and sector steering gear on top of the front wheel; this technology would continue to be used through the F-30, which received an enclosed worm and gear steering joint. This photo illustrates how tractors were used side-by-side with horses in the early days of tractor farming.

This Mogul 10-20 is serving as a snow plow. The early tractors heavy weight and slow-running engines may have actually worked fairly well in slippery conditions. Certainly the machines didn't put unmanageable power strokes to the ground that would cause wheel spin, and ground pressure would have been high. Steering might have been another matter, of course.

Titan 15-30

These tractors were known as "light tractors," evidence that IHC had begun to realize, or at least consider, the fact that the small tractor was the wave of the future. This tractor weighed a sprightly 9,300 pounds, giving it an unheard of power-to-weight ratio of 310 pounds per horsepower.

The tractor debuted as the Titan 12-25 late in 1914, sporting a four-cylinder engine. Shortly after the introduction, the rating was upped to 15-30. Consequently, the Titan 12-25 and 15-30 are one and the same. The 15-30 was plagued with name changes, as the Titan name was dropped in 1917 due to legal action, the result of an anti-trust suit filed against the company. In 1917, IHC was mandated to name all of its products "International." So, the Titan 15-30 became the International 15-30. Perhaps the company's distaste for the mandate is why IHC tractors continued to be marketed by a wide variety of names—Titan, Mogul, McCormick-Deering, Farmall—until the 1960s, when they became more widely known as simply "International" tractors. The Titan 15-30 remained in production until 1921, when it was displaced by the McCormick-Deering 15-30.

This Mogul 10-20 pulling wagons was probably shot this way deliberately to show off the machine's increased power, which came from a half-inch increase in bore. The new Mogul 10-20 featured a two-speed sliding gear transmission that was completely encased and bathed in oil.

This remote setup with a Mogul 10-20 tractor and Deering binders was one of IHC's early experiments. It looked rather Rube Goldberg-ish, and the fact that such a setup pretty much disappeared from production is sufficient evidence that it worked no better than it looked.

The Titan 10-20 was another step toward the general-purpose tractor. It was not smaller and lighter than most, but larger than the Mogul 10-20, which made it better suited for plowing. Less than 20 Titan 10-20s were constructed for field testing in 1915. That fall, a high-tension magneto was added and minor improvements were made to the transmission and cylinder design. The Titan 10-20 was released to the mass market in late February 1916. It was an instant success, selling over 2,000 that year.

The Titan 10-20 brought IHC's standard for success up anther notch, serving on farms for all kinds of tasks. It was the first IHC tractor of which more than 10,000 units were sold in a year (17,000-plus in 1918), and it carried the lineup until 1921, when the McCormick-Deering 15-30 was introduced. IHC produced just over 80,000 tractors from 1918–1920, and over 56,000—70 percent of IHC's total tractor production—were Titan 10-20s. It's interesting to note that the photo above was staged. Photo technology of the day would not freeze action; the fact that the saw blade and belt appear motionless indicates that they were stopped for the photo. Note other photos in this section in which you see the belt and pulleys blurred, and chaff in the air, indicating the photo was taken with action taking place.

Mogul 8-16

Introduced in 1914, the 8-16 was a single-cylinder-powered tractor with a distinctive curved frame that rose up over the front wheels, allowing a tight (for the time) 20-foot turning radius. The tractor was quite narrow at only 56 inches, and smaller than the typical Inter-

This early Titan 10-20 ad titled, "Look, Bill, what Dad bought for you!" characterizes the success of the Titan 10-20. Sales of the tractor exploded in 1918, when World War I ended. Although IHC's tractor sales nearly doubled after the war, they were being slaughtered in the marketplace by Henry Ford. About 133,000 tractors were built and sold in the United States in 1918, and IHC, the number two manufacturer, had less than a quarter of those sales.

Titan and International 12-25/ 15-30 Tractor Production	
Year	Production
1914	13
1915	196
1915	511
1916	60
1917	376*
1918	1,285
1919	1,652
1920	1,068
1921	821
Total Prod.	**5,982**

*Name changed from Titan 15-30 to International 15-30 in 1917.

national tractor of the time. The engine was a horizontal single-cylinder that was hopper-cooled and fired by an ignitor and low-tension magneto. A planetary gear transmission powered the rear wheels through a single left-side chain final drive. The tractor had one forward and one reverse gear.

This Titan 10-20 is pulling an early road grader, a reflection of IHC's desire to get into the construction market. Early Titan 10-20s used the smaller rear fenders shown above. According to C. H. Wendel, Titan 10-20s received larger fenders and a rear platform in 1919.

The 10-20 Titan's horizontal twin-cylinder engine ran on kerosene, which was the most cost-efficient fuel available at the time. Gasoline was more expensive, and was used to start the Titan. A small gas cup above the fuel mixer/carburetor was primed with a few ounces of gasoline. Once the tractor fired and warmed up for a few minutes, the engine was switched over to kerosene.

The 8-16 sold an unprecedented 5,111 machines in 1915, making up the bulk of IHC's tractor production that year. Sales numbers continued to be strong into 1916, with over 8,000 sold. In 1917, the tractor was updated with a larger cylinder bore and a two-speed sliding gear transmission and dubbed the Mogul 10-20. Sales continued to be strong that year, and the tractor was discontinued in 1919, probably due to the popularity of the Titan 10-20.

Mogul 8-16 and 10-20 Production

Mogul 8-16

Year	Production
1914	20
1915	5,111
1916	8,269
1917	665
Total Prod.	**14,065**

Mogul 10-20

1916	25
1917	5,338
1918	3,146
1919	476
Total Prod.	**8,985**

Source: McCormick/IHC Archives, "Tractor Production Schedule"

This shot of a Titan 10-20 powering a threshing machine gives a good look at the larger fenders on the later Titans and also illustrates how photographic technology of the day records action. Note the motion blur of the belt, pulley, chaff, grain, pitched bundle, and even the workers elbow.

Titan 10-20

The Titan 10-20 was the first great success of the IHC tractor line. The size was right, the timing was right, and—thanks to Henry Ford—the price became very attractive. This tractor was not especially innovative, with the standard channel frame, chain final drive, magneto ignition, and two-forward-speed gear-drive transmission. The equipment was hardly earth-shattering, but the package combined all the current technology in a simple, well-built, and relatively reliable package.

Development of the Titan 10-20 began in the Fall of 1914. By April 1915, the first prototype was plowing fields near Milwaukee, and soon after, two more prototypes were sent to Texas for testing. In the summer of 1915, seven more were built and sold. The first of these created a sensation when it successfully completed a 60-hour non-stop plowing demonstration at Carlinfield, Illinois. The Titan was authorized for regular production in 1916, and it was produced at Milwaukee Works.

The Titan 10-20 came complete with a manual that showed how to perform everything from routine maintenance to engine rebuilds. Here, we get a look at one of the Titan's sizable pistons and connecting rods. The engine had a 6 1/2x8-inch bore and stroke that turned at a lazy 500 rpm. Note the mammoth drive chain, which was complemented by an identical unit on the other drive wheel. Also note the adjustable drawbar, which could be moved vertically as well as horizontally.

35

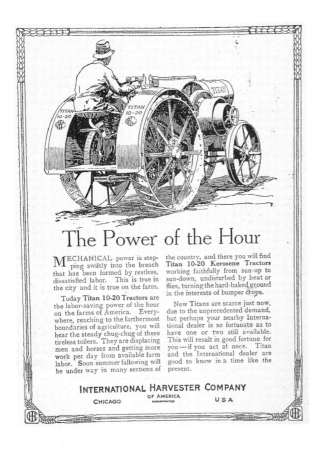

The Power of the Hour

MECHANICAL power is stepping swiftly into the breach that has been formed by restless, dissatisfied labor. This is true in the city and it is true on the farm.

Today Titan 10-20 Tractors are the labor-saving power of the hour on the farms of America. Everywhere, reaching to the farthermost boundaries of agriculture, you will hear the steady chug-chug of these tireless toilers. They are displacing men and horses and getting more work per day from available farm labor. Soon summer fallowing will be under way in many sections of

the country, and there you will find Titan 10-20 Kerosene Tractors working faithfully from sun-up to sun-down, undisturbed by heat or flies, turning the hard-baked ground in the interests of bumper crops.

New Titans are scarce just now, due to the unprecedented demand, but perhaps your nearby International dealer is so fortunate as to have one or two still available. This will result in good fortune for you — if you act at once. Titan and the International dealer are good to know in a time like the present.

INTERNATIONAL HARVESTER COMPANY
OF AMERICA
INCORPORATED
CHICAGO   USA

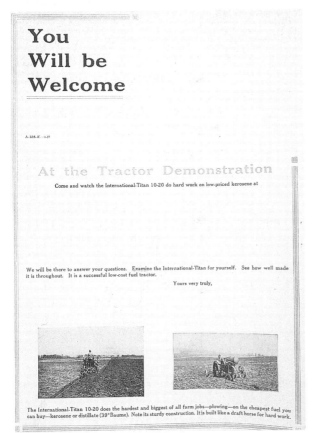

You Will be Welcome

A-335-X—1-77

At the Tractor Demonstration

Come and watch the International-Titan 10-20 do hard work on low-priced kerosene at

We will be there to answer your questions. Examine the International-Titan for yourself. See how well made it is throughout. It is a successful low-cost fuel tractor.

Yours very truly,

The International-Titan 10-20 does the hardest and biggest of all farm jobs—plowing—on the cheapest fuel you can buy—kerosene or distillate (39° Baume). Note its sturdy construction. It is built like a draft horse for hard work.

This 1920 Titan 10-20 advertisement discusses the limited availability of the model. Despite the fact that IHC was getting badly beaten by the Fordson on the sales front, IHC was selling all the tractors it could build. Mass production techniques were cutting-edge technology at the time, and the Fordson forced the industry to either adapt and find ways to mass produce quickly and efficiently or go out of business. According to an article in the September, 1919 issue of *Tractor Farming*, Titan 10-20s were coming out of the factory at the rate of one every five minutes.

The Titan 10-20 had a larger-displacement two-cylinder engine, a bit more weight, and more pulling power than the Mogul 8-16. The 10-20 was rated as a three-plow tractor, which was considered the ideal size. Farmers responded favorably to the tractor, and it sold well until 1922, the last year of production. It's fairly amazing that the tractor sold at all in 1922, as the McCormick-Deering 15-30, a tractor that was light years ahead of the Titan, was introduced in 1921.

The Titan 10-20's engine rested in the chassis horizontally, with the two cylinders parallel. The bearing surfaces were oiled by a Madison-Kipp adjustable oiler, which sent a steady drip of oil down feeder tubes. Carburetion was by a fuel mixer until 1921, when an Ensign JTW carburetor was used. The Titan was started on gasoline, and then switched over to kerosene, and IHC promoted kerosene as the fuel of choice for farming. An IHC advertisement of 1919 read, "Kerosene is the practical tractor fuel. Don't let yourself be led away from this fact. Gasoline is an unwarranted extravagance." At the time, gasoline was significantly more expensive than kerosene, a factor that for some users offset gasoline's superior performance.

The twin-cylinder engine was cooled by a thermosyphon system, which used the engine's heat to circulate coolant from the large water tank to the cylinder head jacket. The water tank system was not the most efficient, but was an improvement over the old hopper-cooled Titans. The engine and transmission were mounted on a steel frame. The tractor weighed in at about 6,500 pounds, which was reasonable at the time.

Power was transmitted to the rear wheels by dual roller chains. Two forward speeds were provided, as well as reverse. The tractors featured small, narrow rear wheel fenders until 1919, when larger full-coverage fenders and an operator's platform became standard.

World War I ended in 1918, but the Titan 10-20 truly went to battle in 1921 (see Tractor Wars sidebar). At that time the Fordson was dominating the tractor market, and IHC slashed prices on the Titan to try and compete with the

This advertisement was released for publication by IHC on May 9, 1921. The ad shows a Titan 10-20 being used in a tractor demonstration. This was another marketing strategy International used to combat the Fordson. The company believed that the Titan was a better machine in the field, and they used demonstrations to drive home the point. Although the Titan sold well enough, it was never able to gain ground on Fordson sales figures. By 1921, Titan sales were slowing and better machines were replacing it.

The Titan 10-20 was powered by a horizontal twin-cylinder engine. Cooling was by thermosyphon, meaning simply that the cylinder's water jacket was the low point in the coolant circuit. As the water in the jacket heated, it rose into the large cooling tank on the front of the tractor and cooler water was forced back into the cylinder jacket. This simple, but effective system required the coolant tank be at least half full to work properly. In this photograph, the mechanic is disconnecting the water return pipe.

This shot illustrates the simple techniques employed by the shade tree mechanics of the day. Farmers used what was available for tools. Here, a couple of timbers serve as a crude lift. Note the good view of the drive chain and sprockets.

cheap, technologically advanced Fordson. The price for the Titan 10-20 was cut from $1,250 to $1,000 in March of 1921. The price was cut to $900 in October of 1921, and slashed to $700 in February of 1922 when Henry Ford cut Fordson prices to $395, a price that he admitted was less than his cost.

The Titan 10-20 gave IHC inklings of the possibilities of the power farming market, and opened farmers' eyes to the idea that tractor farming could be efficient and economical even on smaller farms. It was introduced into an era that saw tractor sales growing in almost unbelievable bounds, rising from 21,000 tractors sold in 1915 to more than 200,000 in 1920.

In those fast times, the Titan 10-20 was a bit of a staid player, although it performed adequately for thousands of farmers. New technology was on the way, and the Titan would turn from state-of-the-art to obsolete in less than a decade.

Famous
Titan 10-20

At
Lowest
Price
Ever
Quoted

$900

ALL former price advances are wiped out by the big reductions made on this three-plow tractor. We believe this is the best buy on the tractor market, barring none.

This is the lowest price ever quoted on the Titan, considering equipment now included (formerly sold extra). March 1, 1921, the price was $1,200. Now it is $900. As this price disregards manufacturing costs, we do not know how long it will be maintained. International 8-16 and 15-30 tractors are also lower than ever before. The 8-16 now sells for $900 complete. The new low price on the 15-30 is $1,750.

All prices f. o. b. Chicago. We can arrange suitable terms. These prices certainly justify the immediate purchase of a tractor. Get yours in time for the horse-killing work of hot weather plowing and the fall and winter belt work.

(Dealer's Name and Address)

The Titan 10-20 served IHC well, and taught the company valuable lessons about mass production and the market potential for small tractors. Its simplicity and relative ease of use won it a favorable following, although the rapidly changing technology of the era made Titans out-of-date in a very short span. The International 8-16 was technologically superior, but was never built in sufficient quantity. The McCormick-Deering 15-30 would appear in 1921, only a few short years later, and was light years ahead of the Titan in technology and function.

Left

Another advertisement released by IHC in 1921, this one dated July 22. The Titan's price was cut to $900. Although IHC certainly cut prices to compete with Fordson, it was also looking to clear out inventory of the Titan 10-20 tractor. The McCormick-Deering 15-30 was released in 1921, and the McCormick-Deering 10-20 was on the way in a few years. Both of these machines were far superior to the Titan, and IHC needed to get rid of the Titans quickly and cheaply.

Titan 10-20 Production

Year	Production
1915	7
1916	2,246
1917	9,044
1918	17,675
1919	17,234
1920	21,503
1921	7,729
1922	2,925
Total Prod.	**78,363**

Source: McCormick/IHC Archives, "Tractor Production Schedule"

This close-up shows a two-piece spark plug. Like everything else on the early tractors, it is built on a massive scale. It also required constant maintenance, as the relatively weak ignition system needed all the help it could get to fire the engine.

Chapter Two

Early Standard Tread Tractors

■

"It is impossible to say whether the tractors we are selling today
will be out of date in four or six years, but it seems quite
probable that they will be."
–International Harvester Company, 1924

The late 1910s were a wild time for the tractor development and a challenging time for International. Technology was changing at an unprecedented speed, and new manufacturers were forming overnight. The feverish growth of the times was similar to the computer revolution of more recent years, with the tractor developing so rapidly that a model became obsolete in a couple of years. The surging technology transformed the tractor from a wheezing beast to an effective tool, and the sales numbers that everyone anticipated emerged. But the combination of the anti-trust suit settlement and the success of the Fordson made the late 1910s and early 1920s a critical, difficult time for International.

Beginning with the International 8-16, IHC's engineering and development work began to bring its tractors above the rest of the industry. More than a decade of experimentation bore fruit with new technologies and refined, effective machinery. The International 8-16 pioneered the power take-off, and was used as a test mule for most of the company's new ideas. The 8-16 also served as the development platform for the McCormick-Deering

15-30 and 10-20, which set new standards for durability and ease of service.

The International 8-16's reception was spoiled by the U.S. Government and Henry Ford. The first blow was from the government to International's dealership network. The anti-trust suit against the company was settled and the company was forced to consolidate dealerships (see Anti-Trust Suit sidebar in previous chapter). Where IHC might have had three or four locations in one town, the settlement required that the company close up all but one.

The government dealt a fearsome blow to International, but Henry Ford would offer an even more difficult challenge. His new tractor, the Fordson, appeared in 1917 and quickly devoured the market. It was light and cheap and backed by a man who was practically a national hero. Despite rising tractor sales, the International Harvester Company was in a life-and-death battle just to stay alive. The company's top weapon should have been the International 8-16, but production woes kept it from reaching the dealerships in sufficient quantities to meet demand. As a result, the Titan 10-20 was brought to the front line.

Left
Beginning in the mid-1910s, the farm tractor began to evolve very quickly. The total-loss oiling and chain final drive of the slow-revving giants were displaced by efficient little tractors with enclosed bearings, power take-offs, and smooth four-cylinder engines. The International 8-16 was the test bed for many of these concepts, and tractors like the McCormick-Deering industrial tractor in the photograph raised the farmer's expectations of what a farm tractor could be.

Above
The International 8-16 was a key player in IHC's struggle to compete with the Fordson, which became known as the Tractor Wars. One of the tactics employed by the company was to revive the practice of field trials and demonstrations begun by the harvester companies in the 1880s. The demonstrations lacked the blood and bile of harvester contests, but the net effect was exactly what IHC intended: to show the buyer that the IHC tractors were superior products. This illustration is the cover of a 1921 IHC field demonstration brochure designed to be handed out at dealerships.

The International 8-16 first appeared in 1916. It used several different engines before a satisfactory one was found. The tractor was not manufactured in volume until 1918, when over 3,000 units were built, and it never really reached its sales potential due to late engineering developments that in turn held up manufacturing. The war effort also slowed IHC's drive to increase production of the model, and it essentially died on the vine. Nonetheless, the model was a hot bed for testing, pioneering the power take-off and gear final drive. *Courtesy of LeRoy A. Baumgardner, Jr.*

International Harvester introduced two new models into that growing market, the McCormick-Deering 10-20 and 15-30. Both were designed to beat the Fordson at its own game, and the result was a couple of machines that were far superior to the Fordson. These tractors were designed with production-line manufacturing in mind, and used the latest technology—enclosed gear final drive, replaceable cylinder sleeves, radiator cooling, carburetors, and more. Although the Farmall is commonly credited as being the tractor that knocked the Fordson out of the domestic market late in the 1920s, the McCormick-Deerings put the Fordson on the ropes.

The McCormick-Deerings also pioneered IHC's first serious attempt to sell industrial tractors. The line would become very successful, as tractors were well-suited to performing all kinds of tasks in industry, and converting the tractors for such use was relatively simple and inexpensive.

The developmental platform for the McCormick-Deerings was the International 8-16, an innovative tractor that, like Rodney Dangerfield, never got much respect.

International 8-16

The International 8-16 was a radical departure for International, with a sleek, streamlined look, a vertical four-cylinder engine, and three forward speeds. It served as a developmental mule for everything from the power take-off to four-wheel-drive to experiments with rubber tires. The International 8-16 was also the first International to be built on a production line.

The channel-frame, chain-drive 8-16 was not the tractor Harvester hoped for, as production difficulties

The 8-16 had a channel frame and used roller-chain final drive linked to both rear wheels. The transmission had three forward speeds and one reverse. This one is shown with a PTO-driven thresher.

kept it from meeting early demand. Once the production line was in place and the 8-16 could be produced in quantity, the tractor's design was dated and the new McCormick-Deering models were being rolled out.

The 8-16 began life in 1914 and, after a couple years of testing, was put into production as the Mogul 8-16 four-cylinder in August 1916. The name was changed to the International 8-16 in 1917, probably as a result of the anti-trust suit settlement, which mandated that International unify its product line.

The 8-16 used several different engines during its production span, all of them being four-cylinder units that ran at about 1,000 rpm. The transmission was a three-speed unit, and final drive was by chain. A high-tension magneto supplied the spark, and a radiator and fan kept things cool, with coolant circulated by thermosyphon.

The International 8-16 had a three-forward- and one-reverse-speed transmission, and a vertical four-cylinder engine with removable cylinder sleeves. The tractor was plagued with engine problems, and three different powerplants were used in the model during its lifespan. The sliding-gear transmission had three forward speeds, a multiple-disc dry clutch, and thermosyphon cooling that used a radiator and fan rather than the simple cooling tank of the Titan 10-20.

The International 8-16 was the first International tractor to go on a moving belt production line. Earlier machines were built on carts which could be wheeled from station to station. The 8-16 was put on the line late in production, perhaps even used as a sort of test mule to sort out the process before the new McCormick-Deering models were produced on the line. *Courtesy of LeRoy A. Baumgardner, Jr.*

Engine Troubles

A variety of glitches kept it from being produced in quantity until 1918. One of the problems was the engine, or engines. Several different engines were used in production 8-16s, resulting in three different serial number series. The first engine had problems with insufficient lubrication. It was replaced, and a new set of serial numbers were assigned. The second engine was apparently under-powered, as it was replaced with a more powerful unit, and a third set of serial numbers were assigned.

It's ironic that the 8-16 was eventually produced on a production line, as difficulties with meeting demand kept sales volume low (although the 8-16 had it's share of engineering problems, as well). The production line, pioneered by Henry Ford with his automobiles, allowed rapid machine construction. For the tractor makers of the 1920s, it was key to meeting the growing demand for farm equipment. *Courtesy of LeRoy A. Baumgardner, Jr.*

One of the engines emerged from the factory with a transmission case that had the disturbing tendency of cracking. The cases used a tube that ran from the transmission to the rear drive chains, cleverly lubricating the chains. Not so cleverly, it introduced cold air into the hot oil of the transmission. If conditions were right, the transmission case could be cracked. A change order replaced the tube with a chain oiler, which was hurriedly retrofitted to the tractors in the field.

Changing engines during production was expensive and raised all kinds of havoc with company balance sheets. Some kind of exceptional force is required to make executives sign off on these kind of decisions, and Henry Ford was undoubtedly that force, since the International 8-16 could have been—and was probably intended to be—IHC's answer to the Fordson.

Competition

The 8-16 was small and light, like the Fordson, and was reasonably priced. The 8-16 weighed about 600 pounds more than the Fordson, and both used four-cylinder engines with a 4x5-inch bore and stroke that ran at 1,000 rpm. The Fordson was rated as a 10-20 and the International as an 8-16, but actual output and pulling power were comparable, according to tests performed by the Agricultural Engineering Department at Ohio State University. Features like removable cylinders, a multiple-disc dry clutch, and a sliding gear transmission made the International a better-built and longer-lived machine as well.

The most significant differences between the 8-16 and the Fordson were the retail price and the manufacturer's ability to produce enough machines to meet demand. From the farmer's perspective, the Ford was cheaper, rated for more horsepower, and available. Factor in the Henry Ford name, and it's evident why farmers were willing to ignore the Fordson's weaknesses and sign on the dotted line.

The Fordson had several shortcomings, but the biggest problem was deadly. The short wheelbase, light weight, and worm-gear final drive made the Fordson flip over backwards suddenly under heavy, sudden loads. Also, the worm-gear final drive heated up the operator's posterior something fierce, and the exhaust note assaulted the ears. Despite this, it was cheap and Ford was set up to build more than 100,000 a year.

Production Problems

The International 8-16's relatively weak sales were certainly linked to the engine difficulties as well as the manufacturing glitches, price restructuring, and engineering changes. All sorts of problems kept the 8-16 from reaching the sales floor in sufficient volume, and the delays led to in-house skirmishes between manufacturing, sales, and engineering. An IHC memo from executive Alexander Legge discusses the problems with open frustration:

"It is now three years since we commenced selling this machine [the International 8-16]. During the first year, I think the delays in progress might in the main be

This International 8-16 is cutting what appears to be alfalfa with a PTO-driven cutter. Although the 8-16 was a benchmark machine, improvements and increased production of the model were shelved in favor of developing an integral frame machine. For IHC, an integral frame was a sturdy, bath tub-like housing that contained the engine, transmission, and final drive. The first I-H machine to use this technology was the McCormick-Deering 15-30, which was soon followed by the McCormick-Deering 10-20. Integral frames would be used in the future, but the most revolutionary IHC tractor, the Farmall Regular, would use a channel frame.

charged to the engineering department, owing to changes in design. During the second year, we might make it fifty-fifty, or perhaps with justice charge a considerable portion of it to the abnormal war conditions,

The McCormick-Deering 15-30 first appeared in 1921, and was a new machine from the ground up. Designed to be built on a production line, it used an integral frame—meaning the engine, transmission, and rear differential housing were housed in a tub-shaped frame—which was stronger and more dust-resistant than previous channel frames. This McCormick-Deering 15-30 and power-driven harvester-thresher is being shown off at the Hinsdale farm, IHC's backdoor test site.

One of the most significant features on the new McCormick-Deerings was the gear final drive and the original names for the tractors reflected that. The first 15-30s were known as International 15-30 Gear Drive Tractors rather than McCormick-Deerings. The name was changed to McCormick-Deering 15-30 in August of 1922, but only for the Canadian and domestic markets. The tractors shipped overseas were supposed to retain the International name. Note that this photo is heavily retouched to read "McCormick-Deering" on the name plate, indicating that this tractor was probably either an early model or a machine intended for export.

Here's an example of IHC's mixing and matching of tractor badging. This 15-30 and Model 11 harvester-thresher bear McCormick badges; no Deering or International. The label on this photo identified the models and read, "Names changed for foreign use."

This McCormick-Deering 15-30 is pulling a competitor's field cultivator. The engine had a 4.5x6-inch bore and the crankshaft ran on ball bearings, an innovation that extended bearing life. The engine ran at 1,000 rpm, used splash and gear-pump lubrication, and was cooled by an enclosed system with a radiator.

as a year ago now we were arranging to devote a considerable portion of Tractor Works manufacturing capacity to government work, making it impossible to make progress on a regular line. However, it will soon be a year since the Armistice was signed, during which period there has been nothing to prevent our going forward with increased production and improved practice."

The memo continues, discussing converting the 8-16 from a chain final drive to a gear final drive. Company documentation shows that a gear-drive 8-16 was considered, but never built. Legge also wrote:

"The tractor may not be the ultimate limit of perfection that we hope to achieve in time, but it has gone through the year with surprisingly few complaints. Dealers who have been fortunate enough to secure a substantial number of them during this season make the statement that very little experting or service attention has been required. In any event, it is good enough so that I feel certain we could be selling a hundred a day if we were making them, yet our product is about one-fourth that number."

A follow-up memo came from company president Cyrus McCormick, who supported Legge's assertions that the onus was on manufacturing to produce more tractors. He balanced this view by questioning whether it was worth

sinking tremendous sums of money into revamping the International 8-16, when its longevity was in question due to a new design (presumably the McCormick-Deering 15-30 and 10-20) that was in the works.

"What will happen . . . cannot be foretold, as we have reached no conclusion as to whether we will continue to manufacture a frame-type tractor or go over to the unit-type. I would like nothing better than to undertake a tractor program of great volume. The present 8-16 is a wonderful tractor, but will it last long enough to equip, say, on a basis of five years of unchanged production?"

Mass Production of the 8-16

McCormick's uncertainty about the 8-16's future was reflected in company actions. International 8-16s were originally built on wheeled carts or other more primitive methods. Henry Ford showed the world how well a continuous, moving production line could work with the early Ford cars, and the rest of the industry scrambled to follow. While the advantages of increased capacity and decreased costs were obvious, the initial investment required to change over an entire line were prodigious.

Part of IHC's plan for the new McCormick-Deering tractors was to build them on a production line. Inter-

The 15-30 was a larger, more powerful tractor, intended for field and heavy belt work. Note the Deering cultivator, most likely a leftover from the pre-1917 days when IHC products were sold under several different brand names. This 15-30 was owned by LeRoy Smith of Kingsden, Kansas.

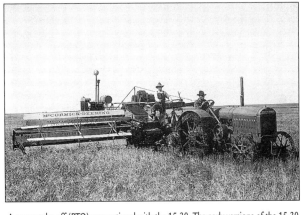

A power take-off (PTO) was optional with the 15-30. The early versions of the 15-30 were apparently geared a bit too high, as factory updates lowered the gearing and strengthened the transmission in 1926. This McCormick-Deering 15-30 and implement were at work near Ford, Kansas.

estingly, the International 8-16 was also built on a production line, at least for a short time. Photos from *Evolution of A Tractor*, published by Stemgas, clearly show 8-16 engines and chain-drive machines being assembled on a production line.

There are several reasons that the 8-16 was built on a production line. One is that the company decided to move forward with mass production despite the 8-16's somewhat dated design. With Ford breathing down the company's neck, International may have considered it of paramount importance to put something on the market in large volume. Considering the huge expenditure required to set up a production line and the relatively low volume of 8-16 sales, this would have been a losing prospect for Harvester.

Another, perhaps more plausible, answer is that the company temporarily built the International 8-16 on the new production line with the intention of converting the line to produce the new McCormick-Deering machines. In this way, the teething problems of running a production line—a totally new process at the time—could be ironed out before trying to get a brand new model out the door as well.

To add an interesting and perhaps confusing twist to the story, early versions of the McCormick-Deering 10-20 were known as the International 8-16 Gear Drive Tractor in company records.

Too Little, Too Late

When the 8-16 could have been selling exorbitantly, the production facilities

The McCormick-Deering 15-30 was offered with a complete line of attachments and options. Vineyard and orchard attachments were available as early as 1922, and rice field equipment was made available in 1923.

did not exist. By the time it was feasible to step up production, the International 8-16's time had passed, both from a market and a company standpoint, and the tractor was more or less abandoned.

Another aspect to the 8-16 was the development of the power take-off (see sidebar). Sold in conjunction with specially-designed implements, an 8-16 could increase efficiency in the fields in an unprecedented manner. It is believed to be the first American tractor sold with a practical rear power take-off.

Rubber Tires

A crude form of a rubber tire was also tested on the International 8-16. This was hardly the first use of rubber tires on a tractor, as the Rubber-Tired Steamer was built in 1871 with rubber-coated steel wheels. The 8-16 used a similar type of tire, as International engineer L. B. Sperry described it in *The Agricultural Tractor 1855–1950*:

"The front wheels were fitted with solid-section rubber tires; the rear wheels with solid-section blocks molded into metal detachable lugs and the blocks were made by the Firestone Tire & Rubber Company." The tires didn't work well on pavement, and the rubber peeled away from the steel lugs, so the idea never made it past the experimental stage.

The Tractor Wars

Like the Titan 10-20, the International 8-16 was used as an agent in the price war against Ford. Prices of the 8-16

This McCormick-Deering 15-30 is at work in Columbus, Ohio. The model was produced as an orchard model beginning in 1924. Standard equipment included a belt pulley, lugs, air cleaner, necessary tools, and front wheel skid rings.

were cut steadily in the early 1920s, from $1,000 in March 1921 to $670 in February 1922. The price cut to $670 has been made famous by Cyrus McCormick III's account of a phone call in which Alexander Legge was told that Henry Ford cut the price of the Fordson below cost. Legge supposedly issued a vehement response, stating that International would meet the price. International certainly needed to respond to Ford's challenge, but the $670 price on the 8-16 probably reflects the company's desire to clear out old inventory to make room for the new McCormick-Deerings as much as it did the desire to compete with Ford.

The International 8-16 was a hallmark vehicle in many ways. Its full-coverage body work, three-forward-speed transmission, and smooth-running four-cylinder engine were all signs of things to come.

The McCormick-Deering 15-30 received a larger bore in 1928, boosting rated horsepower to 22 at the drawbar and 36 at the belt. This 15-30 is at work in the fields of International's experimental farm in Hinsdale, Illinois.

Changing Times

The tractors of the 1910s and 1920s were changing as quickly as the personal computer of the 1980s and 1990s. Farmers were advised to expect to get five years out of their tractors before they were obsolete; in reality, it was often much less than that. Mind you, the five-year-old tractors still worked as well as when purchased; they simply were no longer efficient or compatible.

Even the overlap was remarkable. The McCormick-Deering 15-30 sat in the showroom alongside the International 15-30. The two were generations apart, with the International essentially a refinement of the original Titans and the McCormick-Deering a rough form of the modern tractor. The International still used total-loss oiling for most bearings, a fuel mixer rather than a carburetor, contracting-band clutch, and chain

49

The McCormick-Deering 10-20 was the second model of International's new integral frame machines. It appeared in 1923, and immediately outsold the larger 15-30. Like the 15-30, it used a four-cylinder engine and could be purchased with a power take-off.

final drive. The tractor was obscenely heavy, complex to operate, and nearly impossible to turn around.

The McCormick-Deering tractors were a departure for IHC, and were the tractors some felt would carry the company to the next level. Although the International 8-16 and Titan 10-20 fought the battle against the Fordson, the McCormick-Deerings were IHC's answer to the Fordson. International did not attempt to compete with the Fordson on price. Instead, the company built a machine that was vastly superior to the Fordson. The McCormick-Deerings were long-lived, with roller bearings and rugged construction. They could be serviced easily, due to unit construction that allowed components to be easily removed for repair or replacement. The engine used removable cylinder sleeves, which meant that it could be rebuilt simply, and the final gear drive lasted longer and worked better than the Fordson's worm gear drive. The end result was that the McCormick-Deerings took the advantages of the Fordson—the integral frame and line production—and assembled them with into a high-quality package that was reasonably priced and, with care, would outlive the farmer.

Development of the Power Take-Off

By the time the International 8-16 reached the market, the idea for using the tractor engine's power to operate implements had been around for some time. The first clearly recorded example was Aveling & Porter's steam reaper, which appeared in the December 19, 1885, issue of *Farm Implement News*. The reaper was pushed in front of the steam tractor, with a chain drive running from the steam engine's flywheel to the reaper. The machine was displayed at the Paris Exposition as early as 1878, so the idea was around for quite some time.

The next, and most direct, reference to a power take-off (PTO) appeared on a tractor built by Frenchman Albert Gougis. Made in 1905, this tractor was a home-built machine looking remarkably like a Farmall. Gougis ran a chain from the crankshaft of the engine to a shaft that connected to a McCormick binder. Several universal joints handled flex on the shaft, and the mechanism could be engaged separately from the clutch. In this way, the tractor pulled the binder and powered it. Gougis developed the binder to help farmers save downed grain, and it reportedly worked well for this purpose.

It has been speculated that the idea for the power take-off was sparked by Gougis' device, which was spotted during an International executive's trip to France. A photo in February 12, 1931, issue of *Farm Implement News* shows Gougis operating a McCormick binder with a home-built tractor and crude PTO. Ironically, the design of the home-built tractor bears a remarkable resemblance to the Farmall Regular. The photo was taken about 1906, and it can be speculated that International saw more possibilities in the ideas of Gougis than just a PTO.

Either way, engineer Bert R. Benjamin proposed developing PTO drives for the Titan 10-20 as early as 1917. He reported on a farmer using a combination of several International powered binders, a Titan 10-20, a team of horses, and a Happy Farmer tractor powered by an 8-horsepower Cushman engine. Benjamin pointed out that the farmer could afford to purchase several more Titan tractors if they were equipped with PTO, allowing the farmer to dispense with the expensive and often inefficient powered binders. Benjamin's proposal was received with favor, and a PTO was developed to power the cutter bar and sweep rake lift of the Motor Cultivator. (The Motor Cultivator, a specialized machine designed purely for cultivation, failed miserably, but the engineering work opened the door for the Farmall, a tractor capable of cultivation.)

McCormick-Deerings

The McCormick-Deerings were more than just high-quality machines for International. They represented the future of the company. Ford was hammering International on the sales front, and knocking prices down to bankruptcy-inducing levels. All around IHC, tractor manufacturers were going belly

This International 8-16 is using a PTO-driven corn binder. The idea for the PTO had been around for a long time, at least since the 1880s, but IHC engineer Bert R. Benjamin was the first to make it a commercial success. The PTO was tested on Titan 10-20s, and made available on the International 8-16. The industry quickly jumped on the bandwagon, and the PTO became a standard attachment for tractors and is a fundamental part of the farm tractor.

In 1919, IHC began experimenting with PTO-equipped International 8-16s, and in 1921, the PTO became available as special order equipment on the International 15-30. The new McCormick-Deering 10-20 and 15-30 also appeared in 1921, and the PTO was available on both machines. The Farmall used a PTO as early as 1922, and it became an integral part of the tractor's design.

Despite the fact that the PTO was available in the early 1920s, it wasn't until later in the decade that it was widely known. The rice crop of 1925, imperiled by a wet season in Arkansas, Louisiana, and Texas, was saved by PTO-driven implements and the agricultural world woke up to the fact that the PTO had arrived.

The next hurdle was standardization of PTO shaft rotation speeds, coupling size, and splining. Under the auspices of the American Society of Agricultural Engineering (ASAE), representatives from tractor manufacturing companies met to attempt to standardize the PTO coupling so that tractors and implements from different manufacturers would be interchangeable. It took about five years to become reality, but by 1931 ASAE had mediated a standard for the PTO and it was being applied to any imaginable implement. The PTO continued to develop with tractors, eventually shaking out 540 and 1,000 rpm, the two standard speeds. Later tractors had two PTO couplings, one for 540 rpm and the other for 1,000 rpm.

uptrying to compete with the Fordson. International could not hope to compete with the Titan 10-20 or the International 8-16. Both were decent machines, but the prices were cut to the point that profits were minimal, and neither machine was spectacular enough to draw attention away from the Fordson's attractive price.

IHC was desperately seeking the next great leap, which it needed to survive. The first thought was to convert the 8-16 to a gear-drive machine, but the twisting of the channel frame wouldn't allow the tight tolerances necessary for a gear final drive. In addition, the addition of gear drive still didn't bring the 8-16 up to the level that International management felt was necessary.

Like the McCormick-Deering 15-30, the 10-20's designation was changed early on. It was originally known as the International 10-20 Gear-Driven Tractor. The name was retained for early imports, but domestic models were renamed the McCormick-Deering 10-20.

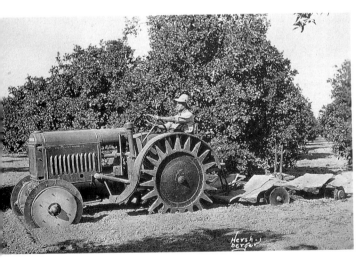

Orchard fenders were one of the earliest options to be added to the 10-20, with fenders and an assortment of lower parts available late in 1923. California orchard fenders that covered the entire upper half of the rear wheels (not shown) became available in 1924. This orchard model is wearing a very odd set of solid wheels and working an orchard near Los Angeles, California.

The 10-20 was initially built with a three-speed transmission; later versions used a four-speed. The 10-20 was built over quite a long production span, from 1923 to 1939. This 10-20's louvered engine covers are off while it is at work on a farm near Wheaton, Illinois.

What the company needed was a high-quality machine that could be built in quantity. A mass production line and a new type of frame were the answers. To do both required complete retooling and the construction of a production line. The investment required was great, but the cost of lagging behind was greater. The McCormick-Deerings were given top priority, and carried the hope for the company's future.

Cyrus McCormick III had this to say: "Two new improved models, the McCormick-Deering 10-20 and 15-

This obviously retouched photo is a shot of either of an early or an exported 10-20. It probably reads, "International" under the retouching, although it could read simply "McCormick" or "Deering." The retouching looks crude on the original photo, but would pass when reduced to a small size and run in a promotional brochure.

30, were introduced which summed up the entire story of Harvester's tractor experience. Millions of dollars were poured into the modern type of labor-saving manufacturing equipment. Production costs were slashed by the means of efficiency gained through elimination of wasted effort."

What McCormick was referring to was modular construction, which simply meant that component groups would be assembled individually. The entire tractor would be put together somewhere else, with each component group simply bolted on. Rather than installing the clutch bit by bit onto the engine, the clutch was assembled as a unit and then simply slid into place when the engine and transmission were mated. This speeded up assembly a bit and, more importantly for the customer, simplified maintenance. Time is money on the assembly floor, and the result was a lower cost to the farmer and higher profit margin for IHC, as well as the ability to meet high-volume demand.

The Integral Frame

The other key aspect of the McCormick-Deerings was the integral frame, which was stronger and better sealed from dirt than the old channel frames of previous models. Keep in mind that what International called an integral frame was not the same as another company's concept of it. The term integral frame can refer to a frame that uses the engine and transmission housing as a stressed member of the frame. The Farmall Letter Series tractors used that type of integral frame.

The integral frame used on the McCormick-Deering 10-20 and 15-30 was simply a big cast iron tub that housed the engine, transmission, and final drive. The axles were bolted to this tub, and the basic equipment was in place. The design was very strong, and sealed bearing surfaces from dust and dirt.

The company believed the integral frame and unit construction, combined with the superior technology of the McCormick-Deerings, made the 10-20 and 15-30 the tractors of the future for IHC. The Farmall threw a huge wrench into that plan, as the efforts of Bert R. Benjamin produced an innovative product that used more traditional construction and a channel frame. The company had to back the obvious winner, but the techniques of modular construction and an integral frame (of sorts) would reappear on the Letter Series tractors, when Benjamin's innovative tricycle design would be merged with the production methods of the 10-20 and 15-30.

The defining intuition into the McCormick-Deerings was offered by columnist Elmer Baker in *Implement and Tractor*. Baker contrasted the McCormick-Deerings to the Farmall by the methods they were developed. The Farmall was the result of one man's vision, while the

The Tractor Wars

One of the major challenges to the International Harvester Company was the entrance of Henry Ford and his Fordson tractor in 1917. The Fordson was light, reasonably powerful, and economical. In addition, it had all of Ford's marketing savvy and tremendous reputation behind it. More importantly, it was sold through Ford's extensive network of car dealerships. Ford soon owned 75 percent of the market, and sold more Fordsons in 1919 alone than most tractor manufacturers had in the past decade.

The key to the Fordson's success was its method of construction, which allowed Ford to price the tractor below the competition. It used an integral frame, which essentially made heavy-duty engine, transmission, and rear drive housings part of the frame. The frame was stronger than the channel frames of the day, and had some advantages on the production line. The production line was also key to the Fordson's success. The tractor was designed for modular construction and could be assembled quickly on a factory line. Ford could crank out hundreds of machines per day for dramatically lower cost than the competition, and was soon doing just that.

The tractor industry had to respond to survive, and most manufacturers simply lowered prices in an attempt to gain some of the market that Ford had essentially created. This was great for the farmers of the day. The lowered initial costs of the tractor made power farming more affordable and improved the efficiency of the farm. Tractors on the farm exploded over the next five years, and Henry Ford was a big reason why.

Ford had convinced the government to distribute his Fordson tractor through government agencies as a war measure, and the result was explosive sales. Cyrus McCormick's commentary in *The Century of the Reaper* is particularly enlightening on IHC's take on Ford's move.

He wrote: "To have convinced worried statesmen and the public that the tractor was a new device twelve years after many tractor builders had attained large production, and that his particular make would prove to be the one solution to the knotty problem of food production, was a supreme feat of salesmanship."

In the early 1920s, tractors sales were dropping industry-wide, and Ford and IHC battled for control of the market in what became known as the Tractor Wars. The first part of the conflict was simply a price war. Henry Ford's Fordson was so economical that tractor manufacturers were forced to drop their prices to sell tractors. Tractors built by IHC saw at least four price reductions beginning in 1921 and ending with the International 8-16 at $670 and the Titan 10-20 going for $700. Despite this, Ford's 1922 decision to drop the price of the Fordson to $395 (which was below Ford's cost!) kept the Ford Motor Company at the top of the tractor sales heap.

While the lowered prices and increased competition brought good things to the farmer, it devastated the industry, and IHC was no exception. Almost overnight, IHC went from owning the market, controlling 39 percent in 1916, to half of that in 1918 (see chart). The Fordson was squeezing IHC, and it also had a catalyzing effect on new manufacturers eager to get a slice of the tractor market pie.

The number of manufacturers peaked in 1921 at 186, an incredible number considering only a handful control the market today, and only one—John Deere—has survived unscathed.

But 1921 was not a good year to be starting a new tractor company. International was fighting for sales, and dropped prices several times that year. They also initiated field demonstrations designed to showcase IHC tractors and convince buyers that IHC tractors were worth the extra money. The weapons were the Titan 10-20 and International 8-16, and it seems they were up to the task of taking on the Ford, as IHC regained a larger share of the sales that year, gaining 12 percent in market share. But Ford wasn't finished.

Ford responded, turning his stranglehold into a death grip by dropping the price of the Fordson to $395, a price he admitted was below cost. For IHC, it was time to do or die. The company cut its prices, as well, selling Titan 10-20s for $700 and International 8-16s for $670. IHC also took the war to the fields, challenging Fordsons to plowing contests. In *Century of the Reaper*, Cyrus McCormick had this to say about the tractor wars:

"A Harvester challenge rang through the land. Everywhere any single Ford sale was rumored, the Harvester dealer dared the Ford representative to a contest. No prizes were offered, no jury awarded merit to one or another contestant. No quarter was given and none was asked. Grimly the protagonists struggled, fiercely they battled for each sale. The reaper war was being refought with new weapons."

In 1922, IHC was not especially successful, losing market share in a market where a buyer could bring home a Fordson for less than $400. The rest of the industry fared worse, with the overnight tractor companies going belly up. Seventy tractor companies failed in 1922, and 13 more dropped out the next year, with less than half left standing in 1925.

But by 1926, IHC had its new McCormick-Deering tractors on the market and selling briskly, and was regaining the dominance of the past. Ford was headed out of the picture, and it would be smooth sailing with the Fordson out of the way. In 1928, Ford bowed out and IHC's new unit-construction McCormick-Deerings helped IHC take control of the market; 55 percent of all tractors sold that year bore the IHC logo. In 1931, IHC's market strength led Cyrus McCormick to write, "When the tractor war was over, the farmers of the world appreciated beyond a shadow of doubt that they would best serve themselves by providing their farms with a tractor rugged enough to resist the shocks of farm use and powerful enough to do all of their work. They knew that there can be no such thing as a good cheap tractor."

McCormick was right at the time, and IHC maintained a dominant market position until 1939, when the introduction of a stunning line of new Farmalls was spoiled by a handshake between Henry Ford and Harry Ferguson that brought the Ford tractor back to the United States.

The second part of the Tractor Wars took place in the fields. Management at IHC realized that it simply could not match Ford's prices and build a quality product. As a result, the company took the battle to the fields. Agents were instructed to find out when Fordson sales were about to take place, and challenge the Fordson representative to a field trial. The IHC weapons were the stodgy but well-built Titan 10-20 and the radical but often unavailable International 8-16. Not the best IHC could build, but the best available at the time. Although the tractors proved more capable than the Fordson, buyers couldn't refuse a tractor built by Henry Ford for less than $400, and IHC lost precious ground.

Below

This chart shows how Ford and International compared in total pro uction and market share. Note that International dominated the market in 1916, then took an almost immediate back seat to Henry Ford's little machine when it appeared in 1917. Note that 1921 saw Harvester pull ahead of Ford, which may have incited Henry to drop the price of his Fordson below cost. The ensuing price war had Ford controlling the market, but International was able to outlast Ford and take control by 1928, when the Fordson was pulled from the domestic market.

Ford vs. International

Year	Total Tractor Production	Total Manufacturers	International Prod.	Share	Ford Prod.	Share
1915	21,000	61	5,841	28%	-	-
1916	29,670	114	11,571	39%	-	-
1917	62,742	124	16,101	26%	259	0.4%
1918	132,697	142	25,269	19%	34,000	26%
1919	164,590	164	26,933	16%	54,000	33%
1920	203,207	166	28,419	14%	58,000	29%
1921	68,029	186	17,762	26%	13,000	19%
1922	98,794	116	11,781	12%	62,000	63%
1923	131,908	93	12,026	9%	100,000	76%
1924	116,838	64	18,749	16%	78,000	67%
1925	164,097	58	32,588	20%	100,000	61%
1926	178,074	69	50,900	29%	NA	NA
1927	194,913	61	55,727	29%	NA	NA
1928	171,469	51	94,148	55%	40,000	23%

Source: IHC, "Tractor Production Schedule'" *The Agricultural Tractor 1855–1950*

The tread width on the McCormick-Deering 10-20 and 15-30 was not adjustable. Narrow tread versions of the 10-20 were available, but this was an extremely expensive way to provide the farmer with the capability to work narrower-row crops.

The 10-20 weighed a bit over 3,500 pounds, approximately 2,000 pounds lighter than the Titan 10-20 and about the same weight as the International 8-16. Lights were becoming more popular in the 1920s, as electric systems steadily improved.

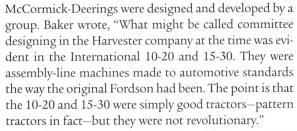

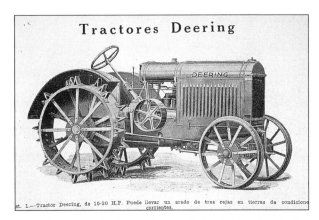

The 10-20 was exported under several different badges, including these Deering-badged units that went to a Spanish-speaking country.

McCormick-Deerings were designed and developed by a group. Baker wrote, "What might be called committee designing in the Harvester company at the time was evident in the International 10-20 and 15-30. They were assembly-line machines made to automotive standards the way the original Fordson had been. The point is that the 10-20 and 15-30 were simply good tractors—pattern tractors in fact—but they were not revolutionary."

This is not to say that the McCormick-Deering 10-20 and 15-30 were not important tractors. They were, in fact, the state-of-the-art in the early 1920s. They were intelligently engineered and well-built, with quality components used throughout. They were light-years ahead of the Titan 10-20, which was considered a good machine as late as 1920. Four years later, the McCormick-Deerings made the Titan obsolete.

McCormick-Deering 15-30

The 15-30 was the first of the McCormick-Deerings to appear. The tractor was essentially a replacement for the International 15-30, with the open field and heavier jobs in mind. The McCormick-Deering was a leap to the next level for tractors, and had features like ball bearings throughout the engine and transmission, decent carburetion, more reliable ignition, and a lower center of gravity. Additions like the power take-off added immensely to the tractor's utility, and it was one of the first tractors that retained its usefulness for a decade or more rather than just a few years.

The two most significant advances on the new 15-30 were the gear final drive and integral frame. As mentioned earlier, International's idea of an integral frame was a frame that was basically a large bath tub-shaped piece, with the engine and transmission dropped in. The final drive was housed in the bath tub frame, but the engine housing was a separate piece. No matter, International's integral frame was many times stronger than the channel frame design, and was sealed to keep dirt out of the engine and drive assembly.

The integral frame also allowed the use of the 15-30's second key advance, gear final drive. Most previous IHC tractors used roller chain final drive. Some were enclosed, but most were open to dirt and grime. The chains needed occasional adjustment, and tension was crucial. Too much and you would wear out the chain and sprockets prematurely; too little, and the chain would jump the sprockets. Oiling was also a black science. Lubrication naturally lengthened the life of the chains, but too much would attract dirt, wearing the chain prematurely. Chain final drive was a less than ideal mechanism, and the gear drive solved the worst of the problems. There was nothing to adjust, the mechanism was fully enclosed and shielded from dirt, and power transmission was positive with little chance for slippage.

The 15-30 was originally called the 12-25 Four-Cylinder International Tractor. The tractor was quickly changed to a 15-30 and geared down a bit. It seems the change in gearing resulted in the power upgrade, as the engine size and equipment were the same. In February of 1921, IHC ordered that a PTO be made optional on the 15-30. The PTO could be added to tractors already in the field, indicating that some 15-30s were built without a PTO. Vineyard editions of the tractor were built for California in 1922, as well.

Most interestingly, the decision to change the name from International 15-30 to McCormick-Deering 15-30 for the United States and Canada was not made until August of 1922. The model was introduced in 1921, making it likely that the first 15-30s were badged with "International" rather than "McCormick-Deering." Only about 200 were built in 1921, but all of them probably carried "International" badging. Also, the tractors exported off the continent continued to use the "International" name. The export tractors also used Deering and McCormick badging.

The engine was a vertical four-cylinder with removable cylinders. The crankshaft ran on ball bearings, an innovation that increased the main bearing's life span. The engine's bearing surfaces were fed oil by a combination splash and gear pump lubrication system. A high-tension magneto provided the spark, with a governor maintaining engine rpm at 1,000. The engine was

The 10-20 Industrial was the beginning of a successful new line for International. Agricultural tractors could be converted for industrial use with little more than a change of wheels, and the tractors proved immensely useful for a wide variety of industrial applications. The first tractor IHC experimented with in this way was the McCormick-Deering 10-20.

The 10-20 Industrial became known as the Model 20. It was introduced in 1923 as a lightly modified McCormick-Deering 10-20, and was available until 1940. This Model 20 was used by New York City for cleaning snow off sidewalks.

started on gasoline and switched over to kerosene once it was warm.

The 6,000-pound tractor sat on an 85-inch wheelbase and could turn within a 30-foot radius. Standard equipment included a belt pulley, lugs, air cleaner, tools, and front wheel skid rings. Priced at around $1,250, the tractor was not cheap, but it was a good value because of its quality design and construction.

Specialty Models and Attachments

In 1923, rice field equipment was offered for the tractor, which consisted of widened wheels with special lugs and special front-wheel tire ring attachments. McCormick-Deering 15-30s were soon after offered as orchard models, which used lower wheels, a shortened air intake, and had the pulley and pulley carrier removed. The California orchard models, released in April of 1924, received the above modifications and rear wheel fenders that covered the top half of the rear wheel and swooped over to meet the hood.

Few tractors were produced in the early years of production, which may have been a result of some early production difficulties. By 1927, production was up to 17,000 a year.

In 1926, the McCormick-Deering's transmission was changed to lower the gear ratios for more drawbar pull. The bevel pinion and shaft, drive bevel gear, low-speed gear, medium- and low-speed pinions, medium-speed gear, and reverse pinion and bushing were replaced. The new transmission was not interchangeable with the old.

Beginning in January of 1928, rubber-skinned wheels were available for the McCormick-Deering 15-30. Such tires were strips of rubber wrapped around steel

One of the unique features of the Model 20 was that the front end was suspended by a heavy-duty leaf spring. This Model 20 was used at the San Diego docks.

The Model 20 could be equipped with pneumatic tires and rims or solid wheels. The solid wheels came in two sizes—40x5 and 40x10—and the larger solid wheels added about 1,500 pounds of weight. This Model 20 is pulling a tanker in Shorewood, Wisconsin, which is near Milwaukee.

The early Model 20 was equipped with a three-speed transmission, while later versions had a four-speed. The industrial versions could be equipped with most of the same options as the regular 10-20.

wheels, providing some relief to the problem of traversing pavement. Such tires were useful for both industrial and orchard applications. Some orchard growers found that steel lugs damaged roots and smooth wheels provided insufficient traction. These early rubber-coated wheels were less than satisfactory for field work. Until Firestone adapted the pneumatic tire to agricultural use in the early 1930s, lugged steel wheels remained the farmer's most efficient choice.

More Power for the 15-30

In August of 1928, the McCormick-Deering 15-30 was given major updates which resulted in a 22-36 power output. The factory continued to call the upgraded model the McCormick-Deering 15-30. Sometime in 1930, the sales department requested the name be changed to 22-36 to reflect the power upgrade. The model was changed on paper to the McCormick-Deering 22-36 for a while, but the name did not stick. As far as can be told, all of the higher-powered McCormick-Deerings are badged as 15-30s.

Increased-power 15-30s are easily identifiable by a bulge in the engine side cowl, over the carburetor.

The additional power came from increasing the bore of the engine from 4 1/2 inches to 4 3/4 inches. The crankshaft and connecting rods were strengthened, and the cylinder head was new, with larger ports. The cooling system was still enclosed with a radiator, but a water pump was added.

The intake and exhaust manifolds were new, and the carburetor was a double-draft unit. One venturi injected fuel, while the other injected water. The crude water injection lessened detonation.

The engine was governed to run 50 rpm higher, at 1,050 rpm. An oil filter was incorporated, and the transmission and rear differential were strengthened. The strengthened parts increased the weight some-

what, as the tractor weighed 6,500 pounds with the standard lugs, pulley, tools, air cleaner, front wheel skid rings, and rear wheel fenders.

The upgraded model and the end of the Fordson in 1928 put some life into sales, pushing unit sales above 35,000 in 1928. In 1933, pneumatic tires became available through special order for the McCormick-Deering 15-30. Production of the tractor tapered off soon after, and the model was discontinued in 1934.

McCormick-Deering 15-30 Production

Year	Production
1921	199
1922	1,350
1923	4,886
1924	7,321
1925	12,978
1926	20,001
1927	17,554
1928	35,525
1929	28,311*
1930	21,891
1931	4,380
1932	1,705
1933	NA
1934	NA
Total Prod.	**156,101**

Source: McCormick/IHC Archives,
*Increased power (22-36) model introduced
1921–32 "Tractor Production Schedule;"
1932–34 figures not available

Industrial models could be ordered with almost any kind of attachment, and International custom-built a wide variety of one-off models. This unique setup was owned by the Edison Light Company of Boston, Massachusetts.

There were apparently some problems with the PTO on the 15-30 and 22-36s, as an upgraded PTO shaft and other parts were released in 1928, although the new part was not publicly announced. Also, some troubles with the rear end led to several new pieces and improved seals to protect against dirt penetration.

McCormick-Deering 10-20

Not long after the decision was made to go ahead with the McCormick-Deering 15-30, IHC decided to build a smaller model of similar construction. Like the 15-30, it used an integral frame and gear final drive. The same high-tension magneto, throttle-type governor, gas/kerosene fuel system, combination splash-and-gear pump engine lubrication, and 1,000 rpm engine speed were used. Cooling was the same, an enclosed system with a radiator but no water pump.

Where the new machine differed was simply in size. It used a smaller bore and stroke at 4 1/4x5 inches. The tractor's dimensions were smaller than the 15-30's in almost every aspect. The 78-inch wheelbase was 7 inches shorter, the 123-inch overall length was 10 inches shorter, and the wheels were 8 inches smaller in the rear and 4 inches smaller in the front. The 10-20 weighed about 3,700 pounds, compared to the 15-30's 6,000.

Early Production

While the official decision to build 10-20s was recorded in August of 1921, it seems none were actually

Below

A Model 20 fitted with an Austin Motor Grader. This one is being used by the State Highway Commission on Road Number 13 near Keskuk City, Iowa.

Another Model 20 grader, this one hard at work pushing snow. The Model 20 was equipped with both foot- and hand-operated brakes.

Options for the front tires included these solid 29x5 wheels as well as pneumatic tires and steel rims. This Model 20 is pulling wagons full of cotton batting.

built until 1923. Note that official or company decisions are documented records of changes and new models. Although company actions may lag behind company decisions, the official decisions are the best source for when new models were conceived and built.

Factory records show several related decisions after the August 1921 decision, all ordering that this new machine be built, the 10-20. The original decision is covered in pen marks, as someone apparently wanted the machine a bit smaller than proposed. It also read, "Do not send copy of Decision to Branch Managers until advised by the Sales Department to do so," indicating that while the company intended to build a 10-20 version of the new integral frame machines, the details were not yet satisfactory. The next decision mentioning the 10-20 shows up in September of 1922, over a year later. The decision specifies that the 10-20, formerly known as the International 10-20, would be badged as the McCormick-Deering 10-20. The report seems to indicate the tractor had not yet been manufactured, supporting the popular belief that 10-20 production began in 1923. On December 22, 1922, another decision came out authorizing production of the "new" McCormick-Deering machine. Again, the branch managers were not to be notified until the sales department gave the green light. Apparently, they did, because over 7,000 were produced in 1923, the 10-20's inaugural year.

Specialty Models

In 1926, the Narrow Tread McCormick-Deering 10-20 was approved for production. Intended for use in orchards and other places that required tractors with a narrower tread, it had a 50-inch rear tread width, which was about 10 inches narrower than that of the standard 10-20. The significance of the narrow tread machines was that altering tread width required new rear cases and significant costs for new tooling, changing production, promotion, and so on. Despite the cost, there were still only two different tread width

10-20s to suit the needs of a globe covered with farmers. This was a problem IHC would look to solve with the Farmall line.

In 1933, the pneumatic tire became available on the McCormick-Deering 10-20 through special order.

Industrial Models

From almost the very beginning, IHC had a knack for getting the most from its tractors. Titan Road Rollers were a classic example of an adaptation of existing machinery to a new market. These machines provided a profitable sideline for IHC due to the fact that engineering and production costs were lower than building an entirely new machine.

But road rollers and graders were fairly complex conversions that would eventually be overshadowed by equipment designed specifically for such tasks. A converted tractor could not compete with a machine tailored to grade or roll roads, and the conversions were not especially cheap or efficient.

About the time the new McCormick-Deering machines were being introduced, IHC began to explore the potential for a simpler brand of specialty machine. Standard tread tractors were useful for far more than simply plowing; the company merely needed to get the tractors into the right location. Rather than complex conversions, a utility tractor could be created with little more than a new set of stickers and wheels.

Despite the simplicity of creating industrial machines, getting into the industrial market was an entirely different matter. With a concentrated effort of advertisements and sales people, IHC put its tractors to work on an incredibly diverse range of jobs.

Promotion

Part of the company's effort was to get articles into newspapers and magazines touting the money industrial tractors saved cities and townships. The articles were written with a slant that is somewhat

McCormick-Deering 10-20 Production

Year	Production
1923	7,117
1924	11,197
1925	18,436
1926	25,021
1927	26,646
1928	30,353
1929	39,433
1930	32,230
1931	10,901
1932	1,852
1933	1,940
1934	1,096
1935	2,960
1936	2,190
1937	2,461
1938	NA
Total Prod.	**213,833**

10-20 Narrow Tread

Year	Production
1925	8
1926	148
1927	183
1928	323
1929	383
1930	207
1931	83
1932	79
1933	40
1934	NA
Total Prod.	**1,454**

Source: McCormick/IHC Archives, "Tractor Production Schedule" 1933–38, *Hot Line Farm Equipment Guide*, 1996 edition

entertaining today; IHC didn't pull any punches with press coverage. This example comes from the *Chicago Daily Tribune* of June 25, 1924: "It has been demonstrated in dollars and sense that skinny old nags and bony old plugs, some lame and some blind, are too expensive to carry on the city pay rolls, even if they have aided many a captain to carry his precinct in a primary or an election." The article went on, lambasting politicians for dragging their feet and costing the city of Chicago as much as $700,000 annually. A series of articles appeared on the topic, and the third installment cited savings of nearly $1.5 million by pur-

chasing industrial tractors. The fact that to save $1.5 million, Chicago would have to place a $2 million order with IHC was downplayed, of course. While today's media are branded as untrustworthy, the subtle slant of modern coverage pales compared to the unabashed slander and outright lies considered acceptable practice for newspapers of the 1920s.

However questionable the press of the day may have been, such articles were simply good business at the time. The tactics worked well, and industrial tractors became a long-standing success for IHC. These tractors were the grunts of the company. They showed up in unusual places, and certainly led more exciting lives than the Farmalls, most of which went straight to the farm. They were also a very profitable sideline for IHC, and the company made such tractors until the bitter end.

Model 20

The McCormick-Deering 10-20 was adapted for industrial use in 1922. The machines were simply 10-20s pulled off the line, and the serial numbers were indistinguishable from other McCormick-Deering 10-20s. At some point in time, this machine was designated the Model 20. Cast iron disc wheels were used front and rear, and the model was sold to industries. All of 23 of these machines were built in 1923. This astounding sales success led IHC engineers to realize that more was required than simply different wheels to make a truly useful industrial tractor. A foot accelerator, suspended front end, high-back seat, underslung muffler, dual rear tires, and rear-wheel brakes were added, yet it was not enough to significantly increase sales in 1924. The suspended front end is not documented in detail, mentioning only the use of four coil springs. What a contraption that must have been. . .

Development continued for 1925, and high-speed (10.4 miles per hour!) top gear and transverse leaf front suspension were added. Front and rear bumpers and an assortment of wheel lugs were added as options. Sales for 1925 are listed as "several hundred" and IHC stated, "there was considerable market for this tractor in modified form." The company responded to the demand by adding an "IND" suffix to the serial number in 1925. In 1926, production of Model 20s reached 1,400 units, and the Model 20 was assigned unique serial numbers that began at 501 and were coded "IN."

Engine and Specifications

The Model 20 used the four-cylinder valve-in-head IHC engine. Bore was 4 1/2 inches and stroke was 5 inches, and the engine was rated to produce 25 horsepower at 1,000 rpm. Removable cylinder sleeves were used, and the crankshaft spun on roller

The Model 20 could be equipped with a power take-off, which is being put to good use here powering a winch that is pulling a stump.

bearings. The engine and transmission were lubricated with a combination oil bath and oil pump system. An oil filter was used, as was an air filter. The engine was cooled by a thermosyphon system that used a radiator and a fan.

Later versions, at the least, used a four-speed transmission. Top speed was about 10 miles per hour, with the three lower gears pulling 2.3, 4, and 7 miles per hour. The intake and muffler were mounted to the left side, and didn't protrude much higher than the hood, presumably for ease of use on the factory floor.

The tractor weighed in between 5,180 to 7,450 pounds, depending on the type of wheels used. Standard equipment included a cushion spring seat, hand and foot brakes, spring-cushioned drawbar, a muffler, and radiator curtains. Options included a belt pulley, 543-rpm power take-off, electric and gas lights, fenders, and a tire pump. In addition, IHC would custom build the tractors. The following modifications were made in the late 1920s to industrial models: special equipment for a dump body type tractor, full reverse transmission, wheels with removeable solid rear tires, Bendix Westinghouse air brake equipment, water muffler attachment, narrow tread tractor for sidewalk plows, and City of New York crosswalk plows

The Model 20 should have been displaced by the I-30 introduced in 1931, but Model 20s continued to be built through 1940. In fact, the first Nebraska Tractor Test of the machine took place in July of 1931. The machine put out 23.01 horsepower at the drawbar in low

Model 20 Production	
Year	Production
1923	NA
1924	NA
1925	NA
1926	1,204
1927	1,842
1928	3,048
1929	4,607
1930	3,397
1931	1,831
1932	715
1933	206
1934	209
1935	173
1936	195
1937	212
1938	120
1939	127
1940	32
Total Prod.	17,918

Source: McCormick/IHC Archives

gear and 29.87 horsepower at the belt pulley. As tested, the tractor weighed 5,415 pounds and was equipped with an IHC air filter, governor, and E4A magneto. A Zenith C5FE carburetor was used.

Model 30

The modest success of the Model 20 was apparently enough to convince IHC that the industrial market was worth pursuing, and a prototype industrial version of McCormick-Deering 15-30 was constructed early in 1929. The "new" machine was dubbed the Model 30 and had the same general features as the Model 20. Production began in 1930, and very few of the machines were built.

An IHC industrial tractor brochure lists the Model 20, Model 30, and I-30. Looking closely at the specs, it appears that the Model 30 is indeed little more than a McCormick-Deering 15-30 with some special equipment. Company records indicate that the Model 30 serial numbers were simply 15-30 numbers stamped with the prefix "HD."

Both of these tractors are experimentals: the machine on the trailer is a Model 15-30 Industrial and the rig in front is an experimental rig that never saw regular production. The 15-30, on the other hand, did make it into production.

Engine and Specifications

The Model 30 used a higher-powered version of the 4 3/4x6-inch four-cylinder engine used in later McCormick-Deering 15-30s. The Model 30 engine was rated for 45 horsepower and was governed to run at 1,050 rpm. The engine used the standard IHC removable sleeves, ball-bearing crank, and combination pressure/splash lubrication. A three-speed transmission was used, with a fairly low top speed of 5.9 miles per hour. The coolant system used a radiator with a fan, water pump, and thermostat.

The Model 30 weighed a solid 9,700 pounds, and swelled to 11,700 pounds when equipped with dual rear tires. The machine outweighed the original McCormick-

This is the Model 15-30 Industrial, which was simply a McCormick-Deering 15-30 with industrial wheels. The 50x10 solid wheels brought the shipping weight of the tractor up to 9,700 pounds.

The W-30 was introduced in 1932, running right into the Depression. As you might suspect, sales volume was low in 1932 and 1933, although it began to pick up in 1934 as the economy began to rebound. This photograph was taken December 27, 1933.

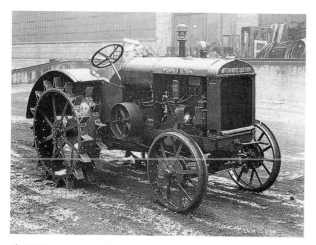

The W-30 was an upgraded version of the McCormick-Deering 10-20, with more horsepower in a similar package. The W-30 was the standard tread counterpart to the F-30, but the two shared little more than the "30" in their model names.

The W-30 used a higher horsepower version of the engine from the McCormick-Deering 10-20. The intake manifold could be switched to be heated or not, allowing the engine to burn kerosene, distillate, or gasoline. Regular equipment included a Zenith K5 carburetor and the International E4A magneto.

Standard tread tractors were most at home in the open field. Ironically, though, the F-30 recorded more maximum pull than the W-30 in the Nebraska Tractor Tests.

The W-30 benefited from new techniques in hardening steel through heat treatment. Aluminum pistons, ball-bearings, and beefy four-bolt main journals added up to an extremely durable lower unit.

Deering by over 4,000 pounds, probably due to a combination of heavy solid wheels and rugged front suspension.

Production ended in 1932, with only 532 Model 30s constructed. This extremely low number makes the Model 30 one of the rarest IHC tractors built, and a great find for the collector.

The Model 20 and 30 seeded the ground for a long line of industrial machines to come. With each new standard tread machine, an industrial variant would be produced. Custom fabrication continued in the industrial line, and these tractors appeared in more unusual and creative forms than any other type of IHC tractor.

The McCormick-Deering machines and their variants were well-built, reliable, and effective farm tractors. They did exactly what a tractor of the 1920s was expected to do better than anyone had reason to expect. But they did not break any new ground. They simply covered the open ground well.

To compete with Ford, IHC needed the McCormick-Deering machines. But to beat Ford, it needed something revolutionary, something no one had seen. Bert R. Benjamin had that tractor under his hat, and after a long battle, he would use it to finally put Ford out of domestic tractor production. But that, of course, is another chapter.

Model 30 Production

Year	Production
1930	48
1931	326
1932	158
Total Prod.	**532**

Source: McCormick/IHC Archives

The W-30 would have been available with pneumatic tires early on, but many of them went out the door on steel. This W-30 and manure spreader are shown near Keeler, Michigan.

W-30

Standard tread tractors were still a priority in the early 1930s, and the McCormick-Deerings were in need of an update. The W-30 was just that; an upgrade of the McCormick-Deering 10-20. The increased-power engine was bumped up to about 30 horsepower, hence the designation.

The W-30s engine put out a little more horsepower than the F-30s. The bore and stroke were the same at 4 1/4x5 inches, but the engine was rated for 31.63 horsepower at the belt, which was 1.3 horsepower more than the F-30. At the drawbar, the two were rated nearly equally. Both engines were governed to run at 1,150 rpm, although the W-30 was rated to run at 1,300 rpm late in production. The change required a different governor spring.

The W-30 engine used a combination manifold that allowed it to burn kerosene/distillate or gasoline. A Zenith carburetor was used, as was an International E4A magneto. A radiator regulated by a thermostat and water pump cooled the engine. Power was transmitted to the transmission via a 12-inch single-plate clutch, and the brakes were hand-operated.

Although the engine was nearly identical to that of the F-30, the chassis was vastly different. The previously mentioned integral frame was used, but the front and rear axle and final drive were all unique to the wheeled 30s.

The transmission is a bit of an enigma, as early company records list a three-speed transmission. At some point in production, a four-speed transmission was adopted. In 1936, a lower-speed four-speed transmission was fit, and

serial numbers were changed with the improvement. The decision to make the change was made early in 1936, but a few of the older units were sold into 1937.

Options for the W-30 included pneumatic tires, high-altitude pistons, a lower low gear, differential lock, and a distillate-burning manifold.

Less than 50 W-30s were built in the first two years of production. The tractor was finally sold in quantity in 1934, when 2,634 rolled out of the factory doors. Sales remained steady until 1940, when the W-30 was being phased out in preparation for the W-6.

The W-30 served IHC well. Although the company was able to use parts and technology designed for the McCormick-Deering 15-30, the cost of building a custom rear drive and front end made the W-30 expensive for the volume of sales produced.

Model I-30

When the W-30 appeared, it was quickly pressed into duty as an addition to the Industrial tractor line as the I-30. It fit neatly in between the Model 20 and Model 30, giving greater flexibility to the line.

The experience the company had with industrial tractors brought a number of improvements to the I-30. The drawbar was strengthened, and built to be more adaptable to mount equipment. Some I-30s were fitted with equipment to perform specialized tasks ranging from landing dirigibles to operating crosswalk plows. The I-30 was produced at Milwaukee Works.

W-30 Production

Year	Production
1932	11
1933	26
1934	2,634*
1935	6,541*
1936	6,236*
1937	7,875*
1938	6,088*
1939	2,560*
1940	560*
Total Prod.	**32,531**

*Number of serial numbers issued that year, which is only an approximation of production numbers.
Source: McCormick/IHC Archives, 1932 and 1933 from "Tractor Production Schedule"

The W-30 was one of the first International tractors in which the cooling was thermostatically controlled. The radiator and fan were common by the 1930s, of course, but most machines still used shutters to control temperature, at least early in the decade.

The I-30's specifications closely resembled the W-30, which was the base model for the machine. The I-30 was slightly smaller than the Model 30, and weighed more than 2,500 pounds less with about 10 fewer horsepower.

The I-30 engine was an IHC valve-in-head four-cylinder with a 4 1/4x5-inch bore and stroke. The engine was rated for 35 horsepower and governed to run at 1,150 rpm. Like most of the IHC line, it used removable cylinder sleeves, ball-bearing crankshaft journals, and splash/pump lubrication. The cooling system used a radiator, water pump, and thermostat.

Options included a belt pulley, 575-rpm PTO, electric and gas lights, fenders, special wheel equipment, and custom-built equipment.

The key to selling tractors was a combination of good equipment and salespeople. International had both, and was the leading tractor manufacturer of the 1930s. John Deere was number two for part of the decade, and the two manufacturers remained the leading players into modern times.

This W-30 is pulling a four-bottom plow near Saskatoon, Canada.

W-40

Introduced into a market hungry for horsepower, the W-40s didn't quite satisfy that need. The initial version, the WA-40 used a heavy-duty integral frame mated to the six-cylinder engine from the TA-40 TracTracTor. Seven experimentals were built for testing in 1934.

The W-40 was first designated as the WA-40, then the WK-40, and finally simply the W-40. Each variant is identified by a unique serial number code, and some bore badging designating "WA-40" or "WK-40."

The WA-40 used a six-cylinder engine with a 3 5/8x4 1/2-inch bore and stroke. The tractor was underpowered, so the WK-40 received a 3 3/4x4 1/2-inch bore and stroke. Both engines were started on gasoline and switched over to kerosene or distillate.

Savvy farmers replaced the stock engine with an IHC Red Diamond truck engine. The 361 and the 401 bolted right in, giving the tractor the increased pulling power farmers were seeking.

The transmission was a three-speed, and the tractor weighed in at about 6,100 pounds.

WD-40

The WD-40 used the same chassis and the four-cylinder diesel engine from the TD-40 crawler. The diesel engine produced about the same amount of horsepower as the six-cylinder kerosene-burning engine, although at a lower rpm of 1,100. The resultant tractor, the WD-40, was released in 1934, and was one of the first production

An I-30—the industrial version of the W-30—owned and operated by the Miller Brewing Company of Milwaukee, Wisconsin. Mike Krenwinkle, foreman in charge of the yards, used this tractor for spotting cars around the brewery from morning 'til night and the tractor was never idle. Full or empty, he could spot three cars at a time without a whimper from the tractor. Krenwinkle said, "Without it, we would be lost."

diesel tractors. The engine used a unique gasoline starting system that switched to diesel once the engine was warm.

Both tractors tested well, and were released in limited numbers for regular production in 1935. The transmissions on the prototypes were a bit fragile, and a strengthened unit was authorized for the regular pro-

A W-30 pulling a six-foot #2 disk harrow in Ontario.

duction machines. Several gears and gear shafts as well as bearing cages and the transmission case were strengthened.

The heavy field tractors sold well for about three years, and died off in 1939 and 1940. At the end of their run, they were replaced by the W-9 series. The W-9 would be the only remaining wheel tractor that was independently designed rather than based on a cultivating tractor chassis.

WA-40, WK-40, W-40, and WD-40 Production

Year	Production
1934	NA
1935	940*
1936	3,679*
1937	2,545*
1938	2,091*
1939	567*
1940	237*
Total Prod.	**10,059**

*Number of serial numbers issued that year, which is only an approximation of production numbers.
Source: McCormick/IHC Archives

The industrial tractor market continued to be a good one for International. The company sold 315 I-30 tractors with plows and cabs to the City of New York to be used for snow removal.

I-40

In 1935, the I-40 and ID-40 were developed. In 1936, production began at Milwaukee Works. These heavy-duty machines were fitted with the standard industrial equipment—front and rear bolsters, solid wheels, and any custom equipment desired by the purchaser. Purchasers, sadly, were in short supply, making the I-40 and diesel ID-40 among the list of rare IHC tractors.

This W-30 is running a thresher near Morris, Illinois. The W-30 was built at the Milwaukee Works.

I-40 and ID-40 Production

Year	Production
1936	20*
1937	98*
1938	58*
1939	94*
1940	79*
Total Prod.	**349**

*Number of serial numbers issued that year, which are only approximations of production numbers.
Source: McCormick/IHC Archives

The big 40s—the W-40, WD-40, I-40, and ID-40—used engines from International's crawler line in a subtly upgraded frame from the McCormick-Deering 15-30. The W-tractors were introduced in 1934, and the industrial versions appeared two years later. This IA-40 is pulling an Adams grader near Macon, Missouri.

As the 1930s drew to a close, the need for more horsepower began to step up, and the influence of industrial designers changed the face of the farm tractor. Most of the major manufacturers were producing row-crop tractors like the Farmall, and IHC needed another master stroke to climb back on top. The next generation of tractors would be just what the company needed, and the beliefs of a man named Raymond Loewy would help the company put the finishing touches on the new tractors they were developing.

The I-40 and ID-40 were not produced in large numbers, with fewer than 500 built. This ID-40 is logging in Tallahassee, Florida. Note the TracTracTor in the background.

The WD-40 was the first diesel tractor tested at the Nebraska Tractor Tests, and produced 44 horsepower at the belt. All of the IH diesels—like this ID-40—used a unique starting system that ran the engine on gasoline until it was warm, when it automatically switched to diesel fuel.

Chapter Three

The Birth of the Farmall

■

"For there came a time when but for the persistence of B. R. Benjamin, the whole idea [the Farmall] might have been abandoned."
—C. W. Gray, 1932

While International and Ford battled to control the tractor market, IHC was in a minor civil war over tractor design. The company had committed great resources to the integral frame and production line construction of the new McCormick-Deering line, and was betting the company future on the success of these new machines. The emergence of a new design, the Farmall, was not greeted with welcoming arms. The Farmall had another strike against it, the dismal failure of an earlier attempt to build a cultivating machine, the Motor Cultivator. With vast resources devoted to building the McCormick-Deerings and a poor track record for the design, company executives were less than eager to jump on board the Farmall train.

With help from the farmers fortunate enough to test experimentals, the sympathetic ear of International executive Alexander Legge, and the impassioned work of engineer Bert R. Benjamin, the Farmall survived to become arguably the most significant tractor in the history of the International Harvester Company.

The McCormick-Deerings were very capable machines, but they were not especially revolutionary. They used state-of-the-art componentry and production techniques, but the basic design of these machines had been around for nearly a decade. The tractors did everything a tractor of the day was expected to do very well, but they didn't do anything unexpected.

The giant leap the times demanded and the industry was striving to build was the all-purpose tractor. Tractor farming was accepted as an improvement, a step forward, but the farmers of the day had yet to be convinced that the horse could be completely replaced on the farm. In fact, the number of horses on American farms was increasing until 1920, and did not drop off significantly during the 1920s. Tractor production soared, but the horse still played an important role on the farm.

So, the tractor that would change the face of agriculture had not appeared in the early 1920s, and it wasn't found among the McCormick-Deerings. IHC had that tractor in the form of a tricycle-design machine developed over more than decade's worth of trial and, more commonly, error. Ironically, the tractor that would be hailed as the first true replacement for the horse came from attempts to build a cultivating tractor. To top it off, IHC took over five years to figure out what it had!

Seeds for the all-purpose tractor were planted before IHC formed. One of these early ideas was Edward A. Johnston's Auto Mower, which he developed for Deering. Johnston was by all accounts a brilliant designer who engineered the International Auto Buggy, the vehicle that pioneered IHC's truck line, and the Auto Mower won a prize at the World's Fair in Paris in 1900.

John F. Steward was another forward-thinking IHC engineer who planted seeds for the Farmall. As early as

---

Left

Although the Farmall became the tractor everyone was reading about, it didn't start out that way. International Harvester had just introduced the McCormick-Deerings, and had put considerable expense and effort into tooling and design. The idea of developing another all-new machine was a bitter pill for management to swallow.

Above

The Farmall's profile was kept low in 1925, and the advertising budget was minimal. The company began to promote the tractor a bit more in 1926, advertising that the tractor would not be widely available due to production limitations (probably true). The trepidation was fading fast by 1928, when this brochure was printed.

75

The Motor Cultivator was not a successful chapter of International's history. It was dangerously tippy on side-hills, and was expensive for a single-purpose machine. The design work on the Motor Cultivator provided some valuable experience, but gave management a distaste for similar machines such as the spindly Farmall.

1902, he was working on a motor-driven harvesting machine. Eight years later, he proposed a multi-purpose tractor to IHC executive Alexander Legge. "What we want is a tractor that will most nearly abolish expensive labor on the farm, both of brute and of man," Steward wrote.

Steward's writing was prophetic, but his relationship with the McCormick-run IHC was not a warm one. Steward was an ex-Deering Harvester Company employee who never forgot that the McCormicks and the Deerings were once bitter competitors.

Motor Cultivator

One of the first machines to result from the search for the general purpose tractor was the motor or power cultivator. Tractors of the time pulled a plow and turned a belt acceptably; what was missing was the ability to cultivate efficiently. The Motor Cultivator was developed to meet this need.

The machine was as simple as its name; it was a self-propelled cultivator. Carl Mott and E. A. Johnston patented a design for a Motor Cultivator in 1916, and set about building experimentals. The quest to build a Motor Cultivator spread across the industry, as most of the major manufacturers were experimenting with some sort of vehicle designed simply for cultivation. In addition to the International model, Allis-Chalmers, Avery, Bailor, and several other companies had motor cultivators on the market in the late 1910s.

The Farmall was engineer Bert R. Benjamin's vision, which he brought to fruition by building the machine around the implement. This version of the Farmall is a later experimental, with all the fundamental pieces in place. It was photographed at Ames, Iowa.

The International Motor Cultivator was of a four-wheel tricycle design, with the two rear drive wheels close together and mounted on a swivel. The machine was turned by pivoting the rear wheels. Out front were two tall, narrow wheels, widely spaced apart. The cultivator hung below the chassis and between the front wheels.

The machine was powered by a four-cylinder engine with a bore and stroke of 3 1/8x4 1/2 inches rated at 12

The Motor Cultivator roots can be clearly seen in this photo of an experimental Farmall. This is clearly a later experimental, possibly of 1921 vintage. The engine is mounted inline, and the final drive is by gear rather than chain. This model appears to be reversible, a feature that was dropped in July 1922.

horsepower at 1,000 rpm. The motor was water-cooled with a radiator and fan that used thermosyphon circulation. The engine was mounted to a channel steel frame, and the entire unit weighed about 2,200 pounds.

The machine was designed specifically for corn cultivation. Early tests of the Motor Cultivator showed that it would overturn when driven on side hills. A nose weight partially solved this problem, but the machine still tipped over too easily. In 1917, the company authorized commercial production of 300 Motor Cultivators. Only 31 made it into the hands of farmers, and they were not well received.

Motor Cultivator Troubles

The Motor Cultivator fared poorly in the fields. It was slow and under-powered, and the wheels broke corn roots. Under ideal conditions, the machine performed adequately. Ideal conditions were relatively rare on the farm. The Motor Cultivator's questionable performance and short supply effectively killed it for 1917. By the time the factory assembled about 100 machines, it was so late in the season that the sales staff felt it could not sell the remaining stock of just over 50 machines.

In 1918, heavier cast rear wheels were added to the Motor Cultivator. The rear wheels were added to offset the machine's tendency to tip. The wheels helped, but the design was inherently unstable. The engine was carried high on the chassis. When the rear wheels were castored to turn the machine, the rear placed a rotating

force on the entire machine. If the Motor Cultivator was turned downhill, it would tip over.

To worsen matters, the 1918 model was again delivered late. Dealers were promised 150 models by June 10. They didn't show up until July 15. By the end of 1918, 301 Motor Cultivators were built.

In August of 1918, the final nail was placed in the Motor Cultivator's coffin. Cost estimates for the 1919 model were high, at over $500 for a machine which would retail for about $650. Revised cost figures came in, and the retail price would have had to be over $800 for the company to make out on the machine. Avery's motor cultivator sold for $540, making the $800 too high for the market to bear. On August 29th, the 1919 order for the Motor Cultivator was canceled.

C. W. Gray, in his report "Notes on the Development of the Farmall Tractor," wrote: "The rock on which the Motor Cultivator finally broke was manufacturing cost. One wonders now how much of that excessive cost was due to the weight which had been added in the effort to make a wrong principle work right. One wonders, indeed, whether the application of some very simple scientific formula should not have disclosed early in 1917 that the Motor Cultivator would probably roll over on side hills. One wonders, again, why, when it was discovered that the outfit would upset, someone did not foresee the weight which would be required to stabilize a tractor so designed must prove prohibitive. Yet we went right on, empirically adding weight until weight killed

One of the biggest stumbling blocks (and there were many), in the Farmall's development was the McCormick-Deering machines. The 15-30 and 10-20 represented the company's vision for the future, using production line construction and integral frames. Due to their existence, management was reluctant to back the Farmall. The Farmall initially survived due to the tenacity of engineer Bert R. Benjamin, but its superior field performance was what eventually made the Farmall successful.

One of the ongoing debates during the development of the Farmall was about weight. Versions ranged from over 4,000 to less than 3,000 pounds. In 1922, several versions were built, including one heavy and one light. The light version was pursued, but final production versions weighed just over 4,000 pounds.

the Motor Cultivator. And there is good reason to believe that the abortive attempt to market the Motor Cultivator all but completely discouraged the management in its purpose to build an all-purpose tractor."

Quest for the General Purpose Tractor

So, the Motor Cultivator was out of the line. Slow, tippy, poorly designed, and over cost, it never really had much of a chance. But the engineering department—especially Benjamin—had not given up on the concept. Years later, Benjamin recalled his feelings on the matter: "There was talk about a new kind of tractor in the industry, but no one had such a machine or even much of an idea on how to start building one. I knew we had to come up with an all-purpose tractor—one with rear

wheels that could be adjusted to straddle two rows of crops and a narrow front with a wheel that would fit into one crop row."

In the late 1910s, Benjamin and his engineers first put these ideas on paper, and began work on an experimental model. Benjamin said, "Working with D. B. Baker, then chief engineer, and John Anthony, who took care of the drafting, we had an operating experimental model within three years."

So began the evolution of the Farmall. In 1920, the drive wheels were shifted from the narrow rear to the wide front. This move was probably prompted by Legge's insistence that the machine, "at least look like a tractor." This version also featured the automatic differential brake that was used on the Farmall. Note also that the "front" and "rear" of the tractor was a slippery concept; the 1920 version sported three forward and three reverse gears and a reversible seat so that it could run either way. Also, the engine was rotated and was now in line rather than transversely mounted.

This machine was known as the "cultivating tractor," and late 1920 photographs show tractors bearing the name, "Farm-all." The Farmall was under way, although it had a long way to go. The tractor was reviewed in an IHC memorandum as too cumbersome, too heavy, the steering action slow, and too difficult to get sufficient gang shift.

Benjamin's Presentation

Despite these shortcomings, Benjamin was still a firm believer in the all-purpose tractor. IHC executives were divided on the topic, and the upcoming release of the all-new McCormick-Deerings did not help Benjamin's cause. Benjamin built his case on a comparison of the International 8-16, the Moline Universal, and a proposed Farmall 8-16. Each machine was evaluated in

The Farmall was introduced in Texas, where the market for the McCormick-Deering 10-20 was weak. The Farmall was well received, as it made just enough of a difference to make cotton farming profitable. This Farmall was photographed near Burlington, Iowa.

In 1925, Harvester sent a group from the general office down to Texas to see what the Texas sales department had to say about the Farmall. The Texas group wanted the tractor put into regular production. When the general office staff balked, Houston sales manager Jim Ryan said, "If you don't adopt it for production, we will organize a company in Houston and build it down here." Needless to say, Farmall production was expanded in 1925.

The original Farmall became known as the Farmall Regular. This one is in its element—cultivation. The spry, maneuverable Farmall turned a belt or pulled a two-bottom plow ably, but the tricycle design offered great visibility and was an ideal setup for working row crops.

how it would operate eleven different pieces of machinery: a manure spreader; a two-bottom 14-inch plow; a double-disk harrow; two drills used as a single unit; a four-row corn planter; a two-row cultivator; a 12-foot mower; 17-foot shock gatherer; 17-foot hay gatherer; binder and shocker; and a one-row corn picker.

The Universal operated nine of the machines alone. The International 8-16 performed four operations without horses or additional persons. The Farmall could operate all 11 implements with only one operator. This was the true strength of the Farmall, and Benjamin had to play to it strongly to keep the project alive.

A film of a Farmall operating a 10-foot shocker and binder at Harvester Farm was shown to IHC executives on December 13, 1920. Immediately afterward, the group met to discuss the fate of the Farmall program for 1921. Most were unenthusiastic about the tractor. Despite the tractor's potential as an all-purpose machine, it was pointed out that the tractor and all of the accompanying implements would be a sizable investment and that using the array of attachments would be complex for the average farmer. Also, the design was too heavy. Naturally, the failure of the Motor Cultivator was brought up as another negative aspect of the project.

Beyond the question of whether or not the farmer would buy such a machine, it was debated whether such a machine could be built. Remember, the Farmall of 1920 was balky, heavy, and slow. Its lineage was the Motor Cultivator, a failed embarrassment. There was little reason to believe a workable machine could be constructed.

First Experimentals

Despite the fact that most IHC executives had little faith in the projected, it was determined that further exploration of Benjamin's concept for a general purpose tractor was worthwhile. Five experimentals were authorized to be built in 1921, at a cost of over $150,000 due to the fact that each example would be built by hand. Benjamin and a handful of engineers working with him on the project were reportedly the only people in the company with much enthusiasm left for the Farmall.

In January of 1921, the authorization for five tractors was changed to two lightweight versions of the Farmall. The Farmall of 1920 weighed about 4,000 pounds. A lighter version was the right direction. Interestingly, the change in authorization was based on a drawing of a lightweight Farmall that Benjamin did not recall, although he assumed it was a pencil sketch.

At the same time, the cultivator was changed to mount to the front of the tractor. According to Arnold Johnson, an engineer working on Farmall attachments,

The Farmall design was most certainly an IHC innovation, but that didn't keep them out of a patent infringement suit. A claim was made about the Ronning patent, which had some similarities to the Farmall design. Harvester's patent department felt the claim of infringement was mainly bogus, and could be avoided by not using shifting cultivator gangs. The company decided to use them, and ended up paying Ronning $1 for every Farmall built, including the F Series.

the switch to a front-mounted cultivator went over well with his department and gained favor for the Farmall concept.

Benjamin kept a steady stream of information flowing to Legge. A document was prepared comparing costs between a farm using eight horses, six horses and a Fordson, and a Farmall and two horses. The figures impressed Legge, and he passed the document around the company.

Benjamin then proposed a version of the Fordson tractor with the front wheels close together and raising the ground clearance in the rear. Such a machine could plow adequately and also cultivate. Benjamin felt such a machine would surely reach the market, and that it was only a matter of whether IHC or Ford built it.

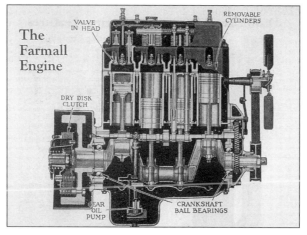

This cutaway from a 1928 brochure illustrates some of the most significant features of the IHC engine. The ball bearings were introduced on the McCormick-Deering 15-30 and 10-20, and increased the life of the engine. Removable cylinder sleeves had been around since the Titans. The basic design of the engine, like the rest of the tractor, is still used today. The engine had a bore of 3 3/4 inches and a stroke of 5 inches and ran at 1,200 rpm. The crank was lubricated by a combination of splash and a gear-circulating pump.

Farmall Under Fire

In the meantime, the company called a special conference to discuss what could be done about Ford. The Fordson was killing IHC in sales, and solutions were hard to find. The Farmall program was discussed as a possible solution, and Alexander Legge sharply criticized the tractor's development. Johnston jumped to the Farmall's defense, and a chorus of lukewarm support followed. Some felt the Farmall could be developed into a better machine than the Fordson, and most thought there was promise in the idea. The result was that 100 Farmalls were ordered to be built for 1922. Also, a new line of implements were to be developed for the McCormick-Deering machines.

The Farmall design continued to evolve, and the order to build 100 was reduced substantially to explore

This McCormick-Deering Number 10 corn picker was part of the extensive development of implements designed specifically for the Farmall. The 25-bushel Number 10 could pick and husk about eight acres of corn in a 10-hour day at 2 miles per hour, or 12 acres a day at 3 miles per hour. In the 1920s, sales of corn pickers were limited, as manual labor was still the dominant technique for corn harvesting.

the new designs. The gangs on the cultivator were designed so that they shifted when the front wheel turned, allowing the operator to easily follow the rows when cultivating. The shifting gangs were an important step forward, but the engineering department staffers were the only proponents of the idea.

Sometime in 1921, the chain drive was abandoned in favor of an enclosed gear drive similar to the type used on the McCormick-Deering tractors. By the close of 1921, demonstrations of prototype Farmalls had gained the tractor some grudging respect, although the sales department was not interested, and Legge stated development was too slow.

Although Legge wrote some scathing comments in his memo, he also made sure Benjamin received enough support. Times were tough for the general purpose tractor program in 1921, and Legge knew that Benjamin was feeling down. Legge told a fellow employee, "Charlie, for heaven's sake go to Benjamin and see if you can give him some help and encouragement. He's got a real job on his hands and we want to see him succeed." Despite Legge's constant criticism of the Farmall project, he believed in the concept and in Benjamin.

The Farmall is Born

In January of 1922, the first official company decision on the Farmall was recorded, and 20 machines were authorized to be built (company decisions are dated company documents ordering engineering actions such as new models, experimentals, and changes). The engine used a 3 3/4x5-inch bore and stroke and ran at 1,200 rpm. A throttle governor and high-tension magneto were used, and cooling was a closed thermosyphon system with a radiator

and fan. Lubrication was splash complemented by a gear circulating pump, and the engine was started on gasoline and then switched over to kerosene. The tractor weighed approximately 3,500 pounds. A PTO and power lift were listed as standard equipment. This machine had a reversible seat and could be operated in either direction. Company records list 17 examples built.

At the time this decision was made, Legge was still skeptical of the Farmall. In a memo to a fellow executive, Legge wrote, "About the only thing we have settled so far is that we have done a very poor job of putting them [Farmalls] together, which suggests that you should try to strengthen your engineering staff." Such stiff criticism reflected the mood of the company.

The day after Legge's memo was written, Benjamin demonstrated a lighter version of the Farmall at the Hinsdale Farm. The machine apparently fared well. Before Legge left Hinsdale, the original order for 20 Farmalls was canceled, and the lighter version Benjamin demonstrated was to be developed further.

The Weight Debate

Early in 1923, the Farmall debate centered on power, weight, and cost. It was felt that the tractor needed to be capable of pulling two 12-inch plow bottoms and needed to weigh about 3,000 pounds. Cutting back features and quality to reduce cost was seen as a mistake. Note that the weight of the Farmall would creep to just over 4,000 pounds by 1925.

The manufacturing arm of IHC was occupied building McCormick-Deering tractors, so the engineering department would have to construct the 1923 machines. Also, it was decided that the tractors needed to be capable of pulling existing implements as well as custom-made units. Beyond the production issues, some feared that the Farmall would harm McCormick-Deering 10-20 sales. A maximum of 25

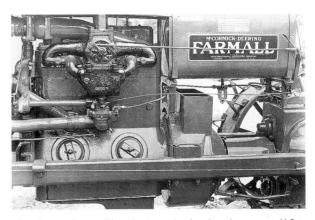

This is the Farmall convertible intake. By opening the valve, exhaust gas would flow around the intake, heating the air-fuel mixture so that the tractor could burn kerosene or distillate. The valve could be closed for gasoline operation, which did not require the intake manifold to be warmed.

McCORMICK-DEERING FARMALL AND EQUIPMENT

FARM WITH FARMALLS

For Lower Production Costs

By the time this brochure was printed for the 1930 season, the Farmall was receiving top billing at Harvester. Concerns about hurting the sales of the 10-20 were discarded for the tractor that had farmers reaching for their pocketbooks and the competition scrambling to build a row crop tractor.

Farmalls were authorized to be built in 1923, along with 25 cultivating attachments. The specifications for the machines were essentially the same as those of the 1922 machine, with the exception of trimming about 300 pounds of weight.

At the same time, Legge was discouraged to discover that the engineering department was developing several types of rear gear drive. He felt the tractor had been developed enough, and that there was not time nor resources for drastic engineering changes. Legge wrote, "I think per-

The Farmall was big news by about 1930, although initial reactions to the tractor were mixed. Although the tricycle design looks natural enough today, it was quite unusual when compared to the standard tread tractors of its day. Alexander Legge, the company president, insisted that the Farmall be designed so it "at least looked like a tractor." A Texas cotton grower said, "It's homely as the Devil, but if you don't want to buy one, you'd better stay off the seat."

with an oiler. Also, fuel capacity was increased to 13 gallons. The new tractor sold for a little less than a $1,000.

The production run was limited to 200 units. The numbers were kept small mainly to avoid hurting sales of the McCormick-Deering 10-20, as the Farmall would sell for the same price. The tractors were sold through dealerships, and each model was closely monitored to determine performance and reliability.

In the showroom, the tractor had some other hurdles to overcome. The tricycle design was unusual at the time, and the Farmall was rather gangly and unfinished when compared to the compact, more graceful lines of the popular standard tractors like the McCormick-Deerings. One Texas cotton grower said, "It's homely as the Devil, but if you don't want to buy one you'd better stay off the seat."

The tractor sold for $950 in 1924, and 200 were built and sold. Throughout 1924, the tractor's performance was lauded. Company executives believed the tractor would probably kill the McCormick-Deering 10-20, but also felt that it would be better for an IHC product (rather than a competitor's) to knock off the 10-20.

Strong Support From Texas

For 1925, the Farmall was again improved. The changes were fairly slight, but covered most of the tractor. A host of systems were simplified, including the gear shift, starting crank, steering gear, front bolster assembly, differential assembly, transmission assembly, and even the tool box. In addition, the wheel hubs and transmission case were strengthened and a muffler and air cleaner were added. The tractor weighed just over 4,000 pounds. International management's reluctance to put the Farmall into production resulted in a better machine. With each delay, the tractor was refined and improved.

Although only 250 were originally authorized to be built in 1925, the demand prompted IHC to build 838 Farmalls that year. The majority of these were sent to Texas, and were sold for $100 more than the 10-20. It was felt that the tractors would sell to cotton growers, and open the market to IHC without hurting 10-20 sales. Interestingly, IHC did not devote an advertising budget to the Farmall. This move reflected the company's desire to avoid interfering with McCormick-Deering sales. The publications of the time reflect the decision, as Farmall ads are scarce and IHC's magazine hardly mentioned the Farmall until 1926.

The reports were again favorable on the 1925 machines. In a company memo, G. A. Newgent responded to queries about how the Farmall was performing in Texas. Rather than reply in his own words, he gathered a few statements from farmers who were using the new machine. They included the following:

"I have used my Farmall eight months and on one occasion it was run six days and six nights without a stop except to refill it with

haps it is true that in the past we have brought out some of our designs a little too hastily; however, this is not true of the Farmall, as you have been building it up and down for five or six years and by this time ought to have a pretty fair judgment as to what is the best and cheapest plan to follow." Whatever the new development may have been, Legge's letter put an end to it.

The 25 prototypes were assembled and sent into the field. Performance reports were favorable. The tractor cultivated efficiently, steered easily, plowed well, was durable, and had respectable power on the belt.

More Improvements in 1924

The tractor was strengthened in an assortment of key areas for 1924. The bolster became a single casting, the bull gear housing was strengthened, and the rear axle was increased in diameter. The drawbar fastening was enlarged. The rear axle roller bearings were equipped

This shot asks more questions than it answers, as it was completely unlabeled. This appears to be a dealership with the Farmall on the showroom floor. The unit bolted to the floor looks like a generator of some kind, although it could also be something that was used to demonstrate the belt pulley. And the little guy in the hat? Your guess is as good as mine. Note the nifty cover over the magneto.

fuel. I have tested it thoroughly and I am satisfied as the purchase of another recently proves."

"Well, I am buying my second Farmall today. When I bought the first last spring I was afraid it would give me considerable trouble as it looked spiderly, but there has not been a cent spent on it and it pulls as well today as it did the day it was delivered to me."

"There are wonderful daydreams and visions possible to a driver of horses."—Letter from a retired farmer, *Tractor Farming*, 1927

"My wife uses a nickel's worth of ice per day and the drippings from the ice box are more than ample to water my Farmall."

Newgent went on to write that the 250 Farmall owners were, without exception, extremely pleased with the Farmalls. He closed with this: "When a farmer buys a Farmall he joins the sales force of the International Harvester Company."

'If You Don't Build It, We Will'

That was strong testimony, but another Texas sales rep had stronger testimony to offer. Several general office men—including representatives from sales, manufacturing, and engineer Bert Benjamin—met with a group of International's Texas salesmen. The Texas representatives wanted the company to build the Farmall for regular production. P. Y. Timmons, the general office manager of tractor sales, said that it might affect sales of the McCormick-Deering 10-20. The response was that the Texas branches didn't sell many 10-20s. J. F. Jones, general office sales manager, commented that if anyone was going to build a tractor that would displace the 10-20, it might as well be Harvester. Lastly, Jim Ryan, manager at Houston, said, "If you don't

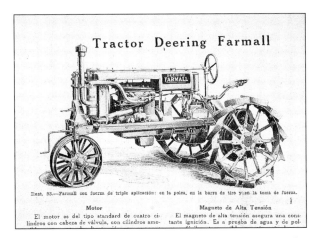

Tractor Deering Farmall

Ilust. 33.—Farmall con fuerza de triple aplicación: en la polea, en la barra de tiro y en la toma de fuerza.

Motor

El motor es del tipo standard de cuatro cilindros con cabeza de válvula, con cilindros amo-

Magneto de Alta Tensión

El magneto de alta tensión asegura una cons-
tante ignición. Es a prueba de agua y de pol-

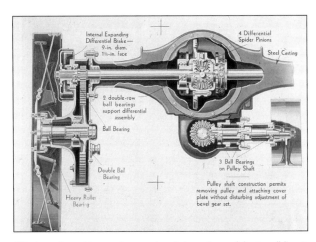

Yes, Virginia, there is a Santa Claus, and Harvester did build a host of tractors that were simply "Deerings." This brochure was printed in Spanish, leading one to believe that these machines were export-only products. International used names as marketing tools, the result being a plethora of designations for each model. The true name for the original Farmall would be the International Harvester Company's McCormick-Deering Farmall (later known as the Regular).

This dropped-rear drive was the strength and the weakness of the Farmall line. It allowed the tractors the high-ground clearance necessary for row crop cultivation. The drive was also heavy and expensive to build. When the competition figured out larger rear wheels would eliminate the need for such a drive, Harvester followed suit. The F-12 was the first of the line to lose the dropped-rear drive, and benefited doubly with a straight axle that made rear tread width adjustment a snap.

The Farmall was nimble and easy to drive compared to the traditional standard tread tractors of the day. The Farmall turned on a dime, partially in thanks to a cable system that activated the inside rear brake when turning sharply. This would spin the tractor around on the rear tire.

Let's Figure This Out

And see how to place

"A Farmall on Every Farm"

———

The farmer has heard of tractors and about tractors for several years—and possibly to him a tractor is just a tractor.

———

The Farmall is more than a tractor—it is all-purpose farm power. It does all the work of any other type of tractor of equal capacity and in addition it will plant and cultivate row crops and supply the power for putting up the hay crop.

———

The time and labor saving effected by using a Farmall is such an outstanding factor—play it up. One man with a Farmall can do the work of two to three men and six to ten horses.

———

But it's not enough to tell the farmer that—you have to show him. Take a Farmall out to his place and let him see for himself what it will do, how much it will do, and how nicely it operates.

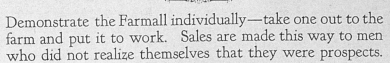

———

Demonstrate the Farmall individually—take one out to the farm and put it to work. Sales are made this way to men who did not realize themselves that they were prospects.

———

The Harvester Company is paving the way through national advertising, direct-mail campaigns, letters, posters, films, slides and other agencies. It's up to you to demonstrate the Farmall on every farm.

———

Sharpen up—get busy and you will have

"A Farmall on Every Farm"

By late in the 1920s, management's initial reluctance regarding the Farmall was quelled by the enthusiastic response of farmers using the tractors. This brochure urges dealers to demonstrate the Farmall. For the time, the Farmall looked strange and getting the farmer behind the wheel was the best way to make a sale. Also, as a Texan salesman said, "When a farmer buys a Farmall, he joins the sales force of the International Harvester Company."

The International Harvester Company sold much more than just tractors, and it was continually searching for successful new lines that fit into its product line. Milkers were such an addition, and could be purchased with a McCormick-Deering engine to power them.

adopt it for production, we will organize a company in Houston and build it down here."

This kind of statement was hard to ignore. Even so, there was still some concern about producing a tractor that competed with the McCormick-Deering. In December of 1925, Legge wrote that although the Farmall production for 1926 would be increased, he felt sales should be confined as much as possible to territories where its current lineup did not sell or work particularly well. Legge's concern was that the sales staff would put all its efforts toward the new Farmall and let down on promoting the other tractors.

Regular Production Begins

In 1926, the Farmall's sales began to take off, and IHC was finally backing the Farmall concept. A new plant was opened specifically to build Farmall tractors. The plant was known as Farmall Works and, once it got started, tractors would roll out the doors at an incredible rate.

The machine received a generous splash of attention in *Tractor Farming*, IHC's promotional magazine. The Farmall was on the cover of the March-April 1926

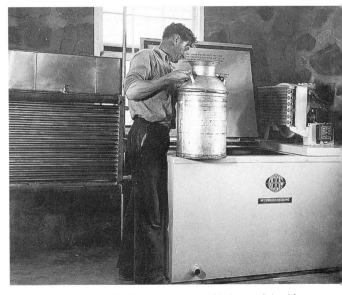

International also built and sold refrigeration equipment. This piece was designed for the barn, but later incarnations would be targeted squarely at the kitchen. The line began in 1935, and it did not prove especially successful.

Harvester had more luck putting tractors into unusual places than putting IHC refrigerators in the kitchen. The Fairway Regular (later known as the Fairway) used wheels that were either smooth or equipped with small spiked lugs to perform an assortment of jobs at golf courses.

issue, and the magazine lauded the merits of the company's "new" machine. "For the last three years, this new tractor has been proving its mettle and merit in considerable numbers in a few limited sections, primarily the Southwest cotton territory," one article read. It went on, "Quantity production is now getting under way, though it will be some time even yet before production can overtake the demand, especially now that the Farmall will be supplied, on order, to any section of the country."

The 1926 machine was again improved, and it certainly benefited from the long development phase. Each year, a few new problem areas were identified and rectified. The result was that, by 1926, the Farmall was a very solid machine.

The Farmall Fires Up

Sales exploded to nearly 25,000 in 1928, and the Farmall was off to the races. It did just as IHC management hoped and feared. The McCormick-Deering 10-20 was pushed aside, as was the rest of the industry.

A narrow-tread version of the Farmall was built to accommodate farmers who required a narrower wheel set. According to IHC documentation, the need for such a tractor was especially great in Argentina, so these tractors are

Farmall Regular and Fairway Production

Year	Production
1924	200
1925	838
1926	4,430
1927	9,502
1928	24,899
1929	35,517
1930	42,093
1931	14,088
1932	3,080
Total Prod.	**134,647**

Note: Several IHC archive documents indicate that Regulars were sold in 1933 and 1934, although exact figures were not available; it is unclear (and doubtful) if tractors were still being built after 1932.
Source: McCormick/IHC Archives, "Tractor Production Schedule"

Putting the Regular on the golf course began quite early in the development of the Farmall. The first golf course wheel attachments were authorized in January 1926, and the narrow tread Farmall received the same option in 1929.

This photo was taken in October 1928 of a Farmall Fairway model cutting grass at Monroe Country Club near Monroe, Wisconsin. Note the backrest fixed to the seat.

probably quite rare in America. The tractor was equipped with a offset rear hub that narrowed the rear tread width from 80 inches to just over 63 inches. The narrow tread was authorized in the spring of 1927. Interestingly, IHC documentation also refers to a 57-inch rear-tread-width Farmall, which may have been a domestic narrow-tread version.

Another special edition of the Farmall was the Farmall Fairway, which was designed for use on golf courses. Smooth wheels were used, as well as offset wheels that narrowed the tread width to 57 inches. In 1929, a set of

lugs was authorized for the golf course machines, probably due to wheel-spin on wet grass or hillsides. The lugs were simply small spikes.

Perhaps the rarest of the Farmall attachment packages was the orchard fenders. These were available from 1931 to 1934, and then were dropped due to lack of demand. This is easy to believe, as the ideal orchard tractor is low-slung, which the Farmall is not.

In 1930, a field change was supplied for early 1925 model Farmalls (serial numbers QC700 to 8821). The

Another Farmall Fairway at work, this one at the Chariton Golf Course in Chariton, Iowa.

Bert R. Benjamin

The design of the Farmall is largely credited to one IHC engineer, Bert R. Benjamin. He designed the tractor at a time when the company was putting a huge amount of available resources into the new integral frame McCormick-Deerings. With the company focused and financially ransomed to the new machines, there was little room or interest for another new design. Benjamin's persistence in forwarding his ideas for the Farmall resulted in a revolutionary tractor that changed the way the entire industry approached tractor design.

Benjamin grew up on a farm near Newton, Iowa, and studied agricultural engineering at the college in Ames, now known as Iowa State University. He began his employment in 1893 with the McCormick Harvesting Company as a draftsman in the experimental department. In 1901, he became Chief Inspector of the McCormick Company, a post he held until 1902, when the International Harvester Company was formed. He continued in a similar position until 1910, when he was named Superintendent of the Experimental Department.

In 1922, Benjamin was named Assistant to the Chief Engineer at the IHC Corporate Offices, which was where he took the Farmall under his wing. He guided the Farmall through a series of set-backs and suffered criticism from those who could pull his funding, and triumphed. The Farmall proved all the nay-sayers wrong, and was perhaps Benjamin's defining moment.

Benjamin may have had a hand in the other farm tractor success story of first part of the century, as well. He was sent to the Ford plant to cooperate on work on the Fordson in 1917. A war board decision designed to increase production put him there. The extent of his contribution is unknown, but it is supremely ironic that he was sent to help Ford, the company that would dominate the industry—and IHC—by the 1920s.

Although Benjamin is best known for his work on the Farmall, he was granted 140 patents in his 47-year career with IHC. His work with the power take-off was another industry first, and the rest of his patents include harvesting equipment as well as a wide variety of tractor advances ranging from shifting cultivator gangs and the drawbar to the seat spring and draft couplings.

Columnist Elmer Baker wrote about Benjamin in a 1959 issue of *Implement and Tractor*. He had this to say: "Then one man, not a committee, got an idea that a tractor that wouldn't displace the horses and mules on a farm was only half of the answer to the farm tractor. So he started to work on units that would . . . cultivate . . . as well as doing the land locomotive work of other tractors.

"That man was Bert R. Benjamin, and he worked for the Harvester company experimental department. He may have had an office on the old 7th floor at 606 S. Michigan Ave., Chicago, but we always found him somewhere around that old shack close to McCormick Works next to the Illinois and Michigan Ship Canal."

In 1937, Benjamin left the corporate offices and was assigned to research work, which he continued until his retirement in 1939. Benjamin was all engineer, as he remained in hands-on positions to the end of his career.

The American Society of Agricultural Engineers honored him with the 1943 Cyrus Hall McCormick gold medal. In 1968, Iowa State University's College of Engineering awarded him the Professional Achievement Citation in Engineering.

Benjamin died in October of 1969 at age 99.

---

change package improved the tractors' durability, especially in dusty conditions. Most of the changes centered around better sealing against dirt. The change was authorized in February of 1930.

Farmalls Sold in 1933 and 1934

According to most documentation, production of the original Farmall ended in 1932. But, an assortment of company documents indicate that a limited number of Farmalls were sold in 1933 and 1934. The most convincing of these is the record of payments to the Ronning family. The Ronnings owned a patent to several features similar to those of the Farmall. The key feature of the Ronning patent concerns the shifting cultivator gangs. The company agreed to pay the Ronning family one dollar for every Farmall Regular, F-30, F-20, F-12, and F-14 sold. Records of the payments for 1933 and 1934 show several hundred dollars paid for Farmall Regulars produced and sold. It seems highly unlikely that the company would make this payment unless the tractors had been sold. More likely than not, a few tractors from the 1932 production run were left over and sold in 1933 and 1934.

Pneumatic Tires Retrofit

Near the end of the Farmall's production run, IHC authorized optional pneumatic tires for its tractor lineup. Although the decision wasn't signed until 1933, after the Regular was out of production, it listed 9.00x36 rear and 6.00x16 front pneumatic tires as additions for the Farmall. It is doubtful that many Farmall Regulars were equipped with these tires from the factory, but dealers and owners almost certainly retrofit pneumatic tires. The attachment number for the rear tires for the Regular was 25711-D; the number for the front tires was 25494-D.

Lift-All Retrofit

A later retrofit was a hydraulic lift, which was authorized in 1945. The lift was a version of the new Lift-All adapted to Farmall Regular, F-20, and F-30 tractors. The part numbers were 350420R91 for the Regular, 350421R91 for the F-20, and 350422R91 for the F-30.

The Farmall design proved to have lasting merit, and the Farmall formed the basis of the IHC lineup for the next several decades. Engineer Benjamin succeeded in his quest and created an all-purpose tractor. The road to his success was filled with potholes and road blocks. C. W. Gray claims the resistance to the Farmall was as much political as it was practical. Benjamin was often the only proponent for the Farmall, and Gray states that Benjamin threatened to leave unless the project received the funding and support he felt it deserved.

History owes a tip of the hat to Benjamin and the Farmall, as both brought in a new era of farm power. The horse, once vital to farming, was gradually replaced with the tractor, and the Farmall was the first tractor designed around and able to fill the horse's shoes. Some debated the merits of replacing flesh with steel, a companion animal with a cold steel beast, but it was impossible to debate the merits of increased productivity and decreased manual labor. The general-purpose tractor had arrived. It appeared in the form of the Farmall.

"A man can earn more money with a tractor than he can idly dreaming behind a slow-moving team of horses."
Tractor Farming, 1927

Chapter Four

Unstyled TracTracTors

"Farm equipment was not selling as well and other products were necessary for the established dealers to remain in business."
—*Implement & Hardware Trade Journal,* 1924

From the beginning, IHC was a diverse company. Its truck line was ample evidence of this alone, and a closer look reveals the company tried everything from cream separators to home appliances. One of the more logical product groups for the company to produce was crawlers. Companies like Holt, Best, and Cletrac demonstrated a definite demand for crawlers in orchards, the giant wheat fields of the Northwest, for logging operations, and on construction sites. The market potential was quite large, and IHC naturally looked to adapt its existing technology to crawlers.

McCORMICK-DEERING TracTracTor

Announcing THE NEW

McCORMICK-DEERING TracTracTor

With Henry Ford out of the way and Farmalls flying out of the showrooms as fast as IHC could build them, the company explored new markets and looked to expand in the late 1920s. Despite an oncoming economic slump, the scare with Fordson was a graphic demonstration of the fact that a large company cannot hang its hat on one or two product areas. For IHC to survive, they had to find success in some alternate markets.

The company experimented with four- and six-wheel design models on the International 8-16, the company's favorite test bed. The prototype tractors were quite popular with those lucky enough to get their hands on one. The four- and six-wheel-drive models were never put into regular production, but they provided some valuable engineering experience with steering a vehicle without turning the front wheels.

The company first experimented seriously with crawlers during the late 1920s. The primary problem with adapting a wheel tractor chassis to crawler tracks was steering. The existing power train could use the rear axles to drive the track if the machine had only to go straight. Turning required separate activation of the left and right track. Stop the left, drive the right, and the tractor would pivot left. Reverse one and drive the other forward, and the tractor would spin in a circle.

To accomplish this, steering clutches were required to drive the left and right treads separately. Ideally, the clutches needed to be progressive as well. While sudden engagement was great for turning tightly or spinning around in corners, gradual turns would require simply letting off on one side or the other rather than total disengagement. To further complicate matters, track brakes were necessary to pivot neatly and to stop the machine.

So, the first challenge was to build a reliable, durable, and cost-efficient method to drive the tracks.

Left

The TracTracTor line was International's line of crawlers, which had its share of ups and downs. This orchard-type T-20 is cutting under Austrian peas with a B-8 offset disk near Talbotton, Georgia.

Above

The first International crawler was known simply as the "TracTracTor." Note that the rear drive sprocket for the tracks is larger than the front. This was in part due to the fact that the steering clutches were housed in that rear sprocket, meaning service and wear were problems.

95

The T-20 was the first of the TracTracTors to be produced in volume, and saw plenty of use pulling combines in open grain fields, especially in the Northwest. Its predecessors were a variety of crawlers adapted from the McCormick-Deering 10-20 and 15-30. The first 50 T-20s, produced in 1931 were badged as Model 15s.

This T-20 is at work on a logging site in North Dana, Massachusetts. The man in the suit was the salesmen for the territory.

The T-20 relocated the steering clutches to the rear of the machine. Logging was one of the more popular uses for the little crawlers, which worked well for skidding logs and clawing their way through muddy or snowy woods.

When IHC got serious about building a crawler, it turned to machines the company knew well: the McCormick-Deering 10-20 and 15-30.

10-20 TracTracTor

The first IHC production crawler began with the McCormick-Deering 10-20. Perhaps the company speculated that a crawler might be a way to salvage the McCormick-Deering chassis after the inevitable loss of sales to the Farmall Regular. Per-

haps the McCormick-Deering was simply well suited to conversion.

Initial experiments were with crawlers that used a French & Hecht track adapted to an existing tractor. French & Hecht built track conversion kits for existing tractors, and gave IHC an existing mechanism to try out.

The company documentation of the 10-20 TracTracTor, or No. 20 as it later dubbed, is sketchy and contradictory. One 1940s document entitled "International Harvester Industrial Power Activities" traces the devel-

The steering clutches are key to any crawler, and take a lot of abuse. The crawler turns by slipping the inside clutch, and the clutches are fully engaged only when going straight ahead. Servicing the T-20's steering clutches was relatively easy, as they were accessible from the rear.

This nearly completed chassis clearly shows that the T-20 used the "bath-tub" style integral frame like the McCormick-Deering 10-20 and 15-30. Note the huge leaf spring in the center, which suspended the chassis. International called the spring an "Equalizer Spring."

The T-20 was just as popular in the orchard as it was for logging operations. The rounded fenders were designed specifically for orchard use. This T-20 is pulling a three-gun Hardie sprayer in an orchard near Escondido, California.

TracTracTor 10-20 Production

(Also known as No. 20)

Year	Production
1928	NA
1929	472
1930	78
1931	975
Total Prod.	**1,525**

Source: McCormick/IHC Archives,
"Tractor Production Schedule"

The T-20 used this generator to power the lighting system. This photo was taken at the Tractor Works in Chicago, Illinois.

opment of the tractors with recollections of engineers. According to that document, IHC began adapting the 10-20 to tracks in 1927.

Another document listing production figures shows that eight of the 10-20 TracTracTors were built in 1925, with a few hundred per year constructed until 1929 and less than a hundred per year in 1930 to 1932.

Total production figures are also contradictory, with *Endless Tracks in the Woods* listing 7,500 10-20 TracTracTors built and simple serial number math indicating about 1,500 were actually made. One company document says that 1,000 were built, while the company production chart from the archives lists 1,454 produced, which is consistent with the serial numbers. The 1924

date seems plausible enough, as the company was well on its way to recovering from the tractor wars at that point. Serial number data fits, as well.

The 10-20 TracTracTors were built at Tractor Works. Problems with the early TracTracTors centered on track roller and bearing wear, mainly because they ran down in the dirt. Steel guards were built to cover the lower rollers, but the ultimate solution would be sealed bearings.

The 10-20 TracTracTor was tested at Nebraska in October 1931. It weighed 7,010 pounds, and was rated at

This T-20 is pulling a power spray rig that is spraying sodium arsenate on Thomson Seedless Grapes to kill vine hoppers, bugs, and Spanish mizzles. The tractor moves along at about 1 mile per hour, and can cover about 25 acres a day. This 400-acre grape farm was in Orange Grove, California.

T-20 production continued until 1939, with about 15,000 machines built. This T-20 is operating a salt crusher at a plant near the Great Salt Lake in Utah.

18.33 drawbar horsepower and 26.59 belt horsepower. The carburetor was a Zenith K5.

The crawler equipment made the TracTracTor about 2,000 pounds heavier than the McCormick-Deering 10-20. The additional weight and the traction afforded by the treads let the TracTracTor pull about twice as hard at the drawbar as the McCormick-Deering. The TracTrac-Tor compared favorably to its crawler competition, as well. It was about 1,300 pounds heavier than the comparable Cletrac, the Model 15. The IHC machine out-pulled the Cletrac by about 20 percent. The TracTracTor also out-pulled the Caterpillar Model 20 at the drawbar, although the Cat pulled at a slightly higher speed.

Despite the TracTracTor's respectable showing, it was never produced in quantity. The machine performed well enough to convince IHC that crawlers were

The TD-40 was a big, powerful machine designed for construction or heavy logging jobs. The machines were huge, weighing in at about six tons, and cost about twice as much as a medium-sized wheel tractor.

The big TD-40 could move snow with ease, as it packed 44 drawbar and 52 belt horse-power under the hood. The gasoline-burning six-cylinder put out similar amounts of power, but didn't have the low-rpm torque of the powerful diesels. The diesel was more popular than the gas version, and production of both models ended in 1939.

These T-35s are operating in oil bath test stations. The lack of badging and the fact that they are being tested make it highly probable that these are experimental or pre-production models.

a viable product, and the company continued to develop new models.

15-30 TracTracTor

The 15-30 TracTracTor was the crawler adaptation of the McCormick-Deering 15-30 wheel tractor. It seemed like a natural for an IHC crawler experiment, seeing as the company was already using the 10-20 as a crawler. Records on these machines are pretty scarce, but according to existing records, experimentation began in 1926 with an adaptation of the McCormick-Deering 15-30 that used brakes at the drive sprockets for differential steering. In 1928, the steering clutches from the 10-20 TracTracTor were adapted to the 15-30-based tractor. Work continued through 1929, and in 1930 the tractor was redesigned with steering clutches and brakes that could be serviced from the rear. You'll remember that steering clutches were the key to the crawlers, and that they were heavily abused and in need of regular adjustment and replacement.

In the document, "International Harvester Industrial Power Activities," this 1930 development work is discussed, as well as the new ability to service the brakes and clutches from the rear. The document also states specifically that the 15-30 TracTracTor was never put into production.

Model 15 TracTracTor

The Model 15 is the most intriguing of the early crawler models. A few photos are shown in *150 Years of International Harvester*, with little information. The machine is distinctly different than the 15-30 and 10-20 TracTracTor, with equal-sized track wheels, and a distinct guard over the pins and rollers.

According to the scant bits of information available, the Model 15 is the missing link between the 15-30 Trac-TracTor and the T-20. More interestingly, it appears that 50 Model 15s were actually built.

The IHC document, "International Harvester Industrial Power Activities," includes the following:

In 1932, the T-20 was joined by the T-40, a larger gas crawler. The diesel version, the TD-40, appeared one year later. The engines were the same four-cylinder diesel and six-cylinder gas units in the W-40 and WD-40. This TD-40 is skidding logs near Winnipeg, Manitoba.

"The smaller model which we then called the Model 15 TracTracTor was completed early in this year [1930] and went into production in 1931 when 50 machines were built. In 1932, full production was started and the name was changed to T-20 TracTracTor."

The "smaller model" is referenced in the section on the 15-30 TracTracTor as a smaller example of the redesigned 15-30. The new design is referred to as the forerunner of the new line of crawlers.

TracTracTor T-20 Production

Year	Production
1931	50*
1932	1,502
1933	475
1934	746
1935	2,108
1936	3,114
1937	4,018
1938	2,036
1939	1,033
Total Prod.	**15,082**

*1931 machines produced as "Model 15"
Source: 1931–33 from McCormick/IHC Archives, Production Number Chart; 1934–on from *150 Years of International Harvester* by C. H. Wendel

A diesel four-cylinder engine is being installed into a TD-35 frame. Like the rest of the crawler line, the TD-35 used an integral frame with the engine and transmission cradled inside. The design sealed the components from dust and dirt, which was advantageous for the grim conditions in which crawlers usually operated.

The final piece of the puzzle is found on the factory production sheet, which lists 50 T-20 TracTracTors built in 1931. The two numbers match, which seems to indicate that the first statement—that 50 Model 15s were built in 1931—is true. Whether they were built as Model 15s or T-20s is undoubtedly the question, but if they truly exist as Model 15s, perhaps one has or will turn up somewhere.

T-20 TracTracTor

As stated above, the T-20 moniker was applied to the Model 15 in 1932. The T-20 was a bit more powerful than the Model 20, and used the F-20 power plant. The little TracTracTor was small and maneuverable, and was used in a wide variety of situations ranging from orchards to logging to grain harvesting. As you would expect, the crawler was more expensive than the wheel tractors. With a price of about $1,500 in 1935, it was about $400 more

The T-35 was introduced in 1937, and was an engine from the TA-40 installed in a chassis that was a bit lighter than the T-40s.

than its wheeled counterpart, the F-20. Despite the high price, the T-20 was fairly popular. About 15,000 units were sold from 1932 to 1939, when the new line of streamlined crawlers choked off the old T Series.

The T-20's four-cylinder IHC engine—which was the same as used in the F-20—had a bore of 3 3/4 inches and a stroke of 5 inches. The engine was rated at 31 horsepower and was governed to run at 1,250 rpm, 50 rpm higher than the F-20. An air cleaner, oil filter, and fuel filter were used, as was a three-speed transmission. The engine was started on gasoline and switched over to kerosene when warm.

The T-20 weighed 6,250 pounds, and came equipped with a 543-rpm power take-off. The T-20 put out about 25 horsepower at the drawbar. Standard tread width was 41 1/2 inches, although a 51-inch wide tread version was available as well.

The little crawler was quite maneuverable, and could be turned in a six-foot radius. A cab, canopy, belt pulley, front pull hook, and other options could be purchased for the T-20 on special order.

TA-40, TK-40, and TD-40

While small crawlers were great for jobs around the farm or smaller logging operations, the construction and logging markets had a need for large, powerful crawlers. For IHC to be player in these areas, it needed a big machine, and the TA-40, TK-40, and TD-40 were the entrants. They were developed early in 1931, and used a six-cylinder engine. The TD-40 used a four-cylinder diesel engine. Both were built at Tractor Works.

In 1933, the gasoline version became known as the TA-40. The diesel TD-40 was introduced. The tractors were improved that year. The six-cylinder engines built in 1937 and after were equipped to

TracTracTor TA-40, TK-40, and TD-40 Production

Year	Production
1932	232*
1933	476*
1934	850*
1935	1,608*
1936	1,910*
1937	1,416*
1938	880*
1939	967*
Total Prod.	**7,631**

Source: *From McCormick/IHC Archives serial number listings, so numbers are approximate; total is from *150 Years of International Harvester* by C. H. Wendel

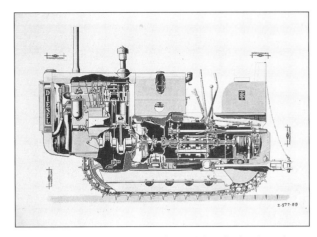

This TD-35 cutaway shows the five-speed transmission, diesel engine, and steering clutches. The T-35 used a combination of steering brakes and the steering clutches to turn.

burn kerosene or distillate. Note that although most company documentation lists the TA-40 and TD-40, advertisements sometimes listed the tractor simply as the T-40 that could be equipped with either a gas or diesel engine.

The TA- and TD-40 were physically larger and much more powerful than the T-20, with the gas tractor rated at 51 horsepower, with 44 horsepower available at the drawbar. The tractor was more than two tons heavier than the T-20, with the gas model weighing 11,200 pounds and the diesel an even 12,000 pounds.

A five-speed transmission was used, allowing the operator to exactly match power to load. Top speed was a galloping four miles per hour. The six-cylinder engine's

This TD-35 was just delivered to a 857-acre farm near McMinnville, Oregon. The crawler is using a McCormick-Deering 24-6 double-disk drill. The man in the tie is the local industrial equipment salesman, and the heavy-set man is the Portland general line manager.

Crawlers were fairly popular in industrial settings. This TD-35 was used by Pan-Am to pull a Bermuda Clipper in Baltimore, Maryland.

bore was 3 5/8 inches and the stroke was 4 1/2 inches. The engine was governed to run at 1,600 rpm. A radiator and fan regulated by a thermostat cooled the big six.

The TA-40 had the smaller 3 5/8-inch bore, while the TK-40 had the larger 3 3/4-inch bore.

The tractor was available in a standard and wide-tread version, and sold for nearly $3,000, making it an expensive vehicle at the time, although not out of line for large crawlers. The TA-40, TK-40, and TD-40 could be equipped with an assortment of Bucyrus-Erie blades, transforming the crawlers into bulldozers. Options included a power take-off, enclosed cab, electric lights, various sizes of track shoes, and a canopy top.

T-35 and TD-35

The T-35 and TD-35 were slightly less-powerful versions of the big 40s. They were introduced in 1937, and were only produced for three years before the styled Trac-TracTors appeared in 1938.

The T-35 used a six-cylinder engine that could be equipped to burn distillate, kerosene, or gasoline. Burning gas, the big six put out 37 horsepower in Test G at Nebraska, using the engine from the TA-40.

TracTracTor T-35 and TD-35 Production	
Year	Production
1937	2,464
1938	1,659
1939	1,464
Total Prod.	**5,587**

Source: 1936 from *150 Years of International Harvester* by C.H. Wendel; others from serial number data and are approximate

The six-cylinder had an 3 5/8x4 1/2-inch bore and stroke, and ran at 1,750 rpm.

The TD-35 used a diesel engine that produced 42 horsepower on the belt at 1,100 rpm. At the drawbar, the TD-35 put out about 37 horsepower. The TD-35 put out about 9 fewer horsepower than the big TD-40 on the belt, and weighed about 1,5000 pounds less as well.

104

Chapter Five

The
F Series

"Estimates of 1932 farm equipment sales from various reliable and
competent sources indicate average purchases of not
more than sixteen or seventeen dollars."
—Howard E. Everett, *Implement and Tractor*, 1933

As the 1920s closed and became the 1930s, times turned tough for the farmer. As always, difficult times for the farmer are hard on for the agricultural industry. Bad times turned worse and became the Great Depression. Farms dried up and blew away, as did tractor sales. Even so, new model development continued almost unabated. The onslaught of power farming, which was part of the rush of technology known as industrialization, could not be slowed by a mere economic catastrophe. Tractor farming was more economical and efficient than horse farming, and the use of the horse was steadily declining as more and more farms turned to tractors.

The manufacturers seemed to deal with the Depression with considerable aplomb. Production was scaled back, and profits slid significantly, but a surprising amount of research and development was continued. Sales were strong for the tractor industry in 1930, at 200,000 units, but dropped off to only 19,000 tractors sold in 1932, the lowest since 1915. Even so, the International Harvester Company introduced the F-20, F-12, and the industrial version of the McCormick-Deer-

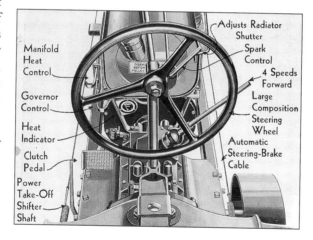

ing 10-20. Obviously, the company was counting on an eventual market rebound. Those predictions would prove correct, although it wouldn't happen until the second half of the decade.

By 1932, International was the number one tractor manufacturer with John Deere number two and J. I. Case third. That order would not change radically through to modern times, as John Deere and International Harvester would remain at the top of the list right into the 1980s.

The 1930s saw some competition show up for the Farmall, as well. Tractor manufacturers saw the success of the Farmall, and looked to build similar machines. Oliver, Massey-Harris, Minneapolis-Moline, Case, and Allis-Chalmers all had row crop tractors by 1930. John Deere was not far behind, and introduced its own row crop tractor.

To respond, IHC first turned to increased horsepower with the F-30 and F-20, and then used a mix of engineering and production savvy and tit-for-tat imitation to build the F-12.

Left

The Farmall line expanded beginning in 1931, bringing new features and more power to the basic Farmall design. The first of the new Farmalls was the F-30, a more powerful iteration of the Regular.

Above

This shows the cockpit of the F-20. The "manifold heat control" was used to switch from burning kerosene or distillate, which required a heated manifold, or gasoline. The radiator shutters controlled (sort of) coolant temperature. The automatic steering cables simply activated the inside rear brake when the front wheel was turned all the way to the right or left.

This F-30 is pulling a McCormick-Deering power spreader. The F-30 provided more power than the Regular in a larger, heavier frame. It weighed about 5,300 pounds, about a ton heavier than the Regular.

The F-12, and later the F-14, were the most significant of the F Series Farmalls. For the first time, the standard tread and cultivating tractors used the same basic power units and similar chassis. The practice was continued to modern times, and saved considerable expense both on the development and the production ends.

The 1930s saw IHC's market dominance challenged and the introduction of several new models spoiled by the ravages of the Great Depression. But IHC was more than up to any challenge, whether it came from other companies or economic slumps. Rather than pull back and wait for times to improve, the company pressed its advantage with more powerful engines and innovative equipment. Tractors continued to roll out of IHC dealerships in impressive quantities, and IHC and the Farmall continued to be the cutting edge of tractor innovation and sales.

Pulling a disc, culti-packer, and a harrow at the Purdue University Experimental Farm near Lafayette, Indiana, this F-30 struts its stuff. The four-cylinder engine was rated for 30 belt and 20 drawbar horsepower, which meant it was capable of pulling a three-bottom plow in most conditions.

The dropped-rear drive on the F-30 was its Achilles heel. Expensive and time-consuming to build, it added weight and cost to the first three Farmall models. It also caused tread width to be adjustable only by reversing the wheels. Note the power lift mechanism mounted to the rear of the differential housing of this F-30.

Farmall F-30

During the development of the original Farmall, which became known as the Regular when the F-30 appeared, an assortment of weights and sizes had been tried; the final version was essentially a medium-heavy version. The experience with a heavier model certainly played a role in the development of the Farmall F-30, a tractor that was simply a larger version of the Farmall Regular.

The F-30 was also confirmation of IHC's worst fears and hopes; the Farmall dramatically slowed sales of the McCormick-Deering 15-30. The sales of the Farmall were so strong that IHC management was convinced to back the concept wholeheartedly, and continue with its successful new design.

The F-30 packed the punch of the 15-30 into a more maneuverable package. It also gave the farmers a reason to replace their McCormick-Deering 15-30s with a new IHC product, which the company had to consider a good thing. The tractor was priced at about $1,150, about $100 less than the 15-30.

The tractor featured a four-speed transmission, one more speed than the Farmall had. At 12 feet, 3 inches, the F-30 was nearly 2 feet longer. It turned tightly, like the original Farmall, but took a 3-foot-larger circumference to do so. Still, a turning radius of just over 17 feet was impressive for a tractor of that size.

The narrow tread version of the F-30 helped for working fields with closely spaced rows. Until the advent of more-adjustable rear hubs, narrow treads were an expensive way for tractor companies to offer the range of adjustment necessary for the wide variety of farms. The F-30 Narrow Tread was authorized in March 1932.

Lighting was experimented with early in tractor development, but it wasn't until later when it became practical to use. Available as an option on the original Farmall and the F-30, as seen above, electric lighting of the 1930s was still a bit short of what was needed to work efficiently at night.

The McCormick-Deering 15-30 turning radius was nearly double that, at 30 feet.

The F-30 weighed about 5,300 pounds, which was 700 pounds less than the 15-30 and nearly 2,000 pounds more than the Regular. The F-30 engine used a 4 1/4x5-inch bore and stroke, making it a shorter stroke and a smaller bore than early McCormick-Deering 15-30s. The F-30 engine ran at 1,150 rpm. The additional 150 rpm was enough to give the F-30 engine more horsepower than the 15-30. Despite the weight disadvantage, the F-30's ability to cultivate and maneuver made it more popular than the 15-30.

The F-30 was available with either a narrow (as shown) or a wide front end. The wide front was authorized in October 1932. This F-30 is pulling a Little Genius plow near Attica, New York.

The high-clearance F-30—also known as the Cane Tractor—was modified to provide higher ground clearance. The model was not authorized until late in F-30 production, sometime late in 1937 or early in 1938. This photograph is dated March 7, 1938.

Early Power Increases

Mind you, the F-30 was originally proposed to be built with a slightly less powerful engine. One of the first decisions on the F-30 concerned an increased-power engine and increased coolant capacity, and that decision received final approval on May 1, 1931. The decision bears a handwritten note stipulating that the serial numbers for the more powerful engines would be AA501 and up. Also, construction of the new engines was to begin at Tractor Works on July 15, 1931. Considering that only 623 F-30s were built in 1931, it's doubtful that any were made with the less powerful engine.

The tractor was equipped with a power take-off and an oiled air filter. The tractor could burn distillate, kerosene, or gasoline. The manifold was switchable, and would route exhaust gas to warm the carburetor. The manifold could be switched over from the dash. Actually, distillate was considered the most economical farm fuel by 1925. It didn't produce nearly as much power as gasoline, but was much less expensive. Kerosene wasn't as economical as distillate, but some farmers still used it, so tractor manufacturers were forced to equip their tractors to burn all three types of fuel.

The F-30 engine also featured a water pump and thermostat. This replaced the shutters used on older models to regulate cooling. An IHC E4A magneto with automatic impulse coupling was also used.

Several specialized versions of the F-30 were built, although information on them is somewhat sketchy. Perhaps the most desirable is the cane tractor, which was a narrow, high-clearance model with a wide front end. The F-30 Cane Tractor and high-clearance models are both known to exist today. Other versions included a narrow tread and wide-front-end narrow tread tractors.

Right
Pneumatic (air-filled rubber) tires were made an option on the Regular and F Series in 1933. Although Allis-Chalmers is credited with debuting pneumatic tires, Harvester was right on their heels. Both worked with Firestone to develop the tires, and both demonstrated pneumatic-tired machines in 1932.

The Farmall developed into a complete line, from the big F-30 down to the little F-12. All three of these models were introduced into the struggling economy of the 1930s, a time when tractor sales for all manufacturers dropped from about 200,000 in 1930 to just 19,000 in 1932. It also marked a decade in which the industry was beginning to catch up to the Farmall and introduce competitive row crop tractors.

The F-20 was the third Farmall model introduced, and was an upgrade of the Regular. Introduced into a weak market in 1932, the tractor sold well when the economy picked up a bit in 1934.

Pneumatic Tires

In 1933, the company authorized pneumatic tires as an option on IHC tractors. The rear tires for the F-30 were 11.25x24s (attachment number 25714-D) and the front tires were 6.00x16s (attachment number 25715-D). Pneumatic tires were a solution to a problem that was becoming increasingly troublesome for the farmer.

Paved roads were becoming more common in rural areas, and lugged steel wheels severely damaged pavement. Laws were passed prohibiting the use of lugged steel wheels on paved roads, and farmers were forced to use planks anytime they needed to cross a paved surface.

Rubber-coated steel bands known as overtires and easily detachable lugs were attempts to solve this prob-

This F-20 is pulling a power spreader near the Purdue University Experimental Farm near West Lafayette, Indiana. The F-20 featured a four-speed transmission and topped out at a blistering 3 3/4 miles per hour with stock gearing. High-speed attachments were available to gear the machine up enough to travel down the road at acceptable speeds.

Farmall F-30 Production

Year	Production
1931	683
1932	3,122
1933	1,222
1934	1,506
1935	3,375
1936	8,057
1937	8,502
1938	1,821
1939	1,020
1940	NA*
Total Prod.	**29,526**

*F-30s were sold into 1940.
Source: McCormick/IHC Archives, 1932 and 1933 from "Tractor Production Schedule"

The F-20 Narrow Tread was designed for use in tighter rows, and was an expensive way to provide the farmer with choices of rear tread widths. The narrow tread version of the F-20 was available early in production, certainly by 1932 and was perhaps introduced alongside the F-20 regular tread. As with other F tractors, tread width was adjustable by flipping the rear rims.

This F-30 equipped with high cane-type wheels is working a 400-acre asparagus field near Rio Vista, California, in 1936. The tractor is more than likely a pre-production model of the Cane Tractor.

Farmall F-20 Production

Year	Production
1932	2,500
1933	3,380*
1934	662*
1935	26,334*
1936	36,033*
1937	35,676
1938	25,268*
1939	13,111*
Total Prod.	**148,690**

*Number of serial numbers issued that year, which is only an approximation of production numbers.
Source: McCormick/IHC Archives, 1932 from "Tractor Production Schedule," 1937 and total from *150 Years of International Harvester*

lem, but were too time-consuming to be practical. Solid rubber tires were in use, mainly on industrial tractors, but they provided poor traction in wet conditions. Chains were a partial solution to this problem, but then the farmer was back to dealing with something that needed to be removed to cross pavement.

B. F. Goodrich experimented with rubber tires that were arched rather than air-filled in 1931, but Firestone provided the solution in the form of the pneumatic—air-inflated rubber—tire. The Firestone tires were introduced on Allis-Chalmer's tractors in 1932, and International demonstrated the same tires on IHC machines that same year.

The pneumatic tires provided good traction in all sorts of conditions, and had the added advantage of an improved

ride for the tractor. In a 1934 test of lugged steel and pneumatic tires, the University of Nebraska Tests found that steel had a slight edge in mowing alfalfa and grass, but pneumatic tires worked more acres per hour while plowing, cultivating, combining, and harvesting crops. Conversely, steel had a slight advantage in fuel economy.

Another advantage of the pneumatic tires was the ability to fill them with water to weight the rear end for traction. Rear wheel weights were commonly used, and water was a simple way to increase rear traction without lugging heavy weights about.

In 1945, the Lift-All was adapted to the F-30 and offered as a retrofit kit with Cylinder Type Hydraulic Lift number 494015891.

The F-20 used an engine similar to that of the Regular with the addition of new intake and exhaust manifolds and a new Zenith carburetor. Bore and stroke did not change. The F-20 engine produced 15 drawbar and 23 belt horsepower when burning kerosene, compared to the Regular's 9 drawbar and 20 belt horsepower on kerosene. The F-20 engine received minor improvements that eked a couple more horsepower out of the engine by the end of production.

The F-20 weighed about 4,500 pounds, just a few hundred pounds more than the Regular. The more powerful engine and bit of additional weight made it better suited for open field plowing without sacrificing the maneuverability and superior cultivating abilities of the original Farmall.

Left
The F-20's wide front axle attachment was authorized in October 1932. The attachment was available for the standard and narrow tread versions of the F-20, F-30, and Regular.

The F-30 proved to be a rugged, maneuverable tractor, and did well for both IHC and the farmer. It was built and sold in respectable numbers until 1939 (with perhaps a few trickling out of the factory in 1940). The tractor slipped out of production when the Farmall tractor line was completely redesigned and the styled Letter Series was introduced.

When compared to its standard tread line-mate, the W-30, the F-30 outsold it at a significant ratio every year except 1934. The F-30 proved that the Farmall design had merits in a larger, more powerful tractor. Although heavy field work had been the territory of the standard tread tractor—and still was with a certain segment of people—the big F-30 was proof that a tricycle tractor could work a field hard and retain the design's ability to straddle rows for cultivating and maneuverability advantages.

Farmall F-20

The next tractor to take the Farmall mold was the F-20, which was an upgrade of the Regular. The F-20 had

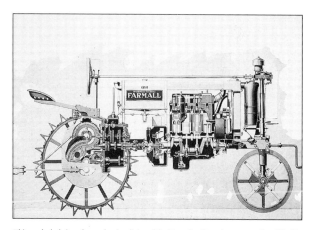

This exploded view shows the simplicity of the Farmalls. Note the power take-off is driven directly off the clutch, and the dropped-rear drive gears. The enclosed steering gear was one of the changes between the Regular and the F-20.

more power than the Regular, and a few more features, and was introduced in 1932, the same year in which Regular production was reduced. The F-20 it was upgraded with more power and some additional features in 1936.

The F-20's transmission used four speeds rather than the three of the Regular, and the engine used a bore of 3 3/4 inches and a stroke of 5 inches. The four-cylinder engine was governed to run at 1,200 rpm and used

This F-20 is pulling a McCormick-Deering combine at Purdue University's Edgewood Farm. Note the odd tread on the early pneumatic tires. Pneumatic tires provided better fuel economy and a smoother ride than steel.

removable sleeves, ball bearings on the crankshaft, and a combination of splash and gear-driven pump lubrication. It also had an oiled air filter. The engine was started on gasoline and could burn either kerosene or distillate. It was cooled with a thermosyphon system consisting of a closed system with a radiator. The clutch was an 11-inch single disk.

High-Clearance Model

In August of 1938, the F-20 Cane Tractor was authorized to be built. The tractor was a narrow-tread F-20 with the addition of a high-arch wide-tread front axle with new steering knuckles, steering knuckle arms, and drag link in the front as well as larger front and rear wheels and foot brakes. The F-20 Cane Tractor was manufactured for use with tall crops. The company decision lists Australia as a key market for this tractor. Interestingly, this tractor could be equipped with a high-clear-

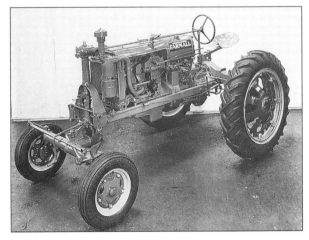

The F-20 Cane Tractor was authorized to be built in 1938. It was based on a narrow tread model, and featured a different front bolster and taller rear tires. According to company decisions, a high clearance version of this model was made available a bit later. Although this tractor is clearly indicated in company documents, it is rare or nonexistent today.

The F-12 was the fourth Farmall tractor, and was first produced in quantity in 1933, although experimentals and pre-production models were released early in 1932 and regular production models were released in October 1932. Early F-12s used Waukesha engines, although Harvester quickly switched to an IHC unit.

ance attachment, which could be bolted to the front end of the F-20 Cane Tractor. This attachment increased front axle clearance over a foot, and widened the front axle tread nearly six inches.

The F-20 Cane Tractor and the high-clearance models are extremely rare in the United States. In fact, these models are not known to exist as of 1996.

Farmall F-12

The F-12 is one of the most significant members of the Farmall line, for two reasons. First, it came without the heavy and expensive-to-produce rear drive mechanism from previous Farmalls. Second, the F-12 was the first to be used as a basis for both the wheel and cultivating tractors. From the F-12 forward, International wheel and cultivating tractors would become increasingly similar. By using one basic model, production costs were cut, engineering time was reduced, and retooling costs were slashed.

By the 1950s, the difference between the standard tread and cultivating tractor would be only a few parts needed to adapt the wide front end and lower the tractor a few inches.

One of the keys to the original Farmall was having sufficient ground clearance for cultivating. International's solution was to use a dropped-rear drive gear mechanism. On each wheel, an enclosed, oil-bathed drive ran from the rear final drive down to the rear hub. This added complexity to the tractor, but increased ground clearance as desired. One of the drawbacks was that tread width was adjustable only by flipping the offset rear wheels.

The engineering stroke of genius that eliminated the dropped rear drive was incredibly simple, not to mention the fact that it was someone else's idea. The Case Model CC and Oliver Hart-Parr Row Crop both simply used larger rear wheels to get the ground clearance necessary for cultivating. These tractors also made more power—about 18 horsepower at the drawbar and 28 on the belt—

than all of the Farmalls except the F-30. For IHC to compete, it needed to eliminate the dropped-rear drive, and it did so with the simple solution of larger rear wheels.

This not only eliminated the dropped-rear drive mechanism, it also freed them from the restraints of a fixed tread width. Rather than fooling with clumsy reversible hubs, the rear axle of the F-12 was keyed so that the wheel could slide freely. The tread width adjusted between 44 and 78 inches. This eliminated the need to produce a narrow tread version of the tractor, another clumsy and expensive way to meet the farmer's needs.

F-12 Roots

The new concepts aside, the F-12's roots resided in early Farmall development. At one point, a lighter version of the Farmall was discussed. In May of 1921, engi-

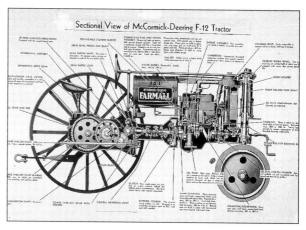

This F-12 schematic shows the features of the little tractor. Note that the power take-off shaft was dropped down a few inches, compared to the F-20. The F-12 engine developed 10 drawbar and 16 belt horsepower when burning gasoline.

Left
One of the F-12's most significant features was the elimination of the gear between the rear axle and rear wheel. By using larger rear wheels, the gear was no longer necessary. This feature reduced manufacturing cost and weight, and was pioneered by the competition.

someone, probably Ford or International, would produce the tractor in the near future.

Benjamin's description was close to that of the F-12, a lighter tractor, weighing around 3,000 pounds, that sold for about $800 when introduced. These specifications closely mirrored those of the early Farmall designs in weight and power.

The company was enthusiastic about the new F-12, and felt it had more market potential than any of the previous Farmalls. The F-12 could be sold more cheaply than previous Farmalls, and Benjamin felt it was more profitable to operate than either animal power or the combination of a plowing tractor (typically a Fordson) and a cultivating tractor.

This F-12 Farmall tractor is used by a rural mail carrier. This tractor is equipped with high-speed gears, and it travels 32 miles on the 65-stop mail route, using 5 gallons of gasoline. The cab is heated by the exhaust. During the summer months, the tractor is used on the farm.

neer Bert R. Benjamin wrote company executive Alexander Legge, suggesting that they build a tractor similar in size and power to the Fordson with a narrow front end. Benjamin's contention was that such a machine could plow as well as cultivate. At the time, it would cost the farmer at least $1,200 to purchase both a tractor to plow and a tractor to cultivate. Benjamin felt the new IHC machine could be sold for about $700. He also felt that

117

The original concept with the F-12 stems from a May 1921 proposal by engineer Bert R. Benjamin. He suggested that a tractor like the Fordson be built with more ground clearance and a narrow front end to allow decent cultivating as well as plowing. Benjamin felt the tractor should sell for about $700, and that either Ford or Harvester would build such a tractor. Over 10 years later, the F-12 was built almost exactly to those specifications.

This F-12 is operated by 18-year-old Juanita Washington of El Cajon, California. She regularly operates the tractor for producing crops on a 25-acre farm. Her mother markets the produce and her brother works in a grocery in El Cajon where some of the crops are sold.

118

The F-12 had enough power for light-duty belt work. It was upgraded with more power and a few subtle changes and released as the F-14 in 1938. The increased power was gained by governing the engine to run at 1,650 rather than 1,400 rpm.

Early Production

In 1932, 25 pre-production F-12s were built and sold. Quite a few of them went to Texas, but the rest were sprinkled around the Midwest and Southeast, with at least one going west to Arizona.

Most of the 1932 and 1933 models used a Waukesha Model FL four-cylinder engine. Later models used an IHC engine. The engine, with a bore of 3 inches and a stroke of 4 inches, turned at 1,400 rpm, and an oil filter and pump were used. The carburetor was a Zenith 93-1/2W, cooling was by thermosyphon, presumably with a radiator, and the clutch was an 8-inch single plate. The transmission was a three-speed, and a PTO and belt pulley were standard equipment. Also standard were an IHC oil air filter and spade lugs.

The tractors must have performed acceptably, because 1,500 more of the same machine were authorized to be built in early December of 1932. Either some kind of problem was discovered with the Waukesha engine or IHC wanted to increase profit margin, because the Waukesha engine was jettisoned only a few weeks later. Late in December of 1932, the decision was made to build a new IHC four-cylinder for the F-12. The engine had a bore of 3 inches and a stroke of 4 inches,

Farmall F-12 and F-14 Production

Year	Production
1932	25
1933	4,355
1934	12,530*
1935	31,249*
1936	33,177*
1937	35,681*
1938	6,425*
Total Prod.	**123,442**

Note: Most 1932 and 1933 F-12s used the Waukesha Model FL four-cylinder engine. Subsequent machines used an IHC four-cylinder engine.

F-14

1938	15,607*
1939	16,296*
Total Prod.	**31,903**

*Number of serial numbers issued that year, which is only an approximation of production numbers.
Source: McCormick/IHC Archives, 1932 and 1933 from "Tractor Production Schedule"

This F-12 wide-tread version features a small fuel tank on the right side of the hood which was used to hold gasoline for starting kerosene or distillate engines.

ran at 1,400 rpm, and was cooled by a thermosyphon system. The engine was equipped with a new IHC 1-inch down-draft carburetor, a Purolator oil filter, and an IHC magneto. The original decision specifies the IHC E4A magneto with a handwritten note stating that the IHC F4 magneto was actually used on the F-12.

Later references to the F-12 and F-14 indicate that both gasoline and kerosene versions of the tractor were made. It does make some sense that the dual-fuel manifold would be left off the machine to help keep the cost down. Use of the IHC engine required extensive changes to the control levers, cooling system hookup, and exhaust and intake attachments. The main frame beams were changed as well. A total of 30 changes were listed on the specifications sheet, undoubtedly requiring a fair amount of retooling and retrofitting.

New Engine in Late 1933

So, the F-12 was given a new engine late in 1933, and sold beyond the 1,500 allotted to be built that year. More than 4,300 F-12s were built in 1933, which was a modestly successful first year. Sales picked up from there, and the F-12 sold over 35,000 in 1937, which was a strong number

The F-12 and F-14 were available with a single front wheel, as shown above. By the end of production, most of the F Series tractors were going out the door shod in rubber.

Right
The W-12 marked the beginning of a trend for International. While the W-30 bore little or no resemblance to the F-30, the W-12 and F-12 shared the same basic chassis. The result was reduced costs on everything from production to parts. This W-12 with a 25-marker drill is near Oak Bluff, Manitoba.

The F-14 above is the upgraded version of the F-12. The major difference between the two was that the F-14 was rated to run at a higher rpm, giving a bit more horsepower. Note that the steering wheel shaft has been raised a bit, and angles away from the hood.

for the time. Certainly IHC was turning a profit on the little F-12, but the numbers were not perhaps as strong as management had hoped. It was successful, but hardly more so than the fast-selling Farmall Regular.

F-14

In 1938, IHC decided to see if giving the F-12 a little more power would put more life into sales. The engine was governed at 1,650 rather than 1,400 rpm, and the gearing was adjusted to maintain the same vehicle speeds. Some additional improvements were made, including raising the seat and steering wheel to a higher and purportedly more comfortable position, adding a heavier seat spring, and moving the clutch and hand brake levers to accommodate the repositioned seat and steering wheel. Also, a new PTO pinion gear was installed.

The diminutive W-12 gained loyal followers with its good performance for its small size. This W-12 tractor is pulling a No. 8-C two-furrow adjustable beam plow. The caption on the original photo reads, "This outfit is owned by Mr. J.S. Hunton, Ancaster, Ontario, who reports that the tractor has plenty of power to pull this plow up fairly steep grades on his farm."

In February of 1938, it was determined that the modified F-12 would be known as the F-14. A belt pulley was added to the list of standard equipment, and the new F-14 was introduced in mid-1938. The decision notes that all F-12 accessories and implements would work on the F-14, with the exception of the Hydraulic Lift Attachment. The Hydraulic Lift Attachment for the F-14 was different than the unit available for the F-12.

Electrics

An electric starting and lighting package for the F-12 and F-14 was introduced in 1937, and modified in 1938. The modifications allowed the battery box to be located on either side of the tractor to accommodate implements. Two different part numbers were used for the kits for gas or kerosene models, but the sole difference between the kits was the choke and governor control brackets.

The W-12 put out about 10 drawbar and 16 belt horsepower, similar numbers to the F-12. The W-12's standard equipment included steel wheels and slightly lower gearing than its siblings, the I-12 and O-12. Like the F-12, the W-12 was upgraded to the W-14 in 1938, with a higher rpm rating giving the tractor a bit more horsepower. This W-12 is pulling a John Deere disc harrow near Manitoba, Canada.

The industrial version of the W-12, the I-12, rode on rubber tires and used a taller third gear than the W-12. The taller gearing and rubber tires made it easier to get around town or the company yard. This I-12 was working at the Missouri Botanical Gardens in St. Louis, Missouri.

The versatile I-12 performed duties in a wide variety of situations. This one is cleaning debris dropped by gravel trucks at the Salman River Cut-Off near Portland, Oregon.

12 Series Production

Year	Production
O-12 and O-14	
1934	580*
1935	534*
1936	651*
1937	984*
1938	621*
1939	406*
Subtotal	**3,776**
Total O-12/ O-14 Prod.	**4,793**
I-12	
1934	263*
1935	200*
1936	550*
1937	970*
1938	209*
Subtotal	**2,192**
I-14	
1938	310*
1939	585*
Subtotal	**895**
Total I-12 and I-14 Prod.	**3,087**

Year	Production
W-12	
1934	853*
1935	675*
1936	737*
1937	1,031*
1938	334*
Subtotal	**3,630**
W-14	
1938	476*
1939	686*
Subtotal	**1,162**
Total W-12 and W-14 Prod.	**4,793**

*Number of serial numbers issued that year, which is only an approximation of production numbers.

Source: McCormick/IHC Archives

In 1939, the F-14 carried on the banner, and sold over 16,000 units, a respectable number. The tractor had carved out yet another niche for IHC tractors, proving that the market would bear a smaller general purpose tractor. The F-12 and F-14 were also the parental units of two of today's most popular, collectible, and useful IHC tractors, the Model A and Model B. Those tractors would appear in 1939, carrying a new look that continued IHC's dominance in tractors.

Standard Tread 12s

The standard tread 12s, as the W-12, I-12, O-12, and Fairway 12 are referred to in this book, were a significant step forward for IHC. From almost the first day IHC began producing tractors, several different divisions or factories built an assortment of similar tractors with different engineering bases. The result was independently engineered and produced machines, requiring different tooling, independent development costs, and non-interchangeable parts. This drove up costs and, in some cases, the tractor lines competed against each other.

Very early in IHC history, all of this was understandable because divisions were formed from independent companies. The animosity between the makers of the Titan and Mogul lines may have been a natural result of the people having battled tooth-and-nail one day and then becoming company bed fellows the next. The internal competition may have spurred some designs, and perhaps even created the Farmall, but the process was not cost-efficient.

With the standard tread and F-12s, IHC could focus on building one basic layout, and fairly easily modify it for both the cultivating and wheel tractors. One engine. One basic frame. Interchangeable parts. Costs down, price down, and, theoretically, sales going up.

The company's theory was correct, and its predictions bore fruit. The standard tread 12s did not sell as wildly as the F-12s, but IHC did not have as many developmental dollars to recover. Modest sales would return a profit, which was exactly why IHC wanted to move to a single base engine and chassis design. Note, however, that the W-12 was still built in a separate facility—Tractor Works—while the F-12 was built at Farmall Works. Despite all the com-

This I-12 is at work at Milwaukee Station. The stunning train is a "Hiawatha."

Another I-12 at work. This one was owned by Forest Home Cemetery of Milwaukee, Wisconsin. Also shown is an International all-steel wagon. When asked why they purchased this equipment, the owners said, "It is fast, light, powerful enough for our work, easy on fuel, and equipped with air tires that can go over the edge of drives, over grass, in fact anywhere without damage."

The 12s were upgraded in 1937 to accept lights, making it likely that this machine was built after that time. The International Harvester badging is especially intriguing, as most photographs show the 12s badged as McCormick-Deerings. This I-12 was photographed working at the Newark Airport in New Jersey.

Regular Production Begins

The field, orchard, and industrial versions of the little 12s were authorized on the same day, December 4, 1933. They were introduced as 1934 models, and all three used the same engine as the F-12, with a slightly different frame.

These tractors weighed about 3,200 pounds, just like the F-12, and used hand-operated brakes and throttle, a three-speed transmission, and an 8-inch single-disk clutch. The frame was a two-piece unit bolted together in the middle. The front axle was a low-slung unit with tapered roller bearings for the wheels, and the rear axle was semi-floating with diaphragm oil seals. Rubber tires were standard, and the cooling system was thermosyphon with shutters on the radiator controlling temperature. A swinging drawbar and pan seat completed the package.

The orchard version bore swoopy fenders and low-slung exhaust and intake pipes, while the industrial had different brakes and drawbar. Both wore rubber tires, while the I-12 had foot brakes and the O-12 brakes were hand-operated. The transmissions in the I-12 and O-12 had a tall third gear, which allowed the little tractor to sprint through the orchard or across the warehouse at just over 10 miles per hour. The W-12 rode on steel wheels, had a farm-type drawbar, and was geared a bit lower for field work.

pany's efforts to bring the two machines to one common base, they were still built on two different production lines in two separate locations. Unified production sites would have to wait for the Letter Series.

An I-12 owned by Twin City Hardwood. The engine in the 12s was the same as that of the F-12, and good for about 16 horsepower at the belt when burning gasoline.

The fourth addition to the standard tread 12s was the Fairway 12, which was simply an O-12 with steel wheels and an I-12 foot brake. The Fairway was designed for—you guessed it—use on golf courses. The Fairway 12 was authorized in April 1934.

In 1936, the 12s were upgraded a bit. The 8-inch clutch was replaced with a 9-inch unit, an agricultural-type seat was fitted, foot brakes replaced the

An I-12 at work with a Hough Shovel at the Farmall Works, which was perhaps the best-known of the International factories. Farmall Works was located in Rock Island, Illinois and was built expressly for building Farmalls. The plant was closed when the agricultural division combined with Case to form Case-International.

hand brake, and the wheels and tires were changed.

The front half of the frame was upgraded in 1937 to accommodate electric starting and lighting. The flywheel, steering gear housing, rear engine support, timing pin, and clutch pedal return spring were new, in addition to the new front main frame. The little 12s provided International with an easily convertible wheel tractor, and made it easier for the company to offer such machines.

The Fairway 12 was authorized in April of 1934, only a few months after the other 12s were approved. This Fairway 12 is at the Aurora Country Club with groundskeeper Ralph Teeter at the wheel.

The Fairway 12 was simply an O-12 with steel wheels and foot-operated brakes. This one is caring for the greens at the Country Club of Virginia in Richmond, Virginia.

Chapter Six

The Farmall A, B, and C

■

"The whole power farming picture has been changed by half a million Farmall
tractors on the job . . . and now comes a brand-new family of
Farmalls to step up farm efficiency all over again!"
IHC advertisement, 1939

As the 1930s drew to a close, the competition was beginning to nip at the heels of the International Harvester Company. The company was the number one producer, but John Deere and Case were both gathering steam. These companies, along with a host of others such as Oliver, Massey-Harris, and Minneapolis-Moline, had row-crop models to compete with the Farmalls. In addition, the farm market slumped a bit in 1938, and IHC's earnings dropped about 33 percent. The climate was not as hostile as the tractor wars of the 1920s, mainly because the use of the horse was finally declining and tractor sales were booming. All the same, IHC needed another stroke of genius to stay on top.

The Letter Series tractors provided just that. The tractors sported innovative features combined with a functional, streamlined look. The gangly appearance of the earlier Farmalls was replaced with the graceful design of Raymond Loewy, one of the era's most prominent industrial designers. The new line was incredibly successful, and was part of a company-wide design move that included a new logo. The new machines were produced for more than a decade, and the basic form endured until 1958, when the round lines of International tractors were replaced with the squared-off look that lasted to modern times. The logo survived until 1985, when the IHC tractor division was merged with the Case tractor division.

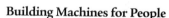

The Letter Series innovation stemmed more from refinement than dramatic engineering breakthroughs, but the end result was revolutionary. The key to the tractor's new design was Raymond Loewy. At the time, industrial designers were changing the face of all kinds of products. Everything from toasters to pop machines to diners were being streamlined and styled. The result was big sales, but the concept represented a fundamental change in the way machines were designed.

Building Machines for People

In the early part of the twentieth century, new technology dramatically changed the way America worked and lived. The automobile and tractor were two of the most obvious innovations, but every facet of people's lives was affected by the rise of power equipment. Manufacturers concentrated on efficient, effective equipment. The tractor changed from a difficult, clumsy beast to an efficient tool. Similar evolutions were reflected in all types of equipment.

The evolution of the machine brought more efficiency and reliability, but the machines were designed for tasks rather than for people. The approach could be seen from all angles. Machines were harsh and jarring in design and, more often than not, unfriendly and uncomfortable to use.

What Loewy and his contemporaries brought to the table was more than streamlined toasters and coffee

---

Left

The Model A was part of the Letter Series, the most successful International tractor line of all time. Over one million of these streamlined Farmalls were sold between 1939 and 1954.

Above

This illustration shows graphically why the Model A was such a great cultivating machine. The operator and engine were offset, which allowed for a great view of the crops being cultivated. International called this "Culti-Vision."

These three—the Model A, Model H, and Model M—were the cornerstones of the Letter Series line. These machines combined the function of a tricycle design with the smooth styling of industrial designer Raymond Loewy.

makers. It was the idea that machines should be designed for people to use. The success of the industrial design movement can probably be credited to the fact that the new machines looked futuristic and exciting. But the significance of the movement was that the machines were shaped to humans rather than vice versa.

Bert R. Benjamin brought in a new revolution by concentrating his engineering efforts on the task rather than the machinery. Loewy helped IHC bring another revolution by concentrating on the operator. The result is a series of timelessly attractive tractors that retain their utility 50 years after their introduction.

The smaller Farmalls were designed for the small farm, and were the most likely to directly replace a horse. By the 1940s, the tractor had turned the corner and more farms used tractors than not. Still, there was a reasonably large contingent of small, low-profit operations using horses. The initial cost of a tractor was one barrier for these farmers, who didn't necessarily have the capital or good standing with the bank to purchase a new machine. Profitability was another factor. A tractor that was too large to perform most of the farm work wouldn't save money even if the farmer had enough money to buy a tractor.

The Model A, B, and C addressed those very concerns. The tractors were economical to run and purchase, agile around the farm, and able to perform a wide variety of tasks. The Model A and B appeared in 1939, debuting with "Culti-Vision" and a complete line of implements. The Model C appeared in 1948 as a replacement for the Model B. The A and C both went "Super" near the end of their production runs, with boosted

The Model A was the smallest of the Letter Series tractors introduced in 1939. It was intended for use on smaller farms, where a more expensive or larger tractor was not cost effective.

Right
The Model A's strong point was cultivating a single row. It was maneuverable and offered an unprecedented view of the ground below. The Model A was designed as a one-row cultivator, with the wide front end straddling a single row.

The Farmall A was fairly powerful for its size, putting out about 13 drawbar and 17 belt pulley horsepower. It was also the right size to do much of the work being done by horses in the 1940s. This Model A is pulling a horse-drawn potato digger on a 20,000-bushel farm. Note that tires are flipped to widen the rear tread width.

This 1940 photograph shows a Model A equipped with Pneumatic Lift-All. The lift was operated by air pressure from the engine exhaust. Pneumatic Lift-Alls reportedly worked quite well when clean, but the hot exhaust gases clogged the mechanism and accelerated rusting.

This Model A was owned by Gene Kenney from Otis Orchards in Washington state. He used the Model A to haul apples from the orchard to the packing house. The trailer shown is a Linderman, which was popular in apple country because the double wheels carried smoothly over irrigation furrows.

The Model A's dropped-rear drive resurrected the problems of limited rear tread width and increased manufacturing cost found on the Farmall Regular, F-30, and F-20. The F-12 solved the problem with larger rear wheels and a straight rear axle, but the drop-drive mechanism reappeared on the Model A. This Farmall A is pulling a disk harrow in a rye field near Eldon, Missouri.

power and new features. As far as IHC tractors were concerned, these machines were super throughout their lifetime, with impressive sales figures and hundreds of thousands of satisfied Farmall owners to their credit.

Farmall Model A and Model B

The Model A and Model B were the lighter and more powerful replacements for the Farmall F-14. In many ways, they were the most innovative of the first group of Letter Series tractors. As with all of the new tractors that year, the models used streamlined sheet metal and smooth lines. The gangly appearance of the previous Farmalls was transformed into a sleek, attractive package.

Beyond the new sheet metal, the most distinctive feature was the offset of the operator and the engine, which truly reflected the industrial design concept; think about the operator first. Ground clearance and tread width are key to cultivating, but neither of these things is worthwhile unless the operator can see what he or she is doing. The result was what IHC called "Culti-Vision." The engine was offset to the operator's left, and the view to the ground was unobstructed.

The tractors also represented a union between IHC's desire to use Henry Ford's manufacturing techniques and the revolutionary Farmall design pioneered by Bert R. Benjamin and company. The roots of their design harked back to Benjamin's suggestion to build a light tractor like the Fordson that was capable of cultivating as well as plowing. The Model A and B were just that, with enough power and weight for light plowing, and adjustable tread width and great vision for cultivating.

More significantly, the two models used the integral frame and unit construction developed for the McCormick-Deering 15-30 and 10-20. The engine, steering gear housing, clutch housing, transmission case/differential housing, and final drive housing were each built as a modular piece. The pieces were then bolted together to effectively become the tractor's frame. The design was strong and efficient and reasonably easy to service.

Engine and Transmission

The four-cylinder engine had a bore of 3 inches and a stroke of 4 inches. The engine was rated at 1,400 rpm, but was controlled with a variable speed governor. The engine was lubricated by an oil pump using an oil filter with a removable star-shaped element. Ignition was a IHC H4 magneto with automatic impulse coupling and an integral grounding switch. The Model A used several different types of carburetors during production, all designed to burn gasoline. The compression ratio was 5.33:1, which was considered sufficient to burn gasoline. The engine was cooled with a closed thermosyphon system and a fan. The Super A-1 used a regular water pump and thermostat.

Ralph Hurst of Madrid, Iowa, does the heavy part of his farming with an F-20 and added a Farmall A for lighter work, the odd jobs, and hauling usually done with horses. He says the F-20 and Farmall A make the best "team" for reducing operating costs on the larger farms.

The clutch was a 9-inch single plate operated by a foot pedal. The transmission had 4 forward speeds, and used 11 roller bearings and 1 ball bearing. One advantage of the increased power was that it allowed a broader range of transmission gears. In top gear, the Model A would pull a blistering 9 3/4 miles per hour. This was a significant increase from the top speeds of previous tractors, which were limited to 3 or 4 miles per hour. Kits

had been offered for several years to install a "road gear" to bring tractor speeds up a bit. The Model A was one of the first to finally receive a top gear suitable for moving the tractor from place to place.

Chassis and Final Drive

Physically, the tractors were small and light. The operating weight of the Model A was just under 1,700 pounds, more than 1,000 pounds lighter than the preceding F-14. The Model A was shorter and a bit narrower than the F-14, as well.

One of the oddest engineering decisions on the Model A and B was the dropped-rear drive mechanism. The simple straight axle and larger rear wheels introduced to IHC on the F-12 provided the advantages of easily adjustable rear wheel tread and reduced complexity. The Model A and B used the same dropped-rear drive found on the Farmall, and experienced the same problems. Rear tread width could

The dropped-rear drive may have been used on the Model A to allow the use of smaller, cheaper rear tires and to provide some extra weight for improved traction. Still, the rear tread width was adjustable only by flipping the offset rear wheels. According to company documents, further adjustment required purchasing wheels with different amounts of offset. If the tires were liquid-filled (a common way to increase traction), the task was a pain even on a small tractor like the Model A. This photograph was taken during World War II and captioned, "Kathryn Mann of Columbia, Pennsylvania, is typical of the many young farm wives who are pitching in during these war days."

For grinding grain, frequently in small quantities, Ralph Hurst finds the Farmall A on the 1-B Hammer mill more economical as well as handier than the F-20. It takes a few minutes longer, but the time is offset by savings in fuel and by convenience since the Model A is already on the job, pulling the wagons. If the grinding were being done in large quantities at one time, he would use the F-20.

Utility versions of the Model A were badged as Internationals, while the agricultural models were Farmalls. The differences were a standard heavy-duty front axle and a foot-operated accelerator on the International models. Note the utility tread rubber tires, which were more common on the Internationals. This International A is hauling barrel staves with a homemade wagon.

smaller rear tires to be mounted. Perhaps the added weight of the mechanisms were intended to improve traction. The answer may never be clear.

Equipment, Standard and Optional

The standard wide front end on the Model A was not adjustable. An optional adjustable front end provided eight settings that ranged in 4-inch increments from 40 inches to 68 inches.

Pneumatic tires were widely used by 1939, and were standard equipment on the Model A and B. All of the Model As used a wide front end and were designed to cultivate a single row. For those who wanted a two-row cultivator, the narrow front-end Model B and BN were offered. The turning radius on the wide front models was 9 feet.

The brakes were external contracting bands on forged steel drums mounted on differential shafts in housings. They were operated by foot pedals that could be depressed separately for turning or together as a unit.

The rubber on the wheels smoothed the ride out a bit, and the new seat helped a bit more. The pan-style steel seat of past machines was discarded for a padded seat covered with cotton duck mounted on a spring. The seat was adjustable, and could be tipped back to accommodate standing. The seat was another reflection of the design of Raymond Loewy. Function was king, and a machine that

only be adjusted by flipping the offset rear wheels and the additional parts added weight and complexity. It's possible that IHC wanted to keep rubber costs down, as using the mechanisms allowed

The high-clearance Farmalls were intended for use with crops with high beds, primarily sugar cane. In the early 1940s, Louisiana was the leading producer of sugar cane in the United States, putting out as much as six million tons of sugar cane in 1943. The Farmall AV shown is preparing a sugar cane field in Louisiana for December planting.

The Shop Mule used Model A, Super A, or Model H components. This is a Shop Mule at work in Havelock, Nebraska.

is operated for hours on end should be comfortable. The advance was undoubtedly well-received.

Power Lifts

Power lifts were becoming increasingly popular on tractors by the 1940s, and the Model A and B had several options. One was a simple hand-operated mechanical lift.

If the A or B owner wanted a power lift, the optional pneumatic lift was the answer. In many ways, the lift was an elegant engineering solution, although it had one major drawback. The lift was powered by exhaust pressure, and provided plenty of lift power without the drain on engine power of a hydraulic lift. The drawback was if the mechanism got dirty (which tends to happen in farm conditions or after 20 or more years of sitting idle), the lift became less than powerful. Regular maintenance kept the pneumatic lift working well, but neglect would bring only misery. The Super A had a hydraulic system to power the lift, and the pneumatic lift was phased out. Although the hydraulics required less maintenance, the hydraulic system soaked up horsepower. Some say that the Model A actually has more drawbar power than the Super A due to this.

Other attachments available for the Model A included a swinging drawbar, belt pulley, power take-off, wheel weights, exhaust muffler, equipment for burning distillate and kerosene, electric lighting, a radiator shutter (which included a temperature gauge), and several different pistons to change the compression ratio for use at higher elevations. Shortly after being introduced, the Model A received a redesigned rear wheel and a PTO shield. Options added later included an electric starter, spark arrestor, optional tire sizes, dual rear wheels, adjustable front wheels, air pipe extension, and an air precleaner.

At the rear of this Farmall AV preparing a sugar cane field near Belle Alliance, Louisiana, for planting is a simple tool bar frame attached to the power lift. The two disc gangs shown can be adjusted for angle and position, or other implements can be attached to the tool bar.

The Farmall B was the two-row counterpart to the one-row Model A. The major difference between the two was the narrow front end, which was designed to ride in the middle of two rows. This Texas farmer is running a Farmall B is using a B-236 cultivator raised by a pneumatic power lift. Note the "Culti-Vision" logo behind the "B" logo on the hood.

This Farmall B is part of the Red Cross Motor Corporation and is at Herbert's Hill Angus Farm in Pennsylvania. The photograph depicts a training and promotional program that IHC called the "Tractorettes." During World War II, the company held classes training women to use IHC tractors and equipment.

Farmall Model B

The Model B was almost identical to the Model A, but was designed to cultivate two rows at a time. The single front wheel went between the rows, while the dual front wheels of the Model A straddled a single row. The B also had a wider rear tread width and a tricycle front end. The Model A and B used the same series of serial numbers with different codes (see production sidebar).

The rear tread width on the Model B was adjustable from 64 to 92 inches, compared to the range of 40 to 68 inches of the Model A. The wider rear end made the B slightly heavier (just under 1,800 pounds). The same attachments were offered for the Model B as for the Model A.

New Engine Package for Model A and B

In 1940, a high-compression package was authorized for the Model A and B. The company decision (a dated company document ordering engineering actions) reads that the option was offered to meet sales demand and to "provide equipment as tested at Nebraska." The wording insinuates that the University of Nebraska may have tested a more powerful Model A or B than the version IHC released to its dealers. Detroit auto makers have certainly been willing to release factory-massaged machines for testing, so it doesn't seem a huge stretch that IHC would send a more powerful machine to the Nebraska test. The fact that the decision was not to be circulated to distributors or even the head office makes it fairly likely that IHC pulled a fast one on the Nebraska tractor test of 1939.

Whatever the cause, the high-compression package was offered late in 1940 or early in 1941. It consisted of

a cylinder head, valve guide, valves, seats, intake and exhaust pipe, and all the necessary gaskets, studs, and brackets. No horsepower figures were on the decision, but it's safe to assume that tractors equipped with the package would match the output of the Model A tested in 1939. The output of tractors not equipped with the package is unknown.

Farmall Model BN

In August of 1940, a new version of the Model B was authorized, the Model BN. The tractor was simply a Model B with a narrower rear tread width. The tread width was adjustable in 4-inch increments from 56 to 84 inches by ordering optional rims with different amounts of offset. According to the factory decision, the parts required to convert a standard Model B to a Model BN were a new left differential shaft, differential housing, platform, and drawbar. The right seat support on the Model BN touches the right fender, while there is a gap on the regular Model B.

Collector Jim Becker notes that the Model BN has several advantages over the Model B. For one, fewer were built, making it a rarer model. More importantly, the slightly narrower Model BN fits into his trailer, while a Model B will not.

A swinging drawbar was available as an attachment. A single front wheel was standard, and the more common closely-spaced dual front wheels were optional.

The BN was narrow and light for a tricycle design tractor and according to company documents, was a bit tippy. It was an expensive solution for the farmer who

This one-off Farmall B with a cultivator is shown working the gladiola fields of the A&W Bulb Company of Fort Myers, Florida. The Model B is converted to a high-clearance model, with larger 4.5x40 tires and a raised front bolster. The company uses 15 tractors for the 1,000-acre operation, including a Farmall M with a front-mounted auxiliary-powered cutter used to chop the tops off of the bulbs.

The Farmall BN was the narrow-tread version of the Model B. The need for a narrow tread model would be more or less eliminated with the Model C, which used a straight axle that was more adjustable than the dropped-rear drive on the Model A and B. This Farmall BN is at work on a farm near Batavia, New York.

worked tightly spaced crops, and tread width adjustment was still a pain. These problems undoubtedly influenced the development of the Model C, which was heavier, wider, and had the easily adjustable straight axles of the larger Letter Series tractors.

Farmall Model AV

The Model AV was the high-clearance version of the Model A. It was intended for use in tending to crops planted on high beds that required additional tractor ground clearance. Sugar cane was the most common crop requiring a high-clearance machine, and cane fields used the higher beds to improve drainage.

The Model AV consisted of a group of additions to the Model A. It was authorized for production in October of 1940. The package consisted of a new front axle, front

International kept production heavy during World War II by both building machines for the war effort and by maintaining a steady flow of tractor production. With a portion of America's work force fighting the war, Harvester maintained that tractors were needed as never before. IHC tractor production was respectable during the war, with 1943 the only year tractor production dramatically decreased.

wheels, rear axle shafts, rear wheels, drawbar, and steering gear housing base. The result was a 5-inch increase in ground clearance, which brought it up to 27 1/2 inches. The front wheels were 4.00x19s, and the rears were 8.00x36s. The transmission gearing was not changed to accommodate the larger wheels, so the tractor traveled slightly faster in each gear than a Model A. Top speed bumped up about 3 miles per hour to 12 3/4 miles per hour. Available attachments in-cluded a swinging drawbar, wheel weights, belt pulley, PTO, muffler, equipment for burning distillate and kerosene, radiator shutters, electric starting, electric lights, flywheel ring gear, double-groove fan and generator pulley hub, spark arrestor, tire pumps, high-compression gasoline starting, and different compression ratio pistons for higher altitudes.

International A

In 1940, the International Model A was introduced. The International was the industrial version of the Model A, and it closely resembled the Farmall Model A. The industrial models were intended for commercial use, and researcher Jim Becker feels that most of them were used as highway mowers. The tractors were certainly marketed to different audiences, and the International Model As show up in all kinds of situations—from orchards to factory applications—in archival photographs.

According to Becker, the major differences between the International A and Farmall A were that the International A used a foot accelerator and the Model A's optional heavy-duty front axle. The diamond-pattern rear pneumatic tires were more common on Internationals, although they became available for any of the Model As.

The convention of stickering industrial or utility versions as Internationals and the cultivating version as Farmalls eventually became common IHC practice. It was unique to the Model A during Letter Series production, but the Hundred Series would use the same convention, replacing the W, I, and O tractors with a standard tread model badged as an International. Orchard and industrial versions could still be ordered, but they no longer had a unique model designation.

Farmall Super A

The Super A was an upgraded version of the Model A that featured a more powerful engine mated with a host of optional equipment that included Touch Con-

The Farmall C was introduced in 1948 as a replacement for the Model B. The tractor was produced in respectable numbers, selling over 20,000 a year in 1949 and 1950. If you include Super C production, over 170,000 Model C's were built from 1948 to 1954.

A pre-production Farmall C with a two-way plow and Touch Control hydraulic lift. Adding hydraulics greatly increased the ability to perform a variety of tasks. Lifting implements easily was the most obvious function, but hydraulics would be used for everything from power log splitters to loaders.

A shot of a Farmall C equipped with a C-18 push-type middlebuster. The operator is putting Touch Control to work lifting the busters out of the ground. This photo was taken in the blackland area of Texas.

trol hydraulics, quick-attach implements, and the universal frame mounting system.

Touch Control

Touch Control hydraulics debuted on the Super A and the Model C. Touch Control was a hydraulic lift that powered implements up as well as down, giving the operator a powered lift at the touch of a lever. Lifts had been around for quite some time, but hydraulics were an up-and-coming development. They eliminated the need for clumsy mechanical linkages to a lift, and afforded great mobility to tractor attachments. Unfortunately, they also required horsepower to run. The horsepower devoted to hydraulics was lost, and the tractor was a bit less efficient at the drawbar. Some even say that a Model A has more pulling power than the Super A due to the horsepower lost to the Super's hydraulic system. Later Touch Control systems had a temperature gauge mounted between the control levers to monitor hydraulic fluid condition. This gauge was used on the Super C and perhaps the Model C as well.

Decals

Super A decals are another interesting topic. Several versions of the decal sets are floating around, with quite a bit of confusion on what was actually used and when. The first issue is the "McCormick-Deering" lettering on the hood. Early Letter Series tractors use "McCormick-

The Farmall C used a straight rear axle rather than the dropped-rear drive mechanism found on the Model A and B. The straight axle required taller rear wheels, but allowed the rear tread width to be infinitely adjustable within a range. It also made adjustment simpler, as the wheels did not have to be removed. Another pre-production Model C is shown above, pulling a C-294 two-bottom plow near Marshalltown, Iowa.

The Model C was intended for two-row work on small farms. Some of the Model Cs were marketed for the less-than-100-acre farms down South.

The Model C engine was the same C-123 unit used in the Super A, which was simply the engine from the original Model A and B with a 1/8-inch-larger bore. This Farmall C with a one-bottom two-way C-189 plow is at work near Bauck's Corners, New York.

The Model C did not use the offset engine as on the Model A and B, but it still offered good vision of the ground for cultivating.

Model A and B Production

Model A, AV, International A, Super A, Super AV, and Super A-1

Year	Production
1939	6,242*
1940	22,023ï
1941	22,950
1942	9,579
1943	105
1944	8,177
1945	18,494
1946	19,739
1947	20,937
1948	15,869
1949	13,805
1950	16,376
1951	27,562
1952	11,334
1953	17,909
1954	5,953†
Total Prod.	**237,054**

*Serial numbers issued
ï International A introduced
§ Super A introduced
†Super A-1 introduced
Source: McCormick/IHC Archives, "Tractor Production Schedule"

Farmall Model B and BN Production
Model B, BN

Year	Production
1939	NA*
1940	12,765**
1941	16,553
1942	6,305
1943	5
1944	7,933
1945	12,951
1946	14,623
1947	20,100
1948	1,921
Total Prod.	**93,156**

*Although 1939 serial numbers were issued, the Tractor Production Schedule lists production beginning in 1940
**Model BN introduced in 1940
Source: McCormick/IHC Archives, "Tractor Production Schedule"

Deering," while later machines tend to have just "McCormick." Researcher Jim Becker has found that original International documentation shows that Deering began dropping off the logo in 1949, although the exact date varied from model to model. Note that the address listed below "Farmall," also changed, probably about the same time as "Deering" disappeared.

Back to the Super A, where two distinctly different "Super A" logos were used. The type commonly found on archival photographs is a white circle around a white letter "A" with a serpentine script "Super" banner behind the letter "A."

The other logo is a filled white circle containing a red letter "A" and red "Super" text in a semicircle within the circular logo and above the letter "A." The second is more commonly seen today, and is the decal most often found for sale. The first, with the wavy "Super" type, is the one Becker feels the factory used on all Super As. Archival photography seems to support his belief, but many other IHC researchers and collectors believe the typical round white logo was used on factory machines as well as the logo with serpentine type.

Universal Mounting System

The universal frame mounting system simplified the farmer's life. Attaching implements to a tractor's frame typically involved bolting on a unique attachment frame for each individual implement. With the universal frame mounting system, IHC attachments used the same mounting frame, and switching implements became easier.

International A (Super)

The International version of the Super A was still known as the International A. It featured all the new Super A bits, plus a beefier Touch Control system with heavier control arms and slightly more powerful internals.

Farmall Super A-1

The Super A-1 used a larger bore to bring displacement of the four-cylinder engine up to 123 cubic inches. Also, it had a thermostat to go with the water pump, bringing the cooling system up to date. The Super A-1 was produced only in 1954. About 2,000 serial numbers were issued that year, so production should have been close to that.

A Farmall C rebedding with a C-18 middlebuster. Note that the main housing was a stressed frame member, with rest of the frame bolting to the front and rear of the housing, as on the Model A and B. Also note the control levers for the hydraulic system are easily accessible on the operator's left.

The White Letter Series Tractors

The white Letter Series tractors are highly desirable items in International tractor collector circles. The tractors were built as part of a promotional campaign in 1950. An article in *Harvester Highlights*, the newsletter of the IHC club, states that white demonstrators were built for three months at the Louisville Plant in Kentucky. The entire line of equipment built at Louisville was reportedly painted white, including, tractors and balers.

Any dealer could order these white tractors, and they were intended to be used as demonstrators. The Cub, Super A, and Model C could for certain be ordered in the white paint scheme, and rumors persist that other models and balers also were finished in white.

The white demonstrator tractors are some of the rarest and most desirable Farmall tractors. This Cub appeared at the Dodge County Fairgrounds in Wisonsin in September of 1950. Bob Steimhorst of Beaver Dam, Wisconsin is shown on the seat. *Courtesy of Daryl Miller of* Red Power

The Farmall Super C was a slightly more powerful version of the Model C. The standard gasoline-burning engine was rated for 24 belt and 22 drawbar horsepower.

A Super C and D-10 corn-picker. The Super C featured disc brakes, a belt pulley, PTO, electric lights and starter, and Touch Control as standard equipment. An adjustable wide front axle, pneumatic tire pump, and magneto ignition were some of the options.

Farmall Model C

Introduced in 1948, the Model C was the replacement for the Model B. It was larger and heavier than the Model B, but used the same narrow front end and was designed to be a two-row cultivator. Like the Model A and B, the Model C was designed for the small farmer who was perhaps upgrading from horses to power farming.

The Model C no longer used the dropped-rear drive of the Model A and B. Instead, the Model C used larger rear wheels and a straight axle like those introduced on the F-12 and used on the Model H and M.

The straight rear axle allowed the rear tread width to be infinitely adjustable within a range, and tread width could be adjusted without taking the rear wheels off. It required larger rear tires, but eliminated the extra tooling and complexity of the dropped-rear drive mechanism. The rear rims also had offset lugs, allowing additional adjustment by reversing the wheels.

The Farmall C engine was the same 3x4-inch four-cylinder used in the Farmall A and B. By governing the engine to run 250 rpm higher, at 1,650 rpm, a couple of extra horsepower were coaxed from the Model C engine. Burning gasoline, output was about 19 horsepower at the belt pulley and 15 horsepower at the drawbar, enough to pull a two-bottom plow in average conditions with ease. The engine used an IHC magneto and a Zenith carburetor.

The engine was the same as that of the Model A and B, but the chassis was significantly larger and heavier. The Model C weighed about 3,000 pounds, significantly heavier than the 1,700 pounds or so of the Model A.

The chassis used the engine and transmission cases as stressed members, like the Model A and B. The front

end bolted to the engine cases, and the rear used straight splined axles that allowed the rear tread width to be adjusted.

The Farmall C also had Touch Control hydraulics, like those on the Super A. Options included a wide tread model, although these are fairly rare. The Model C was quite popular, and outsold the Model A and Super A with production at more than 20,000 units per year.

Farmall Super C

The Super C was an increased power version of the Model C. The increased power came from a bit more displacement found with a larger bore, up from 3x4 to 3 1/8x4 inches. The engines were now rated by displacement rather than bore and stroke, and the four-cylinder gasoline-burning engine displaced 122.7 cubic inches. The horsepower increase was modest, with a gain of a couple of horsepower at both the belt pulley and drawbar.

The Super C introduced International's new double-disk brakes. The disk brakes replaced the drum units, and were covered and sealed from grit. Fast Hitch later appeared on the Super C, along with a plug-in adapter that allowed the use of three-point hitch implements.

Fast Hitch

International's two-point hitch system, dubbed Fast Hitch, was also available on the Super C. This hitch was IHC's answer to the Ferguson three-point hitch. Fast Hitch was a high-quality system, and its advantage over the Ferguson system was the ease of mounting. The operator could simply back the tractor into the implement and go, rather than compete in the wrestling match involved in attaching an implement to Ferguson's three-point system. The drawbacks (for the end user) were that Fast Hitch implements had to be purchased to take advantage of the new system, and the implements could not be used on other brands of tractors.

Model C and Super C Production

Year	Production
1948	15,547
1949	26,338
1950	24,280
1951	37,651†
1952	31,130
1953	29,472
1954	13,753
Total Prod.	**178,171**

†Super C introduced

Source: McCormick/IHC Archives, "Tractor Production Schedule"

Chapter Seven

The Farmall H and M

---

*"First view shows you up-to-the-minute appearances—
the handsome lines of farm power that is practical in the fields."*
—IHC advertisement, 1939

The 1940s and early 1950s were the golden age of the tractor. The horse was nearly gone, and the tractor was king on farms of 100 acres or more. Farmers were working more land than ever before, and molding that land to suit their needs. Machine power was vital to the mid-century vision of successful farming.

For the farmer of 100 acres or more, the Model H and Model M were the ideal tool. The tractors were powerful jacks-of-all-trades, capable of pulling feed wagons and turning conveyor belts as well performing the heavy field work of plowing, harvesting, planting, and cultivating.

The early 1940s were incredibly successful for tractor manufacturers, especially International. Even World War II did not take the shine off the company during this era. Sales dipped in the mid-1940s, but nothing like the slump experienced during World War I. Savvy tractor manufacturers built crawlers for the war effort, and were able to convince the government that tractor production was important enough not to divert material from their production. With the nation's men at war, the remaining farmers needed efficient power more than ever, so the tractor rolled on.

Early in 1950s, with the post-war boom still in stride, IHC's sales of mid-sized and larger tractors would peak, never to reach that pinnacle again. The tractors sold in unprecedented numbers for a full-size tractor. The Model H alone sold nearly one-half million units. The numbers were a result of the fact that farmers were turning to tractors like never before, and the Letter Series was one of the favorites of the time.

During the tail end of Letter Series production, the diesel engine would appear in cultivating tractors. The Super series machines would see the introduction of the independent power take-off, Torque Amplifier, and improved hydraulics. With these improvements, the fundamental functions of the modern farm tractor were in place.

Farmall Model H

The Model H replaced the F-20 with a stylish package that featured all of IHC's latest technology. The Model H and the Model M were based on the same chassis design. Although the two had the same mounting points for implements, they shared very few parts. The Model H was designed to be a two-bottom plow tractor while the Model M was rated to pull a three-bottom plow.

Left

The high-clearance Model MV used the same chassis additions as the Model HV, with a dropped-rear drive mechanism and arched front bolster raising the tractor's ground clearance. The rear drive mechanism consisted of an enclosed, oil-bathed roller chain and gears.

Above

The Super M-TA was a tractor for the future. It featured independent power take-off (IPTO), which kept the PTO spinning independently of the clutch. Torque Amplification (TA) was an International two-speed unit that could be shifted on the fly, allowing the operator to kick down the final drive ratio a bit for more power when needed.

149

This Farmall MV is at work on 350-acre farm near Donaldsville, Louisiana. The Model MV is pulling two wagons loaded with as much as seven tons of sugar cane. The tractor shuttled the cane back to the farm, where it was loaded into semi-trailer trucks and hauled to sugar mills several miles away.

The Farmall H was the styled replacement for the F-20. The industrial design of Raymond Loewy added much more than style. His concept of building the tractor for the operator was applied from top to bottom, with lots of little touches designed to make the tractor easier to use. This Farmall H is pulling a Model Seven disk.

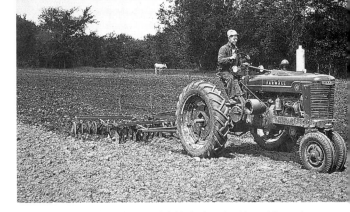

The Farmall H used a chassis that was a hybrid of a channel and integral frame. The front half was a channel that ran along the bottom side of the engine housing, while the housing for the clutch, transmission, and final drive made up the rear frame.

The Model H used modular construction, like the smaller Model A and B. Components could be taken off independently as an assembled unit. This had some advantages when the tractor was being built in the factory, and made servicing the tractor much simpler.

Chassis

The Model H's frame was a hybrid of an integral and beam frame. The rear of the frame was the transmission and final drive housing, while the front was a beam frame that ran from the clutch housing forward to underneath the engine.

The Farmall H was produced in incredible volume, with over 400,000 units sold (including Super Hs). That incredible figure was never equaled by a full-size tractor. It is unlikely that such a large number of a single model will ever be sold again, as modern tractors can perform the same volume of work as several tractors from the 1940s, and the number of farms has steadily dwindled since the 1950s.

The frame design showed touches of Loewy's beliefs. The engine was rubber-mounted to the front frame channels, presumably to make the tractors smoother to operate. A little less vibration would make a big difference over a long day in the fields.

Engine

The Model H's four-cylinder I-head engine used a 3 3/8-inch bore and a 4 1/4-inch stroke and was rated at 1,650 rpm. The engine for the original version was started on gasoline and ran on distillate or kerosene (a gasoline-burning engine appeared in 1940). A variable-speed governor was used. The engine oil was force-fed by an oil pump, and an oil filter strained grit from the lubricant. Air and fuel cleaners were standard, as well. An IHC H-4 magneto and IHC D-10 carburetor were used. The distillate-burning version of the Model H was tested at Nebraska in 1939, and produced 22.14 horsepower at the belt pulley.

The engine was cooled with an enclosed system that used a radiator and water pump. Cooling was adjusted with shutters that could be controlled by a hand crank. Later models used a thermostatically controlled system, with shutters as an available option for cold-weather use.

Transmission and Clutch

The transmission used five speeds, with top gear yielding nearly 17 miles per hour. The top gear was used only with pneumatic tires and blocked out on steel-wheeled machines. A few models were sold with steel when the tractor was introduced, and a significant number appeared on steel during World War II, when rubber was reserved for war use. A lower first gear and taller fourth gear became available as optional equipment.

The clutch was a Rockford 10-inch single disk and was foot-operated. The brakes were external-contracting bands on forged steel drums mounted on differential shafts in housings. The brakes were foot-operated and could be engaged separately or in tandem.

Running Gear

The front axle and lower bolster pivot as a unit. The original configuration of the Model H specified a narrow, dual-wheel tricycle front end, with the wide front end and single front wheel available as options. The standard front tread width was just less than 9 inches.

The rear end used the splined straight axles introduced on the F-12, allowing easy tread width adjustment by sliding the wheels on the splined axles. The rear wheels were reversible as well, allowing a broad range of

A Farmall H pulling a Seaman Tiller in a field of muckland on the Zellwood Farm near Zellwood, Florida. The farm grew mainly truck crops and was controlled by the Beachrut Packing Company. The Seaman Tiller was not well-regarded in most of the country, but worked well in Florida muckland and citrus groves. Note the optional dual rear wheels and wide front end.

Women played a big role in farming from the beginning, and their role increased during World War II. With many of the country's men off to war, the women left behind took over the farming. International capitalized on this with a program they called the "Tractorettes," in which they held training classes to teach women how to use tractors. The program was probably more effective for promotion than training, as women on the farm more often than not already knew their way around a tractor.

rear tread width adjustment from 44 to 80 inches. The tractor weighed about 5,500 pounds.

The cotton duck-covered seat found on the smaller letter series tractors was standard on the H as well. The drawbar was an adjustable quick-attach model. The turning radius was 8 feet, 4 inches, and ground clearance was about 18 inches. Available options for the Model H included starting and lighting equipment, wheel weights, and rear wheel fenders. A temperature gauge and radiator shutter were standard with the distillate engine, and optional on Model H's with the high-compression gasoline engine. A rarer option was the wide tread rear axle, which allowed adjustment from 44 to 100 inches.

Power Lifts

Three versions of Lift-All, International's hydraulic lift, were available for the Model H. The regular lift raised the entire attachment in one movement. A delayed lift was also available, which was used when both front and rear cultivators were mounted. The front implement lifted first, and the back unit a bit after, so the two effec-

Left

The high-clearance version of the Model H was the Farmall HV. A dropped-rear drive mechanism and a high-arch front axle increased ground clearance for work on crops with high beds. This Farmall HV is preparing a seedbed for corn near Belle Rose, Louisiana, with a CIU-12 one-row chopper and a CIU-14 capper attachment.

tively came out of the ground at the same point. The third Lift-All was the selective lift, which allowed raising left and right implements separately. The delayed and selective lifts were attachments to the basic Lift-All.

High-Compression Gasoline Engine

In March of 1940, IHC authorized the addition of a high-compression gas-burning engine for the Model H. Despite the fact that the gasoline engine was not officially released until 1940, a gasoline-burning Model H was tested at Nebraska in 1939. The gasoline-burning Model H produced 19.14 horsepower at the drawbar and 24.28 horsepower at the belt pulley. One suspects that the tractors sent to Nebraska were pre-production machines, and that the publication of the gasoline tests led some to demand gasoline-burning versions for the showroom floor. A somewhat cryptic note on the decision to build the high-compression engine for the Model M lends some credence to this theory, although there is no way to be sure.

In August of 1940, the kerosene and distillate engine was modified to burn distillate fuel only. A kerosene attachment would be offered for those who wished to burn kerosene.

In December of 1940, the position of the controls were moved to the rear of the tractor for easier operation. A bracket was attached to the steering post, and the radiator shutter and magneto ignition switches

The Model H used the modular construction developed for the McCormick-Deering 15-30 and 10-20. Individual components—brakes, clutches, transmissions, and so on—were assembled individually and could be detached as a unit. This helped a bit on the production line, and was most appreciated when servicing the tractors. In this photo, these women are presumably completing their Tractorette training with a quick oil change.

Another view of the Farmall HV at work in Louisiana. The rear drive mechanism lowered the final gearing a bit, dropping top speed from 16 to 15 miles per hour. The HV used stub axles attached to the dropped-rear drive, allowing rear tread width to be easily adjustable. Thomas Dupre of Belle Rose, Louisiana, is driving.

were moved to the new bracket, as was the belt pulley control lever. The starting switch was moved to the platform, near the operator's foot, and the starting switch control rod was eliminated.

Farmall Model HV

In January 1942, a new model designed for cane and high-bed vegetable cultivation was released. The Farmall HV used step-down housings and an arched front axle to provide higher clearance. The front end had a whopping 30 1/4 inches of ground clearance.

The step-down housings provided the arch in the rear of the tractors. Inside the housings, a roller chain transmitted power from the drive sprocket to the rear axle. The housing was sealed, and the chain ran in an oil bath.

The dropped-rear drive used stub axles so that tread width was still adjustable. Additional adjustment was available by flipping the rear wheels, which had offset hubs. If the farmer required more adjustment, optional wheels with varying degrees of offset were available.

The engine, basic chassis, and running gear were the same as the Model H, and the tractor could be equipped with an assortment of special equipment.

Farmall Super H

Introduced in 1953, the Farmall Super H offered some of the new IHC line options, and the engine was punched out for a few more cubic inches and about 18 percent more horsepower. The H's bore of 3 3/8 inches was increased to 3 1/2 inches in the Super H, bumping displacement to 164 cubic inches and

Farmall Model H, HV and Super H, HV Production

Model H, HV

Year	Production
1939	10,151*
1940	41,317
1941	40,927
1942	34,987
1943	21,375
1944	37,265
1945	28,268
1946	25,615
1947	28,382
1948	32,265
1949	27,483
1950	24,681
1951	24,232
1952	16,243
1953	21,916†
1954	10,052
Total Prod.	**425,159**

†Super H introduced
*Serial numbers issued
Source: McCormick/IHC Archives, "Tractor Production Schedule"

The Super H featured a bit more power and more standard features. Introduced in 1953, the tractor was only built for two years. Double-disc brakes were among the new features, and electric lights and starting became standard equipment.

horsepower to 24 drawbar and 31 belt horsepower for the standard gasoline-burner. Torque was up to 267 foot-pounds at 1,046 rpm.

The cooling system was thermostatically controlled, oiling was done by pressurized lubrication, and the oil-bath air filter and replaceable oil filter kept things in the engine clean. The engine was advertised as being equipped with exhaust valve rotators, which were supposed to keep the valves rotating to prevent deposit build-up and extend valve life.

The Super H featured double-disk brakes rather than the drum brakes of the original Model H. The new brakes used a pair of rotating disks in sealed housings. Lights and electric starter were standard, as was a PTO, belt pulley, Lift-All, and the new deluxe hydraulic seat.

Farmall Model M

The Model M chassis featured a more powerful engine fit in a chassis that used the same design as the Model H. The Model M was wider and heavier, and shared the same mounting points for implements. The Model H and M could interchange implements, but very few parts were shared on the actual tractors.

Chassis

As on the Model H, the Model M's rear frame, clutch housing, front frame channels, and upper bolster are bolted together to make a rigid frame unit. The brakes (contracting bands on steel drums) and narrow front end were specified in the original decision on the Farmall Model M.

Engine

The Model M's four-cylinder I-head engine had a bore of 3 7/8 inches and a stroke of 5 1/4 inches. A variable governor was used, and the engine was rated for 36 flywheel horsepower at 1,450 rpm. The engine was started on gasoline, and then switched over to kerosene or distillate. The carburetor was a IHC model with a 1 1/4-inch updraft. Oil pressure was maintained with a gear circulating pump, and the oil filter used the Motor Improvement Company's P-20 star-shaped removable filter.

The engine was cooled with a closed system that circulated water through a flat-tube radiator with a water pump. The water temperature was originally supposed to be regulated with shutters in front of the radiator. In September of 1939, the company decided to use a belt-driven water pump

Fowler McCormick

Fowler McCormick was born in 1898 as the heir of two of the country's most powerful dynasties, the McCormicks of the International Harvester Company and the Rockefellers of Standard Oil.

Fowler had some big shoes to fill. His grandfather, Cyrus McCormick, was the inventor of the McCormick Reaper. Fowler's father, Harold McCormick, became the president of IHC. Fowler's mother, Edith Rockefeller McCormick, was the daughter of John D. Rockefeller, Sr., and an heiress to the Standard Oil fortune.

A man often described as troubled and complex, Fowler did not come to International until 1925, when a six-month stint working incognito for Harvester's Milwaukee foundry and encouragement from his wife and Alexander Legge convinced Fowler that his future was with International.

Harvester groomed executives in the field, and Fowler was no exception. He began as an apprentice working on experimental farm equipment and moved on to sales, where he was moved up to head of foreign sales. He then took over manufacturing operations and, in 1941, he was named president.

One of the largest challenges he faced was the Post-War period. The demand for military equipment had meant a high demand for International, and the company's factories had been cranked up and producing at peak levels. During the post-war period, the company needed to either develop new markets to

Fowler McCormick, president of the International Harvester Company from 1941 to 1946, is shown speaking at the Hinsdale Farm Show held October 13-19, 1945. Fowler was a distinguished company president, and worked his way to the top from a lowly beginning as a student-apprentice making 25 cents an hour.

continue the high level of production or scale back to adjust. Under Fowler's leadership, management decided to expand. Harvester invested nearly $150 million in new factories, product designs, and machine tools. The company was reorganized, and new plants were built and purchased around the country to build everything from crawlers to Cubs to combines.

Fowler's critics would say the expansion was too much and the debt load acquired was too high for the profits that came in, but his personal reputation was that of a good man. John Sucher grew up in Hinsdale, Illinois, on a farm just down the road from the International Experimental Farm. His family was constantly using experimental tractors or watching International test tractors hours upon end in their fields and pastures. John recounts the day when Fowler McCormick came to visit their farm.

"He impressed me when I was just a kid. He pulled up to the farm in a big black limousine. The driver jumped out and ran over to open the door for Fowler, but he would have none of it. 'Forget it,' Fowler said. 'I can open the damn door myself!' He came right out in the cow yard to look over some equipment. There he was, in the cow shit with his oxfords. He didn't care. He was a blue-collar guy."

Fowler was Chairman of the Board from 1946 to 1951, and led the company through one of the most prosperous eras in the history of the company. Fowler McCormick died on January 6, 1972.

The Farmall M was the big tractor of the Letter Series. Rated as a three-bottom plow tractor, it shared the same chassis design as the Model H but had a larger, more powerful four-cylinder engine. Although few parts are interchangeable between the H and M, the two share the same dimensions for mounting implements. The Farmall M above was used in a tillage demonstration held in Mekinnville, Oregon, by a local dealer. The Model M is pulling a Dyrr offset disk harrow.

This Farmall M wide-front is pulling a six-section peg tooth harrow. The dual rear tires were used in soft soil conditions found in Stephen, Minnesota.

The Farmall M, like the Model H, had a five-speed transmission with a very tall top gear intended for road use only. When the machines were factory-equipped with steel wheels, fifth gear was locked out. This Farmall M is at work with a beet harvester near Woodland, California.

and thermostat to cool the engine. This change was supposed to be effective on serial number 501, the first Model M off the line, so all Model Ms built should have had a thermostat. Should is the key word here, as decisions made in the executive boardroom don't always make to the production floor in the desired time. The gas tank held 22 gallons and an IHC H-4 magneto with automatic impulse coupling and integral grounding switch was used.

Transmission

The transmission was a five-speed unit that used roller and ball bearings throughout with the exception of the reverse idler bushings. The tractor would run at over 16 miles per hour in top gear, which was intended for use only on pneumatic tires. The clutch was an 11-inch single-disk built by the Rockford Drilling Machine Company (Model 11 RM).

The rear tread width was wider on the Model M than on the Model H, with the M's tread width adjustable from 52 to 88 inches. A wide-tread model increased rear tread width to from 52 to 100 inches, although that model is quite rare. Ground clearance was the same on the two models at about 16 inches from the rear frame, and both shared the cotton duck-covered seat.

As tested at Nebraska in 1939, the distillate-burning Model M weighed 6,770 pounds (presumably including ballast) and delivered 24.89 horsepower at the drawbar and 34.16 at the belt pulley.

Gasoline-Burning Engine for the Model M

In February of 1940, IHC decided to supply the Model M with a higher-compression engine suitable for burning gasoline. The engine was otherwise the same, with the addition of a new cylinder head that brought the compression ratio up enough to burn 70- to 72-octane gasoline. The intake manifold was designed for gasoline operation, presumably without the fuel-warming system on the manifold for kerosene and distillate. This option was supposed to be available beginning with Model M serial number FBK-18144, meaning it was offered immediately after the decision was made early in 1940.

Interestingly, when the gasoline-burning version of the Model M was tested at Nebraska, it bore serial number FBK-ME533. Either the tractor tested at Nebraska used a prototype gasoline-burning setup, or the note on the decision to offer a gasoline tractor was incorrect. Either way, the gasoline-burning Model M produced a few more horsepower than the distillate machine. At the drawbar, the gas-powered Model M produced 26.23

The Louis Finn 150-acre potato farm near Hicksville, New York. Finn prepared for the possibility of losing some of his five sons to the war's draft by teaching his three daughters to run the equipment.

horsepower with 36.07 horsepower at the belt pulley. Later in 1940, the kerosene or distillate version of the Model M was changed to burn only distillate.

Farmall Model MD

In December of 1940, the Model MD was authorized. As the name suggests, the Model MD was simply a Model M with a diesel engine. The engine used the same bore and stroke as the gasoline and distillate Model M engines.

Starting was significantly different. The engine was started on gasoline with the engine in a low-compression mode. Once the tractor started and was warmed up, it was switched over to diesel fuel and high compression with a hand lever mounted on the rear fuel tank support.

The chassis was nearly identical to the regular Model M.

A hand-written note on the decision specifies that the first Model MD be serial number FDBK-26145. The date January 13, 1941, is also written on the decision. This was quite possibly the date the first Farmall MD left the factory.

Attachments for the Model MD included a 11-inch belt pulley, PTO, swinging drawbar, muffler, pneumatic tire pumps, wheel weights, spark arrestor, fenders, hydraulic power lift, dual rear pneumatic tires, and a low-speed option.

This M-220-L cotton picker was developed as part of International's post-war expansion. Government contracts to build equipment for the war effort had IHC factories producing at full capacity, and following the war, the company had to either expand into new markets or scale back production. The company chose expansion, and a new factory was built in Memphis, Tennessee, specifically to build machinery for Southeastern farmers. This picker is somewhat unusual, as many of the cotton pickers reversed the tractor with the rear wheels in front of the machine. The photo is dated October 8, 1946.

The Model M and Model H used the straight rear axle found on the F-12. The rear tread width adjustment was simply a matter of sliding the wheels on the axles. The A&W Bulb Company of Fort Myers, Florida, uses this Farmall M with a front-mounted auxiliary-powered cutter used to chop the tops off of the gladiola bulbs.

The Farmall MV at work on a sugar cane plantation in Louisiana. Both the M and the MV were available with D-248 diesel engines, and were known as the MD and MDV. The diesels had the same bore and stroke as the gasoline/distillate engines, and used a unique gasoline starting system.

Farmall Model MV and MDV

In January of 1942, the company authorized the Farmall MV and MDV, high-clearance versions of the Model M. The Model MV used the distillate engine used on the Model M, while the Model MDV used the same diesel engine found in the Model MD.

A wide front end was used, with an I-beam forged axle mounted in the center to allow it to pivot. The axle was arched to provide additional ground clearance, and the front wheels were larger than those on a Model M. The rear was arched with a dropped-drive mechanism similar to the one used on the original Farmall. The rear tires were of similar size to the standard tires on the Model M. The final drive gearing was changed so that the five-speed transmission drove the MV and MDV at slower speeds. Top speed was about 15 miles per hour on the MV, and about 16 miles per hour on the MDV.

Farmall Super M

By the 1950s, IHC was looking for ways to breathe some new life into the Letter Series. The line was by no means sagging, as 1950 was a record year for the Model M, but the farmer's appetite for power was slowly but surely increasing. The additions of hydraulics and an

The Super M was introduced in 1952. The bore of the engines were increased 1/8 inch, resulting in 264 cubic inches of displacement. Another result was increased power. The Super M also received disc brakes, standard electric starting and lighting, and more.

increasing number of PTO-driven implements and tools were cutting into the amount of power available to drive the wheels, and 35 horsepower didn't stretch as far in 1950 as it did 10 years earlier.

The road to more power for the Model M took the predictable route; the Super M engine's bore was enlarged 1/8 inch to 4 inches while the stroke remained 5 1/4 inches. The result was a 264-cubic-inch engine that ran at a maximum of 1,450 rpm as the Model M. The engine was tested at Nebraska in 1952, and put out 33 drawbar horsepower and 44 horsepower on the belt pulley, an increase of over 8 horsepower. The gasoline engine produced 363 foot-pounds of torque at 991 rpm.

The diesel version was based on the same 264-cubic-inch engine. Like the gasoline engine, it produced peak horsepower at 1,450 rpm. The Super MD engine used a 12-volt system, and produced 350 foot-pounds of torque at 1,080 rpm. The diesel machine put out a similar amount of horsepower on the belt and at the drawbar.

The Super M was also tested on LPG gas. The engine's compression was bumped up to 6.75:1 to burn LPG, and the result was more horsepower and torque. The Super M produced 371 foot-pounds of torque and 40 drawbar horsepower when burning LPG.

Note that IHC began noting displacement of its engines, going so far as to code them according to displacement. Also, the Nebraska Tractor Tests began measuring torque as well as horsepower. Torque is actually a better measure of pulling power, as it represents an engine's ability to increase rpm rather than simply the amount of power put out at a given rpm.

Horsepower Ratings

Tractors' horsepower ratings are often not that impressive when compared to the amount of power in

Tractor Wars, Round Two

Henry Ford seemed to have a penchant for causing trouble for IHC. His Fordson nearly put the company out of the tractor business entirely, and the Ford-Ferguson 9N took the shine off IHC's stunning debut of the Letter Series tractors. The Letter Series machines had it all: style, power, famed IHC reliability, and the latest bells and whistles. What they didn't have was the Ferguson System. Henry Ford got that, for a handshake no less, and was using it to jump back into the domestic tractor market.

The Ferguson System, or three-point hitch, was dreamed up by Harry Ferguson. It is ironic that it debuted on a Ford, because it solved the very problem that made widows of so many Fordson operators' wives. The Fordson was a bit light to plow well, so farmers would often connect the plow high up on the rear differential to improve traction. Great for hard soil, but if you hit a rock, look out. If the plow was stopped dead, the tractor would ratchet itself up and around. If the driver wasn't quick to either grab the clutch or leap off to the side, the tractor would pile drive the operator head-first into the ground.

What Harry Ferguson's system did was use a three-point mounting system that also forced the plow into the ground. In this case, though, the lever pushed down on the front wheels of the tractor. If you hit a rock, the front wheels would be pressed down on the ground. The system had some downfalls—erratic draft when plowing deep—but it was a tremendous improvement over what was on the market in 1939.

The concept was much like the one that led to creation of the Farmall: build the machine around the implement. In the case of the three-point hitch, the implement became an extension of the tractor. An ingenious system, and a patented one. Ford and Ferguson were the only ones who had it, and they were exploiting it to full measure.

Sales of the Ford 9N were substantial, with more than 30,000 sold per year from 1940 to 1942. The numbers were about one-third of IHC's sales of the Letter Series in those years, but about equivalent to sales of the Model H.

While IHC was looking for a hitch system of its own, Ford and Ferguson's famed "Handshake Agreement," in which they decided to join forces to produce Ford tractors with the Ferguson system, fell apart in 1947. Ford jettisoned Ferguson and launched a revised version, the 8N. Ferguson responded with a $340-million lawsuit and his own tractor, the Ferguson. Ferguson eventually won the lawsuit, and was awarded $10 million.

Ford and Ferguson's antics aside, the Model 8N began selling in big numbers. In 1948, Ford sold nearly 100,000 units. In 1949, sales of 8N topped that figure. While IHC was still selling significantly more total machines, no single IHC model approached sales of 100,000 in a year. Ford maintained a rate of sales close to that torrid pace until the mid-1950s, and did not leave the domestic market this time. While IHC remained the leader, the number of Fords pouring into the market had to bring up bad memories of how close the Fordson had come to driving IHC right out of the market in the 1920s.

vehicles of similar size. Considering that a decent V-8 engine in a 4,500-pound pickup truck puts out well over 200 horsepower, the Model M's 46 belt pulley horsepower in a 5,500-pound package sounds dreadfully under-powered. One factor is that the M's horsepower is measured differently, with the truck engine's

Farmall Model M Production
Farmall M, MV, MD, MDV

Year	Production
1939	6,739*
1940	19,190
1941	23,387
1942	12,921
1943	4,789
1944	20,338
1945	7,606
1946	15,763
1947	26,321
1948	28,641
1949	33,166
1950	35,373
1951	41,381
1952	30,056†
1953	45,543
1954	26,924§
Total Prod.	**378,138**

Source: McCormick/IHC Archives,
"Tractor Production Schedule"

*Serial numbers issued
†Super M, MD, MV, MDV introduced
§Super M-TA, MD-TA introduced

The Super M-TA was produced only in 1954, although the 400 and variants were not a whole lot different. The Super M-TA was the beginning of a quest for more horsepower and gear choices that would continue until modern times.

figure typically taken at the crankshaft. Even so, the truck engine is putting out more than twice the horsepower of the tractor engine.

Gearing is a factor, but the real story is torque. Whether burning gasoline, diesel, or LPG, the Super M engine pumped out a torque peak of more than 350 foot-pounds at about 1,000 rpm. As any big-block muscle car enthusiast can attest, 300 or more foot-pounds of torque is serious power. The Super M was a powerful tractor in its day, capable of performing any task the average farm could dish out. The tractor still is relatively powerful. The obscene amounts of power put out by modern tractors overshadows the fact that the Super M is still a capable machine, and more than enough for most daily tasks.

Super M-TA

The Super M-TA was a sign of things to come for IHC. It featured the company's latest innovations—Torque Amplification and an independent power take-off.

Torque Amplification (TA) was a high-low range that could be shifted on the fly. The drive was a planetary gear unit located between the engine clutch and transmission. Engaging it reduced tractor speed by one-third, giving the operator more pulling power to work with. The addition of TA was the beginning of increased flexibility in tractor transmissions, as manufacturers strove to give the farmer enough gear selections to match power output perfectly to load. The closer the match, the more quickly and efficiently the tractor could perform a task.

The independent power take-off (IPTO) was a simple concept that was complex to apply. The idea was to make the PTO engagement independent of clutch engagement. Previous PTO drives ran off the transmission, which was the most convenient place to find power in the rear of the tractor. An IPTO system was engaged entirely separately from the clutch, with a lever. To do this, power had to transmitted directly to the rear of the tractor, bypassing the clutch. This was accomplished by driving the PTO directly from the flywheel on the Super M-TA.

The Super M-TA was produced in 1954 only, and was the forerunner to the Hundred Series. A diesel version was also available, and was known as the Super MD-TA or Super M-TA Diesel.

Chapter Eight

Styled Standard Treads

"Where farming was once a life of sheer drudgery, power farming
has made it a dignified business."
—*Implement and Tractor*, 1946

The styled standard tread tractors were all about standardizing the line. The W-4 was the standard tread version of the Farmall H and the W-6 was the companion to the Farmall M. This practice cut costs in production and design, as well as simplified things for the parts man at your IHC dealer. Instead of stocking four different sets of piston rings, only two were necessary. By the time you stock enough common replacement parts for a tractor, cutting the number of parts to stock by a third or more added up to significant space savings on the shelves. More importantly, the styled W tractors were built at Farmall Works, alongside the Letter Series Tractors.

Standard treads were steadily but not wildly popular. The tractors were well-suited to plowing, industrial, and orchard work. The low height worked well to sneak under orchard branches or through factories. Loewy styling and the latest features of the Letter Series Farmalls made the W-4, W-6, and W-9 solid additions to the IHC tractor line when they were introduced in 1940.

The gas and kerosene engines for the W-4 and W-6 were taken directly from the Farmall H and M. The WD-6 used the diesel engine from the Farmall MD, and the

diesel and gas engines in the W-9 were from the Trac-TracTor line. The frame differed in that the H and M had front and rear channels that bolted to the block, while the W-4 and W-6 used front and rear gray iron frames bolted together. Mounting pads were cast into the frames, allowing attachments to be hung at several points. The distinction was fairly subtle, but the most important difference was that many of the parts were interchangeable.

Among the more interesting facets of the standard tread tractors were the names. As always, IHC was interchanging names to place on the tractors. The W tractors were first McCormick-Deering machines, then just McCormick machines with the new Loewy-designed "IH" logo on the side. Forty years after the merger, the names of the founding companies were still floating around. Actually, this probably had more to do with marketing strategies than anything else. Whatever grand scheme the company used to name the tractors, the orchard tractors fit into a similar plan to the W machines and bore McCormick-Deering early and McCormick with the IH logo later in production.

The industrial tractors—the I-4, I-6, and I-9—bore the International name, and had for most of the time. Interna-

Left
The styled wheel tractors ushered in a new era for International, an era that was begun with the W-12. The Four and Six Series shared a basic common design with the Model H and M, just as the W-12 shared components with the F-12. This WD-9 is pulling a harrow plow in New Hamburg, Ontario.

Above
Part of the orchard package was a panel covering the engine, again to keep branches and such from snagging. Note the low-slung lights. This O-6 is disking a citrus orchard near McAllen, Texas.

The smaller of the so-called wheel tractors was the Four Series, which included the W-4, I-4, and O-4, all of which were introduced in 1940. This I-4 is pulling a homemade lumber trailer attachment in Milwaukee, Wisconsin. The sturdy tractor hauled 150,000 board-feet of lumber per day with this setup.

The I-4 was the industrial version of the W-4, and the two were very similar. The industrial version used a foot accelerator. The tractor used the same engine as the Model H, and weighed about 5,700 pounds, slightly heavier than the Model H. Horsepower at the belt pulley was nearly identical to the Model H, but the W-4 had a little more power at the drawbar. This I-4 is working at the Bison Lumber Company in Buffalo, New York.

tional was used more or less consistently with first industrial machines and, beginning with the hundred series, all of the standard tread tractors were Internationals.

It seems that not as many of the styled industrial tractors were intensively modified as with previous industrial models. The company advertising doesn't push custom machines, and photos of heavily altered machines are scarce in the archives.

The standard tread tractors were the first IHC tractors to neatly merge wheeled and row crop production, a practice that became common. The tractors made lower production runs feasible and profitable, and were another example of IHC ingenuity bringing good equipment to the market.

Four Series

The W-4 was the standard tread version of the Farmall H, of course, and used the same C-152 engine. The four-cylinder unit was started on gasoline and ran on kerosene or distillate. It used a variable-speed governor and was rated for 21 belt pulley horsepower at 1,650 rpm. As with the Farmall H, a high-compression gasoline-only version of the engine was released soon after the model appeared. The transmission was the same five-speed, with fifth a tall road gear that was locked out when used with steel wheels. The tractor was geared slightly lower than the Farmall H, with a 14-plus miles per hour top speed. The usual IHC filters for fuel, air, and oil were provided. The engine was cooled by a radiator and water pump system, but early models used shutters rather than a thermostat to control coolant temperature.

The front axle was a forged I-beam that pivoted on the front bolster. The steering mechanism differed from that of the Farmall H. On the Four Series tractors, it was a drag link that extended along the left-hand side of the tractor. Forged steel steering knuckles pivoted in bronze bushings in the ends of the front axle. The rear axles were mounted in removable housings. The tractors were reasonably light, at about 3,800 pounds with single rear wheels, and about 5,500 pounds with dual rear wheels. The heavy-duty option, which included beefier front and rear axles and hydraulic brakes, added about 600 pounds more.

The basic standard tread, the W-4, was the first model that appeared. It was approved for production in March 1940. The orchard version, the O-4, was approved shortly thereafter, in April 1940. The O-4 was the same machine with the addition of smooth body work and swoopy fenders that prevented damage to trees as the tractor slipped through the orchard. An underslung muffler and air intake and a hand clutch completed the package, keeping the machine low and compact. Orchard models also have the distinct advantage of stylish good looks. Considering the fact that they look Buck Rogers-ish today, they must have made quite an impact in their time.

The other Four Series was the International I-4, the industrial version of the W-4. The sturdy I-4 could be equipped with dual rear tires (which were, as you probably know, actually quad rear tires, but never mind), rear work and travel lamps, front and rear wheel weights, and hydraulic remote control.

In 1953, the Four Series went Super, and each tractor was labeled with the "Super" on the decal on the front of the hood. Under the hood, the new C-164 engine was up to 164 cubic inches by increasing the bore 1/8 inch. Horsepower took a corresponding jump, up to about 30 horsepower at the belt when burning distillate and 33 on gasoline.

The 0-4 was the orchard version of the Four Series. Like the industrial models, orchard models were quite similar to the W-4. The most noticeable feature is the swoopy fenders, designed to keep branches out of harm's way. This photograph was taken in the lower valley of the Rio Grande.

Orchard tractors were to tree farms what the Farmall was to a crop farm, as the orchard models performed all sorts of tasks. The O-4 used a hand-operated throttle and clutch.

Model O-4, OS-4, W-4, I-4, and Supers Production	
Year	Production
1940	213
1941	2,741
1942	1,888
1943	1,759
1944	3,705
1945	2,799
1946	1,893
1947	2,822
1948	2,975
1949	2,973
1950	3,186
1951	3,519
1952	2,385
1953	2,566
1954	444
Total Prod.	**35,868**

Source: McCormick/IHC Archives; Tractor Production Sheet

Six Series

The first of the Six Series machines to appear was the W-6, which was the wheeled counterpart to the Farmall Model M. Just as the Model H and M shared a common chassis design, the Four and Six Series machines were much alike. The significant difference was the engines, especially the diesel engine available in the Six Series. The increased power had the tractor rated to pull a three- to four-bottom plow or an 18-foot single disk.

Engine

The base model was the W-6, which was authorized for production in November 1939. Production records show that it hit dealership floors in 1940. The tractor used the distillate- or kerosene-burning engine from the Model M, which was the 3 7/8x5 1/4-inch four-cylinder. A variable governor was used, the engine was rated for 31 horsepower at the belt and 24 horsepower on the drawbar when burning distillate fuel. The original cooling system used a radiator and water pump with shutters to regulate engine temperature, although later models used a thermostat. As with the Model M, the high-compression gasoline engine was offered as an option in mid-1940 for all Six Series tractors.

Orchard tractors also used low-slung exhaust and intake pipes, keeping them from hooking the trees as the tractor slid under the trees.

This 0-4 is at work with an offset disc in Orange County, California. The little tractors were able pullers, with 17 drawbar horsepower in second gear when burning distillate.

Interestingly, in July 1940 IHC decided to authorize offering a kerosene-burning attachment for the standard Six Series and Farmall M tractors, despite earlier models clearly marked as capable of burning distillate *or* kerosene. It's possible the earlier engines did not burn kerosene well, and the kerosene attachment addressed that problem. The end result was that all standard Six Series tractors were rated to burn distillate. To burn kerosene, at least according to IHC, you had to purchase the kerosene-burning attachment.

The chassis and running gear were similar to those of the Four Series. The transmission was a five-speed, with a tall fifth gear locked out on steel-wheeled tractors. The clutch was an 11-inch Rockford Drilling Company single-plate unit. The brakes were external contracting bands on

The Six Series were the wheel tractor versions of the Farmall Model M. Early Four and Six Series tractors used the typical radiator and water pump cooling but used shutters to regulate temperature. Later versions used a thermostat to control coolant temperature. This WD-6 is shown near Medina, New York.

drums. The Six Series tractors weighed in at about 4,800 pounds with single rear wheels, about 1,000 pounds heavier than the Four Series tractors.

WD-6

The first variant to be introduced was the WD-6, the diesel version. Authorized in February 1940, it should have been on the farm by the harvest season of that year, and in significant numbers by Spring 1941. The D-248 engine was also used in the company's small crawler, the TD-6. The four-cylinder engine used the same bore and stroke as the kerosene/distillate engine, and was started on gasoline. Despite the similar displacement, the diesel put out a few more horsepower than the standard W-6 engine, with the WD-6 pumping out 33 horsepower on the belt and 26 horsepower at the drawbar.

The diesel version of the W-6 was known as the WD-6. It used the same D-248 diesel engine as the Farmall MD, and was authorized for regular production in February 1940. This WD-6 is pulling a three-furrow Model 8C adjustable beam plow and plow packer.

This O-6 orchard model is being serviced on a Gainesville, Florida farm. The tractor is hitched to a McCormick-Deering manure spreader. The farm has a seven-year tung tree grove as well as a herd of Aberdeen Angus cattle.

The chassis, clutch, and transmission were identical to the W-6. The cost was slightly higher, but the increased efficiency and horsepower of the diesel engine should have made it a popular choice with farmers. No differentiation was made in serial numbers, so production figures are not available.

O-6

The next model to appear was the O-6, the orchard version. As with the O-4, the keys to an orchard model were streamlined fenders and underslung exhaust and intake pipes. The kerosene/distillate engine was used on the O-6, while the OD-6 used the D-248 diesel engine. The O-6 was authorized for production in mid-December 1940, making it available early in 1941. The other Six Series machines were the industrial versions, the I-6 and ID-6, which were introduced in 1940.

Supers

The Six Series went Super in 1952, with engines providing increased power. The horsepower gains were found with an increased bore, up to 4 inches, with the same 5 1/4-inch stroke. The standard engine became the C-264 gasoline burner, and horsepower was up 8 horsepower at the belt to 41 and increased 7 horsepower on the drawbar to 33. Bear in mind that the increases are magnified by the fact that the new engine burned gasoline, which produces 5–10 percent more horsepower than distillate.

The D-264 diesel engine used the same bore and stroke as the gas engine, and put out the same amount of horsepower. The diesel equipment was a few hundred pounds heavier, but otherwise the Super W-6 and Super WD-6 were nearly identical.

The last variant of the Six Series was the TA versions, the Super W6-TA and Super WD6-TA. Like the

This outfit is owned by T. E. Topham & Sons of Riverside, California, who sell fertilizer for citrus groves. They also own extensive acreage of citrus in that area. Jim Topham of the company said, "The economy of operation in using International Harvester tractors and trucks has been very gratifying to us. That is why we now operate two O-6 tractors to replace the McCormick-Deering O-12s that had given us countless hours of satisfactory service."

This O-6 is pulling a trailer loaded with organic fertilizer (steer manure) in a Valencia orange grove near Riverside, California. In October 1944, the OS-6, was authorized for production. In September 1945, the ODS-6, the diesel was authorized. The OS-6 differed from the O-6 in that the fenders were off the W-4 and the hood side sheets were omitted.

This W-9 is shown with "squadron" hitch pulling a Caldwell weed chopper, which was popular equipment for pasture improvement, to chop down weeds and small palmettos, and also to follow disking. The W-9 is at work near Arcadia, Florida.

Super M-TA, these two tractors incorporated torque amplification and live PTO. Produced only in 1954, these were a sign of things to come for IHC. Only about 3,000 or fewer of these tractors were built, making them extremely collectible.

Nine Series

The Nine Series brought additional power to the farmer, and offered the farmer the simple improvement of a larger tractor with more power. The Nine Series were big, open-field tractors that used powerful engines from the crawler series, and had an integral-frame chassis design to meet the demand for more powerful tractors. It's no coincidence that these machines were the best-selling of the styled standard treads; the farmer was demanding more and more power on the farm.. A combination of an increase in

driven implements, larger implements, and changing tastes made horsepower the key to selling tractors, especially in the 1950s and 1960s. The Nine Series were an early IHC entry into the horsepower race that would ensue.

W-9

The first of the Nine Series, the W-9, was introduced in 1940. Like the Nine Series precursor, the W-40, the W-9 used the same engine as the T-9 crawler, the C-335. That engine could be equipped to burn gasoline, kerosene, or distillate, and pumped out 44 horsepower at the belt and 36 horsepower at the drawbar. The diesel engine was actually quite similar, with identical bore and stroke (4.4x5.5 inches) and similar horsepower output. Diesel Nine Series were indicated with a "D" in the model name (WD-9, ID-9, etc.).

Model O-6, OS-6, ODS-6, W-6, WD-6, I-6 and ID-6 Production

Year	Production
1940	287
1941	2,558
1942	1,513
1943	1,180
1944	2,584
1945	4,852
1946	3,273
1947	5,322
1948	5,251
1949	5,498
1950	4,735
1951	5,875
1952	3,838
1953	6,627
1954	3,089
Total Prod.	**56,482**

Source: McCormick/IHC Archives, "Tractor Production Schedule"

This WD-9 used a 335-cubic-inch diesel engine, which used IH's somewhat unusual system of starting on gasoline with a low-compression system that was switched over to a high-compression setting to burn diesel when the engine was warm. In a 1950 Nebraska Tractor Test, the WD-9 put out 51 horsepower at the belt pulley and 37 at the drawbar.

The W-9 was the largest International wheel tractor, and the Nine Series appeared in 1940. Unlike the Four and Six Series, the Nine Series chassis was unique rather than based on another model. The four-cylinder 335-cubic-inch gasoline/distillate/kerosene and diesel engines were shared with the T-9 and TD-9 crawlers. This W-9 is pulling stumps prior to leveling land in Florida.

All used the same chassis and running gear. The transmission was a five-speed, and ran through a 12-inch single-plate clutch. As with the rest of the IHC line, fifth gear was locked out on tractors with steel wheels. The magneto was an IHC H-4, and the carburetor was also an IHC unit, a Model E-13. The cooling system used a water pump and radiator and shutters initially, with later models using a thermostat without the shutters.

Optional equipment for the Nine Series machines included a PTO, swinging drawbar, pneumatic tire pumps, wheel weights, and a wide assortment of steel wheels and rims and pneumatic tires.

A Nine Series tractor was the largest, heaviest machine in the IHC line, weighing in at about 10,000 pounds with fluids and weights. The weight and horsepower translated into sheer pulling power and traction in any conditions.

WD-9, WR-9, and WDR-9

Six models of the Nine Series were built, the regular W-9 and WD-9, the rice field special WR-9 and WDR-9, and the industrial I-9 and ID-9. Perhaps the most unusual of these were the Rice Field Specials.

The Rice Field Special versions of the W-9 and WD-9 were authorized in August 1944. The original WR-9 and WDR-9 were on steel, probably due to World War II restrictions on using rubber, and used 6x4-inch spade lugs. It's doubtful the steel wheels worked well in the extremely soft soil in rice fields, and the wide, deeply lugged rubber tires shown on this WDR-9 were preferred.

The Rice Field Specials were equipped with wider rear tires to keep the 7,000-plus-pound tractor from burying itself in boggy soil. This WR-9 is pulling a Model 98 McCormick-Deering six-bottom disk plow on an Orlando, Florida, farm that houses 1,100 head of Brahmas.

The industrial version of the Nine Series was available in gas or diesel versions. All of the standard tread industrial machines—the I-4, I-6, and I-9—could be bought in "heavy-duty" versions, which were equipped with sturdier rear axles and hydraulic rear brakes. This ID-9 is in the Osceola National Forest near Sanderson, Florida.

This MRS Special is a bit of a mystery. It was probably a Mississippi special model. The Super Nine Series was introduced in 1953 and used an engine with a larger bore to bump horsepower up a bit.

Nine Series Production
I-9, ID-9, W-9, WD-9, WR-9, WDR-9, and Supers

Year	Production
1940	0*
1941	1,764
1942	1,263
1943	1,220
1944	5,765
1945	5,868
1946	5,373
1947	6,235
1948	6,247
1949	9,485
1950	6,937
1951	7,231
1952	5,815
1953	4,773**
1954	3,662
Total Prod.	**74,141**

*IHC documents conflict on 1940 production; serial numbers are listed for that year, but the production chart shows no Nine Series tractors built in 1940.

**Super Nine Series production began in 1953

Source: McCormick/IHC Archives

Rice fields are moist and loamy, and require tractors with high horsepower and good traction. The Nine Series were well-suited to the task, and the original Rice Field Special was equipped with steel wheels with large spades for traction. Ensuing models used wide pneumatic tires with deep lugs, which must have worked much better than steel.

Super Nine

The Super Nine tractors used an increased bore to bring displacement up to 350 cubic inches. The four-cylinder engine had giant pistons, with a 4 1/2-inch bore and 5 1/2-inch stroke. The engine could be equipped to burn gasoline, diesel, kerosene, or distillate. The pistons were aluminum, and the cylinder sleeves were replaceable. The diesel engine used fuel injection and had a compression ratio of 15.6:1. The powerful engine put out 530 foot-pounds of torque at 1,039 rpm. The Super Nines were introduced in 1953. Essentially the same tractor was produced until 1958 as the 600 and the 650, which were simply Super Nines with slightly different standard and optional equipment.

The Nine Series demonstrated IHC's vision. It was the most successful of the wheel tractors, and was what the farmer of the day wanted and needed; more horsepower. Although horsepower was not yet the deciding factor in a purchase, it would be one of the most important considerations from the late 1950s to modern times.

"It's no coincidence that the Nine Series were best-selling of the styled standard treads; the farmer was demanding more and more power."

Chapter Nine

Styled
TracTracTors

∎
---

*"By improving the efficiency of the convential wheel, the track-type tractor furthered
man's ability to apply mechanical power to challenging tasks."*
—Reynold M. Wik, *Benjamin Holt & Caterpillar*, 1984

When Raymond Loewy was styling International products, the TracTracTors received the same smooth, functional styling as the Letter Series tractors. The first to be restyled was the big fuel-injected TD-18, with prototypes floating around as early as 1938. The next to be styled were the new T-6, T-9, and T-14. The two smaller crawlers were part of IHC's efforts at integrated production, as the T-6 shared componentry with the Model M and W-6, and the T-9 shared parts with the W-9. A few of the machines were introduced in 1939, and the full line was put into production in 1940.

All of the new crawlers featured replaceable cylinders and main bearings, with the cylinders constructed of heat-treated sleeves machined to fit on the

outside and honed and polished inside. The engines used oil pumps and lubricated bearings, and were cooled with a thermostatically controlled radiator and water pump system. Steering clutches and brakes were used for steering, as with previous TracTracTors. Most of the models were available in a narrow- and wide-tread version.

Available options included cabs, electric lights and starting, a variety of track lugs (often called "grousers"), cutaway drive sprockets for heavy mud,

radiator shutters for cold weather, and an assortment of guards, bumpers, and shields.

T-6 and TD-6

The T-6 and TD-6 were the crawler counterparts to the Model M and Six Series. They used the same engines, but the chassis was quite different. The crawler chassis was heavier than the tractors, weighing about 7,000 pounds dry.

The T-6 used the gasoline, kerosene, or distillate engine, while the TD-6 used a diesel unit. Both had a five-speed forward and one-speed reverse transmission, with top forward speed at a blistering 5.4 miles per hour. They were available as both wide- and narrow-tread machines, with a 40-inch tread for the narrow model and 50-inch for the wide tread model. When tested in 1940, the gasoline-burning T-6 produced 33 belt and 25 drawbar horsepower on gasoline and 31 belt and 24 drawbar horsepower on distillate. The TD-6 produced 31 belt and 22 drawbar horsepower when burning fuel oil. It was rated to pull a two- to four-bottom plow.

The T-6 and TD-6 received larger engines in several later variations, known as the Series 61 and Series 62. The small crawlers were replaced with the T-4, T-5, and TD-5.

Left
When International's wheel tractors were upgraded in 1938 and 1939, the TracTrac-Tors also received a makeover. This International brochure from 1944 shows the entire crawler line, from the little TD-6 to the giant TD-18.

Above
The largest crawler in the International line when introduced, the TD-18, was billed as the most powerful crawler on the market. The big machine weighed over 22,000 pounds and the 691-cubic-inch six-cylinder cranked out 71 drawbar horsepower. This TD-18 is pictured dwarfing a Model A tractor.

T-9 and TD-9

The T-9 and TD-9 were the counterparts to the Nine Series. The crawlers weighed about 10,000 pounds, and were available in narrow (44-inch) and wide (60-inch) tread widths. Like the smaller crawlers, five-speed forward and one-speed reverse transmissions were used, with top forward speed at 5.3 miles per hour.

The T-9 gasoline engine produced for 41 horsepower at the belt, 32 at the drawbar when burning gasoline. Rated to pull a three- to five-bottom plow. The T-9 used the same C-335 engine as the Nine Series wheel tractors. The T-9 was produced from 1940 to 1956.

The TD-9 engine was rated for 39 horsepower at the belt, 29 horsepower at the drawbar when introduced. It used the D-335 engine, the same that was used in Nine Series diesels. The TD-9 was produced from 1940 to 1956. During that time, the engine's power output was slightly increased. When tested at Nebraska in 1951, power was up a couple of horsepower at the drawbar and the belt.

In 1956, the Series 91 was introduced. The engine bore was increased to bring the four-cylinder diesel's displacement up to 350 cubic inches. The compression ratio was 16:1, and horsepower was up to 43 horsepower at the drawbar and 55 at the belt when tested at Nebraska in 1956.

In 1959, the Series 92 TD-9 came out with a new turbocharged six-cylinder 282-cubic-inch engine. The new engine used a 18:1 compression ratio and brought horsepower up to 66 at the PTO and 44 at the drawbar. The Series 92 was replaced by the Series B in 1962, and production continued through at least 1973. At some point, the TD-9's name was changed to the Model 150 crawler, probably around 1969 when the new Model 100 and 125 crawlers were introduced.

TD-14

The original TD-14 was produced from 1939 to 1949. The tractor was significantly larger than the TD-9, weighing about nine tons with weights and fluids. The TD-14 was available in a wide or narrow tread, with either a 74- or 56-inch tread width.

The original version of the TD-14 was produced from 1939 to 1949. The four-cylinder 461-cubic-inch diesel engine produced 52 drawbar and 62 horsepower at the belt pulley when tested at Nebraska in 1940. The transmission had six forward and two reverse speeds, with top forward speed at 5.8 miles per hour.

The TD-14A was produced from 1949 to 1955. The Series 141 TD-14 was produced from 1955 to 1956. The engine size remained the same 461 cubic inches. The Series 142 was introduced in 1956, and production ran until 1958. It also used the same-size engine, but power output was up due to an increased rpm rating. The TD-14 put out 61 drawbar and 83 belt horsepower when tested at Nebraska in 1956.

TD-15

The TD-15 was the replacement for the TD-14. Introduced in 1958, production ran until 1973. The TD-15 featured a new 554-cubic-inch six-cylinder diesel engine. Tested at Nebraska in 1960, the new engine brought the TD-15 up to 77 drawbar horsepower (PTO horsepower was not tested). The increase was not that substantial, considering the engine was much larger than the older TD-14 powerplant. The tractor's weight with weights and fluids was up substantially, at more than 12 tons. A 12-volt electrical system was used.

TD-18

The development of the TD-18 began in the mid-1930s, when the company experimented with a large crawler. It seems that five machines were at least talked about, the T-80, T-65, TD-65, T-60, and TD-60. The development was discussed in "International Harvester Industrial Power Activities" as follows:

"Development of this larger tractor [the TD-18] started early in 1934, when the Engineering Department built the T-80 which had the same rear-mounted steering arrangement as the T-20 and T-40 models. During 1935, we developed and built the T-65 with many improvements but in general along the same lines as the T-80. Then in 1936 we brought out the T- and TD-60 in which the steering clutches were essentially of the current production. In 1937 and 1938 this design was further developed and streamlined and was then known as the TD-65."

In *150 Years of International Harvester*, a drawing—not a photograph—is shown of a TD-65. The crawler is obviously styled. Although its difficult to tell without a size reference in the drawing, the TD-65 gives the impression of being quite large, with the platform and seat high off the ground and relatively

The T-6 and TD-6 were smaller machines, weighing about 7,000 pounds and putting out about 30 drawbar horsepower. The original T-6 and TD-6 used the same engines as the W-6 and WD-6. In a version known as the 61 Series, the engine's bore was increased. The 62 Series T-6 and TD-6 used a different engine entirely.

The TD-9 was the next rung up the crawler ladder, weighing in at nearly 10,000 pounds and producing about 40 drawbar horsepower. The original T-9 and TD-9 used the same engines as the W-9 and WD-9. Like the T-6 and TD-6, several versions were built, with the 91 Series receiving larger bore engines and the 92 Series and B Series receiving an entirely new engine. This TD-9 is pulling a Dyrr offset disk harrow.

The TracTracTors used a water pump and thermostat by 1944, with radiator shutters available for cold-weather use. Cabs could also be added to make winter operation more tolerable. This TD-9 hauling logs in the frigid winter of La Peine, Quebec, is equipped with optional hood side doors and a radiator guard.

small on the big machine. Author C. H. Wendel refers to a listing without production figures in IHC documentation, which is probably different than the text above. These few scraps of information give a tantalizing look at the development of IHC's large crawler, the TD-18, which was introduced later with the other styled crawlers.

The TD-18 was larger than any tractor the company had produced previously. It was built in several versions from 1939 to 1957, with each iteration producing more horsepower. The engine was a six-cylinder diesel rated for 85 horsepower on the belt and 70 drawbar horsepower (later versions had more, with over 109 horsepower on the belt). The tractor was huge compared to anything else the company built, weighing in at over 10 tons. The tracks were 84 5/8 inches long and 18 inches wide, which put 3,046 square inches of track on the ground.

The six-cylinder diesel engine had a bore and stroke of 4 3/4x6 1/2 inches. The engine featured Bosch fuel injection, full-pressure lubrication, and removable cylinder sleeves and main bearings. The engine was cooled with a thermostatically regulated radiator, water pump, and fan system, with shutters optional for cold weather.

TD-24

The TD-24 was International's grand entrance into the construction business, and it debuted a host of new features in a 18-ton package touted as the most powerful in the industry. The TD-24 suffered some problems when it was introduced, but carried the construction banner for IHC capably for more than a decade.

The TD-14, like the TD-6, -14, and -18—was available in two different tread widths known as narrow and wide. This TD-14 is at work near Spokane, Washington.

The TD-14 had a six forward- and two reverse-speed transmission and a top speed of nearly 6 miles per hour. A four-cylinder 461-cubic-inch diesel powered the crawler. This TD-14 with a Bucyrus-Erie angle dozer is skidding Ponderosa and Yellow Pine logs near Spokane, Washington.

The TD-24 was produced from 1947 to 1959. The power output was stunning for the era, and is still substantial today. International advertised that the TD-24 was the most powerful crawler tractor in the industry. When tested at Nebraska in 1950, the tractor was too powerful for the dynamometer so belt horsepower could not be tested. The tractor recorded a stunning 138 drawbar horsepower. Power output rose steadily as the model was developed, and the 1954 edition cranked out 155 drawbar horsepower at the Nebraska text, and the 1957 machine was up to 163 horsepower at the drawbar.

The crawler weighed about 20 tons, and was powered by a 1,090-cubic-inch six-cylinder diesel that carried 28 quarts of oil in its sump. The tractor used an unusual 24-volt system and a 317-pound crankshaft.

Planetary Power Steering

One of the new features on the TD-24 was what International called Planetary Power Steering. This feature combined hydraulically controlled steering clutches with a two-speed range similar in function to the Torque Amplifier introduced on the Super M-TA. The dual-range unit could be engaged on the fly, allowing shifting under power. The two-speed unit was coupled to a four-speed synchromesh transmission, giving eight speeds in forward or reverse. The synchromesh transmission was nearly unprecedented in the 1950s, and International tractors did not receive synchromesh transmissions until the 1980s (which was late compared to the rest of the industry).

The two-speed system could be utilized for gradual turns by dropping one track to the "low" position and the other to "high." This provided power to both tracks while turning. To pivot, the inside track was stopped and only the outside driven, which was the typical method of turning a crawler.

Troubles with the TD-24

Despite all these advances, the TD-24 came out with some flaws and, according to Barbara Marsh in *A Corporate*

Tragedy, was an embarrassment for IHC. The TD-24 apparently broke down quickly, and Marsh contends that the TD-24 problems badly tarnished IHC's reputation in the heavy equipment field, damaging the company's attempts to compete with Caterpillar and the big Allis-Chalmers crawlers.

The TD-24 was hardly the last of the TracTracTor line, as IHC crawlers continued to flow off factory floors in a fairly steady stream. It is the end of the crawler story in this book, tragically. The line was headed a bit south after the TD-24, and times got increasingly tough for the entire agricultural equipment industry. At one point, IHC was selling crawlers at a 10 percent loss, banking on service parts to make up the difference. The strategy may have worked, but that's a hard way to make money. The tough times took their toll, and the late 1960s and early 1970s saw mergers become the rule of the day for tractor manufacturers. Where once there had been over 180 tractor manufacturers in the United States, there would be only a handful left by 1970. A key to keeping IHC afloat

The TD-14 was good for about 55 drawbar horsepower and weighed over 15,000 pounds. All crawlers could be equipped with a wide variety of tread lugs, as well as cabs or simple cages like on this TD-14.

During World War II, International crawlers were recruited for duty. This brochure depicts the company's crawlers at war.

was the crawler line, although their positive impact on profitability lessened after the ill-fated TD-24.

TD-25

The TD-25 was introduced in 1959, and was the replacement for the TD-24. The big TD-25 used a turbocharged 817-cubic-inch six-cylinder diesel to crank out a prodigious 187 drawbar horsepower. The crawler weighed 26 tons and used a synchromesh eight-speed transmission. A 24-volt electrical system was used, and the crawler was produced until at least 1973.

TD-30

The TD-30 was another monstrous crawler designed for the construction market. It was introduced in 1962, and production ran until 1967. The TD-30 used the same basic engine as the TD-25, although the new crawlers were larger, at about 29 tons. The TD-30 was available with either a power-shift or gear-drive system.

The TD-30 six-cylinder engine in the power-shift model was both turbocharged and intercooled, and was rated for 320 horsepower. The same six was used in the gear-drive model, but without the intercooler, resulting in a rating of 280 horsepower. Both engines displaced

817 cubic inches and used fuel injection, four-valve heads, and a massive oil cooler.

The power-shift drive was similar to the drive used on the TD-24, and was a torque converter coupled to several hydraulically-controlled clutch packs. The result was similar to that of an automatic transmission, with four simple speeds and the dual-range Planetary Power units controlling forward and reverse motion. The power-shift model used a hydraulic fluid cooler, and had more horsepower than the gear-shift model. The torque drive ate up the extra power, making the two models comparable in drawbar performance.

A synchronized gear transmission was also offered. The transmission was a four-speed unit, and the addition of the Planetary Power units from the TD-24 gave eight speeds in forward and reverse. A huge 16-inch dry-disk clutch transmitted power from the engine to the transmission, and the synchronized transmission allowed gears to be shifted while the crawler was moving.

A complete line of construction attachments was offered, including dozer blades, rippers, push plates, and all sorts of guards and cages.

T-340 and TD-340

Produced from 1959 to 1965, the 340 crawlers were used the engines from the diesel and gas 340 tractors. The crawlers weighed about 3 1/2 tons with fluids and weights. Like the earlier crawlers, the 340 crawlers were available in a wide- or narrow-tread model, with tread widths of either 38 or 48 inches.

The 135-cubic-inch gasoline engine in the T-340 was rated for 35 belt and 31 drawbar horsepower. The compression ratio was 8:1, and early models used a 6-volt ignition (a 12-volt was used by 1963). The four-cylinder engine could be run to 2,000 rpm.

The 166-cubic-inch diesel engine in the TD-340 tested at 32 drawbar and 36 PTO horsepower at

This TracTracTor was put to work soon after World War II. It was painted olive drab rather than red, and hauled out over 2 million board-feet of lumber.

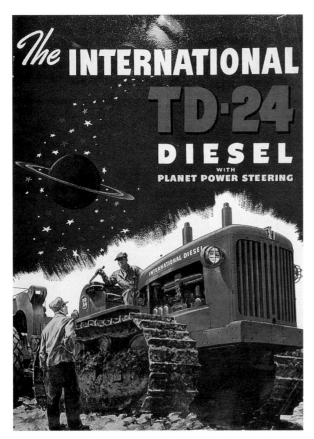

The TD-24 was a monstrous machine designed for construction and large logging outfits. The crawler weighed over 37,000 pounds, and was powered by a 1,090-cubic-inch six-cylinder diesel rated for 155 drawbar horsepower. With 101 inches of track on the ground, the TD-24 produced 38,600 pounds of pull at the drawbar in first gear. The crawler used an eight-speed (forward *and* reverse) transmission, and a 317-pound crankshaft. Despite a host of bells and whistles, a weak transmission in early versions of the TD-24 hurt International's reputation in the heavy crawler market.

Nebraska in 1960. The larger diesel was also a four-cylinder, but bore and stroke were completely different. The compression ratio was 19:1, the higher ratio necessary to burn diesel.

The transmissions were five-forward and one-reverse-speed units. The 340 crawlers could be equipped with either a Torque Amplifier or a Fast Reverser. The Torque Amplifier allowed on-the-go shifting between a high and low range, as on previous International tractors. The Fast Reverser gave an instant reverse gear that was 22 1/2-percent faster than the forward speed selected. Both options could not be mounted on the same machine.

Regular equipment included double-disk brakes, a cigarette lighter, tachometer, heat and fuel gauges, and a swinging drawbar. Options included a three-point hitch, "live" hydraulic system, independent 540-rpm PTO, lights, radiator shutters, and an assortment of guards.

T-4, T-5, and TD-5

The T-4, T-5, and TD-5 were the smallest crawlers in the line, and were introduced in 1959. The tractors used

a derivative of the engine from the Super C in a 3 1/2-ton frame. Don't be fooled by the fact that these crawlers weight just as much as the more powerful 340 crawlers. Weight is often an asset in a crawler, as it increases traction and drawbar pull in most cases.

The smaller T-4, T-5, and TD-5 do lack the more sophisticated hydraulic system available on the 340s, but the smaller machines compared favorably to the competition. John Deere, Case, and Oliver all had crawlers of a similar size, and the International T-4, T-5, and TD-5 have more power and more or equal pulling power. They also had more standard transmission speeds.

T-4

The T-4 used the same C-123 engine as the Super A, rated to run at a maximum of 2,000 rpm. The T-4 put out 21 drawbar and 27 PTO horsepower when tested at Nebraska in 1960. The crawler was equipped with a Torque Amplifier.

T-5

The T-5 used the 135-cubic-inch engine, which looks to be a longer-stroke version of the Super A engine. The slightly larger engine revved to the same 2,000 rpm, and produced a little more horsepower, generating 29 at the drawbar and 36 on the PTO. The T-5 was tested in 1960 and was equipped with a five-speed transmission and a Torque Amplifier, like the T-4.

TD-5

The TD-5 used a 144-cubic-inch diesel engine from the B-275 tractor. The fuel-injected four-cylinder diesel used a 21:1 compression ratio, and produced 30 drawbar and 35 PTO horsepower. The TD-5 tested in 1960 was equipped with a five-speed transmission with a Torque Amplifier, just like the other two small crawlers.

With more than 84 inches of track on the ground, the powerful TD-18 put out nearly 19,000 pounds of drawbar pull in first gear. Equipped with a six forward- and two reverse-speed transmission, the crawler topped out at about 6 miles per hour.

Late Crawler Production

Model Name	Years	Est. Prod.*
T-4	1959–60	NA
T-5, TC-5	1959–60	NA
TD-5	1959–60	NA
T-6 and TD-6	1940–56	38,550
T-6 and TD-6 (61 Series)	1956–59	2,500
T-6 and TD-6 (62 Series)	1959–69	3,920
Total T-6 and TD-6	1940–69	44,970
TD-7	1969–74	1,040
T-8	1969–74	1,030
T-9	1940–56	10,920
TD-9	1940–56	59,800
TD-9 (91 Series)	1956–59	6,990
TD-9 (92 Series)	1959–62	6,000
TD-9 (Series B)/150	1962–74	10,030
Total T-9 and TD-9	1940–74	93,740
TD-14	1939–49	26,260
TD-14A	1949–55	12,540
TD-14A (141 Series)	1955–56	2,250
TD-14 (142 Series)	1956–58	4,010
Total TD-14	1939–58	45,060
TD-15 (150 Series)	1958–61	3,500
TD-15 (151 Series)	1961–62	680
TD-15	1963–73	21,150
Total TD-15	1958–73	25,330
TD-18	1939–49	22,040
TD-18A	1949–55	11,110

Model Name	Years	Est. Prod.*
TD-18A (181 Series)	1955–56	2,450
TD-18 (182 Series)	1956–58	2,760
Total TD-18	1939–58	38,360
TD-20 (200 Series)	1958–60	2,500
TD-20 (201 Series)	1961–62	470
TD-20	1963–73	23,000
Total TD-20	1958–73	25,970
TD-24	1947–55	7,500
TD-24 (241 Series)	1955–59	3,630
Total TD-24	1947–59	11,130
TD-25 (250 Series)	1959–62	1,290
TD-25 (Series B)	1962–71	3,000
TD-25	1968–73	1,900
Total TD-25	1959–73	6,190
TD-30	1962–67	690
100	1969–73	690
T-250	1963–73	6,440
125	1969–73	1,000
T-340 and TD-340	1959–65	8,030

*Production figures are number of serial numbers and do not include the last year of production. These figures are only rough approximates and are rounded off.
Source: Crawler Serial Line Numbers, IHC, 1973. NUMBERS ARE ONLY VALID TO 1973.

The crawlers were available in three tread widths of 38, 48, and 68 inches. The tractors had a standard five-forward and one-reverse-speed transmission that could be equipped with a Torque Amplifier. Two versions of live PTO could be ordered, the standard type and what they called the constant-running PTO. A two-position clutch allowed the operator to depress the clutch part way and disengage the wheels but not the PTO, while depressing the clutch all the way disengaged the engine and the PTO. International called this two-position system a constant-running PTO.

Several different hitch and hydraulic options were offered. A three-point hitch was available with an assortment of hydraulic systems to control just the hitch or a remote implement and the hitch. A straight swinging drawbar was offered as well. A four- or five-roller frame and an assortment of track shoes were also offered.

This TD-18 is equipped with a WO18 winch hoist and KA80 medium arch used to skid out trees large enough to test the big machine.

Chapter Ten

Cub and Cub Cadet

■

"It was a bad guess, but it was in the right direction."
Engineer Gordon Hershman, on IHC's estimate of selling 5,000 Cub Cadets per year.

The Farmall A, B, and C were designed to fit the needs of the smaller farmer who was perhaps making the change from horse farming to tractors, and the Model H and M satisfied the typical farmer. The Cub and Cadet were targeted at an entirely different group and were in some ways more important to International's future than the more traditional tractors.

Opening new markets was crucial for IHC, especially in the Post-War Period. For one thing, the company had geared up production during World War II, building crawlers and bombs and more for the government. With that demand suddenly gone, the company was left with a large work force that would have to be scaled back unless the company expanded. The company chose expansion, attacking new markets like milk coolers, construction equipment, and even some appliances such as refrigerators and air conditioners.

The company also looked to expand coverage in existing markets. One of the trends that had to concern tractor manufacturers was the fact that the number of farms without tractors were dropping off. In the 1920s and 1930s, horse use was still prevalent, and manufacturers had to figure out how to build a tractor that

would successfully replace the horse. The market was almost limitless, and sales potential was huge.

The sales potential of the post-war era was even larger, as the tractors of the 1940s were enough of an advance that most farmers found replacing the tractors of the 1920s or 1930s with new machinery was a profitable move. Also, there was still a respectable percentage that hadn't turned to power farming. An incredible 1.5 million tractors were added to farms in the United States between 1940 and 1950, but that trend simply could not continue. Once most of the farms had a modern tractor, the sales volume would drop. Savvy tractor manufacturers, like International, were aware of this. The only way to keep moving machinery was to develop radical new technology or cater to farming niches. The bigger tractors entered the horsepower race and received new developments, but the key would be selling tractors to people who didn't have them yet. So the tractor line was broadened to include more special equipment for rice farming, cotton growing, sugar beet producers, and orchard farmers. New plants were built just to cater to these types of markets, and new equipment was designed that performed these tasks more efficiently than ever before.

Left
The Cub was somewhat of a departure for International. The name most likely was inspired by early advertising the referred to the Model A, H, and M as three "bears" for work. This Cub is equipped with a Cub-22 Mower.

Above
Part of the success of the Cub Cadet lawn and garden tractor was the extensive line of attachments and implements available for the machine. This is the quick-attach snow blower, shown at work on an early snowstorm in September 1972.

183

The Farmall Cub was introduced in the fall of 1945, and promoted heavily across the country. This woman is trying a new Cub out at a huge showing of International tractors and equipment held at IHC's Hinsdale Experimental Farm in October of 1945.

While searching for farming niches, International must have discovered the fact that more than three million farms still didn't have tractors. Small farms of less than 50 acres did not typically have a tractor. Some of these farms were vegetable, tobacco, and livestock farms. Many of these farmers were part-timers and had another source of income. This huge untapped market was the target for the Cub.

Some say that the Cub was built for tobacco farmers. Although the Cub was indeed built for small farms, and tobacco farms were typically about 25-acre operations, the tobacco farm was only a small portion of the market. The Cub was designed to be small and cheap enough to lure new buyers who perhaps dreamed of a tractor for their little operation, but found previous models were too big and expensive to be practical.

The Cub Cadet was a direct outgrowth of this approach. Once the smaller farmer had a tractor, who was left? The home owner, of course, and most of the residents of the United States were in this category. Better yet, the Cub Cadets were the type of vehicle that gets replaced every few years. The Cub Cadet was the beginning of America's move to lawn tractors, a machine that is hard to imagine living without today. But it all began with the Cub.

The Cub was designed for farms of 40 acres or less. Economical to purchase as well as run, they were used to gain entry to some of the smaller farms—particularly tobacco farms—of the Southeast, although they were marketed across the country. This Cub is on a turn-table display at the Kentucky Hotel in Louisville, Kentucky.

Farmall Cub

The Cub was the left hook of IHC's one-two combination for the late 1940s. The little tractor was a great cultivator, could pull small implements, and was dirt cheap to purchase and operate.

The parade held during the annual Rodeo and Stock Show held in Ballinger, Texas, featured livestock, cowboys, cowgirls, and this Farmall Cub pulling a float loaded with Cub Scouts. International put Cub Scouts and Cubs together at county fairs and the like, all in an effort to promote the simple, friendly nature of the little tractor. In the end, the Cub put the tractor on farms that could not profitably use larger machines.

The Cub was seen as early as October of 1945, when it was one of the star attractions at a show at International's experimental farm in Hinsdale, Illinois. The Cub was heavily promoted in 1946, and was introduced as a 1947 model. It was produced as the Farmall Cub until 1965, when the Farmall name was dropped in favor of International. The International Cub was built in various forms until 1979.

A New Machine

From the name to the introduction hoopla, the Cub was aimed squarely at a new and different market. The rest of the line bore letters or more utilitarian names. The Model M just sounds big and powerful, and later models had especially manly names. "Super M-TA" just has a ring to it that tells you this is a heavy piece of equipment. Not to mention the Titans, Moguls, and even the Farmall had names that connoted work and power. This was not so with the name, "Cub."

Early Letter Series advertisements referred to the larger machines as the "bears." With this in mind, one can see where the Cub name originated. With the first letter of the alphabet already assigned to a small tractor, the company could not go smaller alphabetically. But "Cub" was a natural for the progeny of the "bears" and fit with

the concept that the Cub would be marketed to a group of people who previously considered tractors to large and expensive for their farms.

The Cub was introduced with trumpets blaring and flags waving. Cubs appeared in parades. Cubs were put on display in banks and at fairs. Several promotions piled herds of Cub Scouts on the little tractors. Promotional banners and displays proclaimed how easy it was to use, and how affordable it was. The archival photographs show a disproportionate number of women operating Cubs. Not all farm women, either. These are not the advertising agents' vision of a hearty farm woman, but women in heels and skirts and looking completely unlike a woman who knew her way around a tractor. Are you starting to see a pattern here?

All the signs indicate that IHC's management—a very bright group—knew exactly what they were doing with the Cub. They knew that there was a huge, nearly unlimited market of folks out there without tractors who could surely use one to haul garbage, till the garden, maybe even cut the grass. Owners of large country homes and smaller farms were the starting point, obviously, and the next stop was suburbia. And the way to get into these smaller places was through the

The Cub used the offset design of the Model A and B to provide the operator with a relatively unobstructed view of the ground below.

person who really controlled the money spent in the household—the woman of the house. Early market research showed that—at least in the automotive industry—buying decisions the domain of woman of the household, despite the fact that the man was more likely to write the check.

So, the newest tractor from IHC had a friendly name and was promoted with kids, in banks, at parades, and anywhere else the general public (rather than just farmers) gathered. The company was attempting to bring the tractor to a new group of people, and management believed the company could do so in large numbers. In 1947, a corporate brochure celebrating the 100th year anniversary of the invention of the reaper touted the Cub as a rising star. Production was expected to top 50,000 per year, and Louisville Works, where the Cub was built, was gearing up to meet that anticipated demand.

International tracked the first 10,000 Cubs sold very closely and came up with some fascinating statistics. Over half of the Cubs went to vegetable, grain, and livestock farmers, with only 3 percent going to tobacco farmers. The tobacco myth was shattered by this statistic. If the company had actually built the Cub with tobacco farmers in mind, the sales to them were a dismal

failure. If the tractor was intended for small farms, the tractor was a smashing success. About 75 percent of the Cubs went to farms of less than 50 acres. The Cub tended to be the only tractor owned, with 67 percent of the buyers not owning any other tractor. Also, nearly half of the Cub owners weren't even full-time farmers.

International knew it was backing a winner with the Cub, and did everything possible to see it succeed. The phenomenal success of the Cub was no fluke.

Cub Nuts and Bolts

The Cub used the same integral frame construction as the Model A and B, with the engine, transmission, clutch, and rear differential housings serving as the frame. The rear tread width was adjustable from 40 to 56 inches, and the relatively tall, wide front end and arched rear differential gave generous ground clearance. Like its fellow Farmalls, the Cub was well-suited to cultivating, and could pull a single 12-inch plow with relative ease.

Engine

The engine was an IHC 60-cubic-inch four-cylinder L-head with a bore of 2 5/8 inches and a stroke of 2 3/4 inches. The relatively short-stroke engine was rated to

The Cub was well-suited to mowing. This one is cutting grass in an apple orchard in Madrid, Iowa. Owner Joe Spence bought the Cub specifically to mow the orchard.

A Cub with a Model 170 Planter. The Cub's 60-cubic-inch four-cylinder engine was built with many of the features that made its larger siblings so reliable. Three-ring pistons, hardened valves, crankshaft and connecting rods, and a roller bearing transmission gave the engine a long working life. The Cub did, however, use the simpler thermosyphon cooling (rather than a thermostat and water pump) and did not have removable cylinder sleeves.

Like the Farmall A and B, the Cub was a useful addition to a larger farm. Its small size and great fuel economy made it ideal for simple farm jobs.

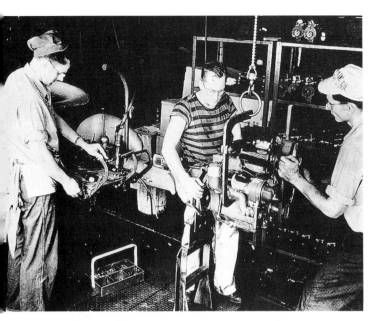

The Cub was built on a production line, naturally, as most of the IHC tractors were in the mid-1940s. The photo above offers a good view of the frame, which was essentially the engine and transmission housing. The engine is being bolted to the clutch housing, and the brake pedals are being assembled at the same time.

run at a slightly higher rpm—1,600—than the larger, longer-stroke engines of its siblings. The engine used an IHC J-4 magneto and an IHC carburetor. The little engine did not use removable sleeves, and produced about 8 horsepower on the belt and 6 horsepower at the drawbar. Fully equipped, the Cub weighed all of about 1,300 pounds.

The caption says that this is the first Farmall Cub off the line at the Louisville Works. The photo is not dated, unfortunately, although it is probably later in 1945. Louisville Works was a converted Curtiss-Wright aircraft plant in Louisville, Kentucky. It was purchased near the end of World War II and expanded by IHC to cover more than 1.7 million square feet. The factory employed more than 6,000 people.

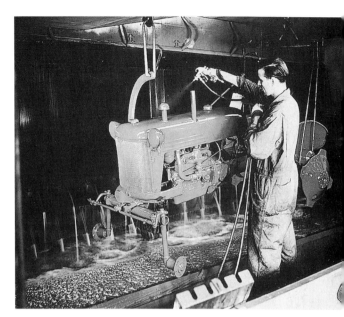

Painting tractors was a bit crude in those days. This photograph was marked with a note that the painter is supposed to be wearing a mask. Perhaps someone should mask those headlights, as well.

Options

Options included a power take-off, belt pulley, adjustable front axle, electric lights and starting, swinging drawbar, and exhaust muffler.

Hydraulics

The original Cub probably didn't have the touch control hydraulic system available as an option, although it became available in 1948. An original parts book owned by researcher Jim Becker does not list hydraulics as an option. Later parts books show Touch Control hydraulics available on the first Cubs, indicating that the hydraulics were made available as a retrofit early Cubs.

The hydraulic system on the Cub was similar to that of the Super A and Model C, although it was a one-valve system rather than the two-valve of the larger machines. These options were part of IHC's package approach to the Cub. The Cub featured a full line of implements and attachments. The unique one-armed scoop is one of the most distinctive and prized attachments, but everything from cultivators and plows to utility wagons were offered for the Cub.

A Brief History of Styles

Researcher Jim Becker has compiled a serial number listing and brief list of style changes on the Cub. The following information was supplied courtesy of Becker. The original style Farmall Cub was built from 1947–1954. When the new Hundred Series tractors were introduced, the Cub was restyled as well and Fast Hitch became an option. A white grille was added a few years later, most likely in 1956. In 1958,

A Cub cultivating cabbage in June of 1946 in the Boston, Massachusetts, area. Note that the Cub used the dropped-rear drive mechanism, requiring the wheels to be flipped to adjust rear tread width.

The Cub could use a host of custom-made implements. This Cub is pulling a Number 100 Manure Spreader.

Cub Lo-Boy

In 1954, IHC produced a lowered version of the Cub, the International Cub Lo-Boy. It was produced until 1968, with just under 24,000 built.

The eventual replacements for the Cub Lo-Boy were not offset machines, but they were a continuation of the line. The Cub 154 Lo-Boy was the replacement for the original Lo-Boy. The 154 was a standard Cub with the rear end turned 90 degrees to lower the rear end. The front was lowered to match. Due to these changes, implements and attachments for other Cubs will not fit the Cub 154 and derivatives. The 154 was built with lawn use in mind, and the most common implements are the mowers and snow removal equipment. The Cub 154 Lo-Boy appeared in 1968, and was produced until 1974.

The replacement, the Cub 185 Lo-Boy, was produced from 1976 to 1977. A subsequent machine, the Model 184, dropped the Cub name entirely, but was built from 1978 to 1981.

Modern Cub Derivatives

In 1981, the line was expanded to include the 234, 244, and 254. These three tractors were in production through the mid-1980s, as Case-International continued to produce them until 1985.

the Cub was restyled again, with a new grille with large horizontal bars. That design carried through to 1963, when the grille was squared off to match another new line of International tractors. Sometime in 1964, the Farmall Cub became the International Cub and the standard color changed from red to yellow. In 1975, the Cub was redesigned, got a bit more horsepower, and was again painted red and white. That basic design was used until 1979, when the Cub was finally discontinued.

One of the advantages of the Cub was good fuel economy. This is Louis Volk of Sylvania, Ohio, fueling his Cub. He reported plowing 12 hours with his Cub and using only 8 1/2 gallons of gas.

The Cub Lo-Boy was introduced in 1954. It was available both as a Farmall and an International. Some of the Internationals were painted yellow. No matter how long you stare at this black-and-white photograph, it seems impossible to tell if this is a red or yellow tractor.

The Cub was produced in several variants from 1947 to 1979. Over that span of time, it featured a number of facelifts. This particular machine was built in the 1960s.

The 234 was powered by a 52-cubic-inch three-cylinder diesel engine rated for 15 horsepower. The tractor came in two- and four-wheel-drive models, and the standard transmission had six forward and two reverse speeds. The 234 Hydro used a two-range hydrostatic transmission. A 540-rpm PTO, lighting, and gauges were standard, and the tractor could be equipped with a loader, snow blower, rotary tiller, harrow, several different mower decks, and front and rear blades.

The 244 and 254 used larger three-cylinder engines, 60 and 65 cubic inches, respectively, and had three-range three-speed transmissions that had nine forward and three reverse speeds. The tractors were rated for 18 and 21 horsepower, and had standard 540-rpm PTOs that could be quickly converted to run at 1,250 rpm. Both

For a smaller airport, the Cub was an ideal addition. Note that this Cub's hood decal reads only "McCormick," rather than "McCormick-Deering." About 1949, "Deering" was dropped from the logo on the Cub.

The more modern Cub Lo-Boy was just as useful as its predecessor, the Cub. This Cub Lo-Boy 154 is using a front-mounted blade in September 1972.

The Cub Lo-Boy was a descendant of the original Cub. This one is toting a Shriner through the streets of Chicago, Illinois, 28 years after the first Cub was introduced in 1947.

were available in two- and four-wheel-drive models. The standard three-point hitch could be equipped with hydraulic draft control.

International carried all three of these models until 1984, and Case-International sold them as the 234, 244, and 254 through 1986. In 1987, the tractors were dubbed the 235, 245, and 255, and were sold as such through 1990. In 1991, horsepower was bumped up for each model and the line was labeled the 1120, 1130, and 1140. These tractors were built through 1993.

Signs of the Future

Tractor development in the late 1950s was mainly refinement rather than the radical jumps of the 1930s, and the basic tools for the job were in place by 1954. Even in modern times, a tractor equipped with torque amplification and a live PTO can perform most of the jobs on the farm with aplomb. Due to the incredible durability and

The 254 was another Japanese-built tractor, also powered by a three-cylinder diesel engine. The 254 was rated for 21 PTO horsepower, and the transmission was the same unit found in the 244. Like the 244, the 254 was available with two- or four-wheel-drive. *Scott Satterland Collection*

When the Cub Lo-Boy disappeared from the line in 1982, the Japanese-built 244 was part of a line of small International tractors that replaced the Cub. The 244's Mitsubishi three-cylinder diesel engine was rated for 18 PTO horsepower. The transmission was a three-range three-speed unit, yielding nine forward and three reverse speeds. The PTO ran at either 540 or 1,250 rpm, and a fully synchronized transmission was available as an option. This tractor stayed in the line, later as a Case-IH tractor, until 1993. *Scott Satterland Collection*

ease of rebuilds, the tractors of the 1950s could be kept at work for nearly indefinite periods of time.

Farmers could do the job well with existing equipment, so the return for purchasing a new tractor began to diminish after the mid-1950s. Selling tractors to farmers no longer brought in the tremendous profits of the 1940s and early 1950s. Tractor manufacturers had to diversify to survive, and find products that were either exploring new markets or in need of regular replacement. For IHC, the Cub was a tractor that began to meet that need, and the Cub Cadet would become one of those products that filled both a new market and was a renewable resource that would keep selling in large numbers.

The company's forays into other markets were less successful, and cost the company more money than it made. There was, of course, the company's truck line, which was a steady producer, but the crawler and construction equipment lines were touch-and-go as far as profits. In addition, the tractor market was becoming a more difficult arena. The future for tractor companies presented some tough challenges, but IHC had an ace in the hole with the first Cub and, later, the Cub Cadet.

Cub Cadet

The Cub Cadet was the right answer at the right time. The Farmall Cub cracked the door to putting tractors into the hands of home owners, and the Cadet burst it wide open. The Cadet was a lawn tractor, built and designed to mow lawns and perform simple tasks around the yard. What made the Cadet special over the years was IHC's approach of bringing the features from the larger models to the little Cadet. Home owners were treated to Hydrostatic

Cub Cadet Production 1961–67	
Cadet (original)	
1960	NA*
1961	19,091
1962	26,051
1963	14,264
Total Prod.	**59,406**
Cadet 70, 71, and 72	
1963	2,901
1964	12,747
1965	7,434
1966	6,686
1967	3,867
Cadet 100, 102, 104, and 105	
1963	1,271
1964	16,656
1965	24,779
1966	14,106
1967	12,766
Cadet 122, 123, 124, and 125	
1965	43
1966	19,478
1967	27,408

Note: Although Cadet was produced until 1985, IHC records available at time of publication only list production numbers through 1967.

Source: McCormick/IHC Archives, "Tractor Production Schedule"

Cub Production

Year	Production
1947	10,847
1948	46,483
1949	41,705
1950	21,918
1951	23,001
1952	17,829
1953	17,128
1954	7,029
1955	7,217
1956	4,573
1957	6,158
1958	7,052
1959	3,533
1960	2,408
1961	2,656
1962	1,345
1963	2,070
1964	1,657
1965	2,099
1966	2,016
1967	1,780
1968	1,976
1969	1,887
1970	1,959
1971	1,679
1972	2,075
1973	2,165
1974	2,905
1975	2,967
1976	2,214
1977	1,277
1978	1,027
1979	362
Total Prod.	252,997

Model Names and Years Produced

Cub Lo-Boy	1955–68
Cub 154 Lo-Boy	1968–75
Cub 185 Lo-Boy	1976–77
Model 184	1978–81
Model 274 Offset	1981–84
Model 234	1982–86
Model 244	1982–86
Model 254	1982–86

Source: McCormick/IHC Archives, "Tractor Production Schedule;" *Farm Tractors 1975–1995* by Larry Gay

The 274 Offset was the replacement for the 140, and it appeared in 1981. It was built by Kimco, a company that was a joint effort between IHC and Komatsu. It used a three-cylinder diesel engine rated for 27 PTO horsepower coupled to a dual-range transmission with eight forward and two reverse speeds. The 274 did not make the leap to Case-IH, and production ended in 1985. *Scott Satterland Collection*

drive, power take-off, and a line of implements built especially for working the garden, plowing and blowing snow, and other home tasks.

The Cadet provided IHC with an almost unlimited market, and was one machine that it was able to sell in large numbers year after year. When it was introduced, the company didn't really know what it had, as IHC engineer Gordon Hershman tells it. "Ben Warren was the product manager then. He thought they oughta' do about 5,000 a year, something like that. Of course, you know, we made tens of thousand of the damn things each year. It was a bad guess, but it was in the right direction. A lotta' other stuff we had was a bad guess in the wrong direction."

The Cadet was quickly assembled, using as many common parts as possible. According to IHC engineer Harold Schram, the early versions of the Cadet didn't actually work that well. Schram helped put together the original Cadet, and stayed with the lawn and garden group for many years. "I was part of the group that was assigned the job of putting together the first Cub

This 1974 display shows off the 500,000th lawn and garden tractor built. The company's first such machine, the Cub Cadet, was first built in 1961.

Cadet. The original concept was to use the fuel tank off the Cub tractor as the hood in order to commonize parts. When they put it together, it did not work that well. I think there were six or seven of us working on it. We built the first prototype about one month from the time we started."

The first version of the Cadet went into production in November 1960, but it was the second version that really made the company stand up and take notice. Schram continues, "Then the second model of the Cub Cadet came out and that turned out to be a success, more than anyone had ever dreamed. In 1962, my boss went to the Harrisburg farm show and he came back all excited about a Bolens tractor that had a U-joint drive for the attachments. I was given the job of seeing what I could do with the Cub Cadet. That's when we designed a Cub Cadet where we took the belt drive out of the tractor. So it became the first garden tractor that did not use belt drive."

Gear drive helped, and Hydrostatic drive came to the Cadet in 1965. The tractor was produced in a wide variety of forms until IHC sold the Cub Cadet garden tractors to a subsidiary of MTD in 1981. Cub Cadet garden tractors continue to be built by this company, and are often available at Case-IH dealerships.

And a Tractor For All . . .

In many ways, the Cub and Cub Cadet were just as significant as the Farmall. The Farmall brought the tractor to the average farmer, while the Cub put tractors on small farms. The Cub Cadet completed the circle by bringing the tractor to the average home.

With the Cub, the small farmer found a tractor that was economical to purchase and run as well as small enough to perform all sorts of daily tasks previously reserved for a horse or man. Today, thousands of similarly sized tractors are at work on small farms, hobby farms, and estates around the country, although most of the modern machinery is foreign-made.

The Cub Cadet took the next step and brought all the conveniences of the power farm to the lawn and garden. All of a sudden, the home owner discovered a useful machine that could perform mundane tasks, fit in the garage, and didn't cost more than the family car.

Just like the Farmall, these two small tractors changed the way people viewed tractors and expanded the role of the tractor in our world. The Cub and Cub Cadet are not hailed with the same reverence as the Farmall, but they have been a part of more peoples lives than perhaps any other type of tractor.

Chapter Eleven

Hundred
Series

■

*"Modern farmers had to be convinced that new equipment
would make them more money and that usually translated into "BIGGER."
—Farm Implement News, 1956*

During the mid-1950s, the tractor market saw incremental changes that were signs of what was to come for the next 40 years. Agricultural technology reached a plateau, with improvements becoming more subtle. Tractors of the 1950s were efficient enough to do most tasks on the farm, and farmers no longer needed to buy a new tractor to farm effectively. The tractors were sturdily built, with the parts that wore out designed to be easily replaced. With a little maintenance and care, a Letter Series tractor could outlast the farmer.

To sell additional tractors, the industry had to meet the demand that existed, which was for more power and accessories. This required intensive research and development, yet with decreasing sales as the reality. The industry was putting more money in to selling tractors, and selling less when they were successful. By the 1960s, selling 10,000 units of a new model in a year was remarkable.

With profit margins cut to the quick, the inevitable economic slumps proved disastrous for tractor manufacturers. Heavy equipment suffered similar woes, and sidelines such as crawlers and payloaders could not be relied on to carry companies through hard times.

The Quest for Power Begins

The demand for greater power matured in the mid-1950s. Most farmers had replaced their horses by this point. In fact, most had replaced the old machines with a more modern 1940 or later tractor. So sales of mid-sized and larger tractors began to drop off in the late 1950s. Naturally, there was still a demand for new tractors. A certain segment of any market will always be looking the latest and greatest, and the demand was for more power and more options. The two were complimentary, as increased hydraulics required more horsepower. Forty horsepower is quite a bit when it is all devoted to driving the wheels. It gets short when you add in powering a hydraulic loader, turning the power take-off (PTO), and powering the brakes and shifting.

The usable power of the increasingly popular diesel engines were a partial solution, and the aftermarket offered big piston and turbocharging kits. The kits brought the horsepower up plenty, but often overpow-

---

Left

The Hundred Series tractors reflected the first major revision of the International tractor line since 1939. The Hundred Series models were introduced beginning late in 1954. The Farmall 400 was a Super M-TA with the additions of new hydraulics and power steering. This 1958 LPG 400 is pulling a Model 21 cotton stripper near Lubbock, Texas.

Above

Only a few years after the hundred series was introduced, International came out with another "new" line. These tractors received a "50" at the end of their model designation, but were not changed much outside of the new red-and-white paint scheme. This 350 Utility High-Clear had a few improvements over the 300; a little tuning squeezed a few more horsepower out of the engine and there were subtle changes to the hydraulics and Fast Hitch.

NEW McCORMICK
Farmall 100
with *Fast-Hitch*

The 100 was the new version of the Super A. The main change between the two was the list of standard equipment, which included hydraulics and Fast Hitch, International's slick two-point hitch.

ered the clutch, transmission, and so on. More problems could be created than solved with a 60-horsepower engine in a machine designed for 40.

The manufacturers' response was to add more options and a little more power on existing lines. By fine-tuning rather than developing new machines from the ground up, retooling and engineering costs were kept manageable, and the companies could be profitable in a tighter market. This is not to say that the new additions weren't significant. The tractor continued to become a more efficient farm tool. The roots were simply more recognizable.

Hundred Series

The Hundreds represented further refinement of the breed, with upgraded styling, a little more horsepower, and a host of new equipment. The chassis of each came from the Letter Series introduced 15 years previously, with some new sheet metal that gave the Hundred Series a cleaner look.

The Hundreds also represent complete integration of utility, wheel, and cultivating tractors. The Farmall tractors were the cultivators, while the International tractors were the utility and standard-tread tractors. The cultivators were the standard taller-tricycle or wide-front tractors, while the utility and wheel tractors were lower to the ground with a solid, wide-front axle.

The first group of Hundreds appeared as the 100, 200, and so on, but IHC went through a phase where the name was changed every third or fourth year. The "new" machines received additional numbers (130, 240, 350, etc.), and the plethora of models made the line a bit confusing. Nevertheless, each "new" model resulted in a spike of sales, which seems to be the driving force behind renaming the tractors each year.

The significant features of the Hundred series had already made their appearances on the later Letter Series tractors: Touch Control hydraulics, independent power take-off (IPTO), and Fast Hitch (IHC's two-point hitch). Two of these three—the hydraulics and live PTO—were improvements that would last. Fast Hitch would eventually be written out of the play by the three-point hitch, simply because it became the standard for the industry.

Live PTO simply kept the PTO turning when the clutch was disengaged. Previously, the PTO did not turn until the clutch was let out. The advantages are obvious, but the application was not that simple. Power had to be transmitted directly from the engine to the PTO, bypassing the clutch and transmission. To do so required more housings and more moving parts to wear out, but the results were well worth the effort.

Fast Hitch Development

Fast Hitch was IHC's attempt to answer the Ferguson three-point system on the Fords. Ferguson's system was effective and popular. After Ford and Ferguson split up, the three-point became available to any manufacturer, but it wasn't available for free. The long tradition of IHC using in-house equipment—carburetors, magnetos, and so on—was not about to be dropped to use a feature that was developed on the Ford.

Fast Hitch was the company's response. The engineers developed it to solve the Ferguson system's problem of erratic draft. The plow wouldn't come right out of the ground, but it would vary in depth as soil conditions

The Super H was replaced with the 300, which received both the Torque Amplifier and the independent power take-off introduced on the Super M-TA.

changed. Fast Hitch solved that problem, but the buyer didn't seem to care.

In 1945, Gordon L. Hershman came to IHC from the military, where he worked on hydraulics for firing rockets from ships in World War II. He ended up working on Touch Control hydraulics and then developing a hitch to compete with the Ferguson system. He explained that the engineering group felt that the Ford, or Ferguson, hitch was too erratic. "If you were plowing a field and got into heavy going, it came out of the ground. If you were trying to plow 8 inches deep, and you were in different soils in a field, the damn thing would be 8 inches sometimes, and other times it'd be 4 inches. We didn't think that was much good. That's why we came up with the Fast Hitch."

Besides the advantages of improved draft control, Fast Hitch was also much easier to hook up. Engineer Robert Oliver also worked on developing hitches, and recalls that Fast Hitch was well received because of easy access. "The tools were getting bigger and bigger, and it was much easier to hitch up than to pound those links on with your heel, or reef those tool around to get 'em lined up. With Fast Hitch, you could just back in, pick up, and go. It was very popular."

Despite the advantages of Fast Hitch, the buyer still preferred the three-point hitch, so IHC looked to develop a three-point hitch. The company looked closely at existing three-point hitch designs, and built its own system with an eye toward avoiding the weaknesses of the Ferguson hitch.

The improved hitch featured Traction Control, which allowed the operator to vary the amount of ground pressure on the rear tires with four different settings. The system was mechanical, and automatically matched ground pressure to load in any of the four settings. The problem of erratic draft control was solved. "It could go over the terrace and the tool never left the ground. It had the best regulation curve in the industry," Oliver said.

This Farmall 400 is pulling a Model 100 grain box and Model 20 corn picker at International's experimental farm in Hinsdale, Illinois. Beginning with the Hundred Series, Farmall machines were the row crop versions, while the International models were standard tread utility tractors.

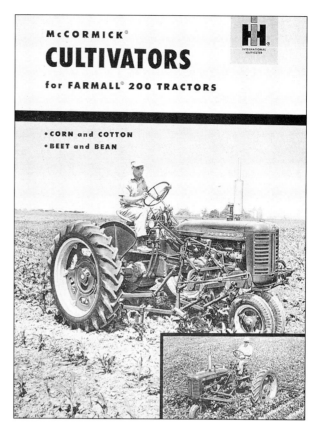

The Farmall 200 was the upgraded version of the Super C. The 200 featured hydraulics, Fast Hitch, double-disc brakes, and a rear wheel tread adjustable from 48 to 80 inches. The tractor could be equipped with a narrow or wide front end.

Fast Hitch was slowly phased out as the three-point hitch became an industry standard. International had a three-point of its own, and it was one of the better systems available. Business as usual.

100 Series

The 100 Series were basically Farmall Super As with a few new features, slightly more power, and new badges. The tractor was built as the 100 from 1954 to 1956, as the 130 from 1956 to 1958, and as the 140 from 1958 to 1979. Although the machine was refined and restyled along the way, the chassis and engine design was not significantly changed in an amazing production span of 40 years.

The Farmall and International 100 engine was the venerable C-123 unit used in the Super C and Super A-1. It was equipped to burn gasoline, which was the standard by that time, but could be equipped to burn kerosene or distillate. The 100's engine produced 18 belt and 14 drawbar horsepower. The Farmall 130 engine put out a little more power, at 20 belt and 16 drawbar horsepower. Although horsepower kept climbing incrementally over the years, the same bore and stroke was used.

Power was transmitted with a 9-inch dry-disk clutch, and the transmission was a four-speed. The same replaceable cylinder sleeves and ball and roller bearings were used, as well. The rear wheel tread was adjustable

The big 600 was a derivative of the W-9 and, like the W-9, was available with diesel and gas engines. Rated as a five-plow tractor, the 600 featured power steering, double-disc brakes, Hydra-Touch hydraulics, a 350-cubic-inch four-cylinder engine, and a shipping weight of about 6,000 pounds. Interestingly, an independent power take-off or Torque Amplifier was not available on the 600.

from 40 to 68 inches, and the optional front was adjustable from 44 to 64 inches. The tractor weighed about 2,600 pounds.

By 1958, the cooling system used pump circulation and was thermostatically controlled, leaving the Cub as the last in the line to use a thermosyphon system. Earlier tractors (A, B, Super A, Super A-1) used thermosyphon cooling with an optional booster pump.

Options and Attachments

The 100 Series came from the factory with a bevy of standard equipment that included Fast Hitch, Touch Control hydraulics, fenders, non-adjustable front end, battery ignition, lights, and a muffler.

Other options included a belt pulley, PTO, rear light and tail light, exhaust valve rotators, foot accelerator, radiator shutters, wheel weights, and a host of custom implements and drawbar attachments. A Farmall 100 Hi-Clear was available, as well, with the same host of options and attachments.

Hydra-Creeper

One of the more interesting options was "Hydra-Creeper," which allowed the tractor to crawl along at speeds of 1/4 to 1 mile per hour at full throttle. This attachment was used for transplanting crops or for pulling equipment when harvesting, all primarily for smaller vegetable, flower, or tobacco farms. The unit consisted of a hydraulic pump that was driven by the PTO. The hydraulics drove a chain and sprocket that were geared extremely low. With Hydra-Creeper engaged, the regular transmission was used, but speeds in each gear ranged from about 0.2 miles per hour in first to 1.1 miles per hour in fourth. Hydra-Creeper could be disengaged at will, allowing normal operation of the transmission. To use the PTO, the unit had to be disconnected.

The 100 Series never lit the world on fire with sales like the Model A and B, but they sold steadily over an unrivaled span of years, with nearly 100,000 machines rolling out the door. These tractors are an ideal size for a hobby farm or residence, and have become increasingly popular with collectors as well.

200 Series

The 200 Series was the upgraded version of the Super C. The Super C already had Touch Control hydraulics, so the 200 was not really much of a change. The 200 was produced from 1954 to 1956, the 230 was produced from 1956 to 1958, and the 240 was produced from 1958 to 1962. Both Farmall and International 200 Series tractors were produced, the distinction being the Farmall was the cultivating tractor and the International was the utility tractor.

The 200 series used the same C-123 engine as the 100 Series, but the 200 put out 22 belt and 16 drawbar horsepower. Where the increased horsepower came from in the C-123 engine is not clear, although piston speed is listed in an IHC brochure as being higher, making it likely that additional rpm yielded the increased power of the 200. The engine cooling was thermostatically controlled, and it was equipped to gasoline with kerosene or distillate equipment optional. Horsepower increased slightly as the model progressed through the years.

Electrall was one of the more unique IH optional attachments. With it installed, the tractor became a mobile generator, capable of supplying power to all sorts of equipment. Despite the seeming practicality of Electrall, it never really caught on.

Farmall and International 100, 130, and 140 Production

Farmall 100

Year	Production
1954	?*
1955	9,990
1956	8,585
Total Prod.	**18,575**

*Serial numbers are listed for 1954, but production schedule shows none built that year. Models were built, but the production sheet simply records it a bit differently.

Farmall and International 130

1956	?*
1957	6,946
1958	2,821
Total Prod.	**9,767**

*Serial numbers are listed for 1956, but production schedule shows none built that year. Models were built, but the production sheet simply records it a bit differently.

Farmall and International 140†

1958	1,386
1959	5,183
1960	3,678
1961	5,188
1962	4,480
1963	3,844
1964	3,157
1965	2,810
1966	3,532
1967	2,620
1968	2,554*
1969	2,394*
1970	2,124*
1971	2,181*
1972	1,902*
1973	2,213*
1974	4,003*
1975	3,050*
1976	3,066*
1977	2,272*
1978	1,433*
1979	NA
Total Prod.	**63,070***

*Production numbers from 1968-on were calculated by subtracting serial numbers, which is a good estimate but not exact.

†These numbers come up about 973 short of other totals. The 1958 to 1967 production of the International 140 may not be included in IHC documentation. *Source*: 1958–67 from McCormick/IHC Archives, "Tractor Production Schedule"

The 200s were equipped with IHC's new double-disk brakes, which were enclosed and mechanically operated. Other standard equipment included a temperature gauge, lights, and electric starting, Touch Control hydraulics, Fast Hitch, muffler, and rear tread width adjustable from 48 to 88 inches. Options include the Hydra-Creeper, combination PTO and belt pulley, hydraulic remote control, hour meter, and a high-ratio third gear.

Touted as ideal for a farm of 80 to 120 acres, the 200 filled the niche of an affordable smaller tractor with enough power to pull two 14-inch plows and perform all the tasks necessary on a smaller farm. Lifetime sales of the 200 Series were over 30,000 units, and ended in 1961 for the Farmall 240 and in 1962 for the International 240.

300 Series

The 300 Series was the descendants of the Model H and the Four Series. Like the rest of the Hundreds, new sheet metal, more power, and more options were the order of the day. These mid-sized tractors were available with a Torque Amplifier (TA) and "live" or independent PTO.

The 300s were built from 1954 to 1956, with the 350 built from 1956 to 1958. The 340 was built from 1958 to 1963. An International 330 (but not a Farmall 330) was built in 1957 and 1958. As with the smaller tractors, the Farmalls were the cultivating tractors and the Internationals were the standard-tread utility tractors.

Horsepower was up from the Super H, with 34 belt and 27 drawbar horsepower when burning gas. The engine could be equipped to burn kerosene, distillate, or LPG. The 300's C-169 four-cylinder engine had a slightly larger bore than the Super H's C-164 engine.

Continental Engine in Model 350

According to an article in *Antique Power* magazine, a Continental diesel engine was available for the 350. IHC documentation shows a 193-cubic-inch diesel for the 350, and a 166-cubic-inch diesel engine for the 340, indicating a probable switch to an International engine for the 340. The 166-cubic-inch engine was also used in the

Farmall and International 200, 230, 240 Production

Farmall and International 200

Year	Production
1954	?*
1955	7,576
1956	6,150
Total Prod.	**13,726**

*Serial numbers are listed for 1954, but production schedule shows none built that year. Models were built, but the production sheet simply records it a bit differently.

Farmall and International 230

1956	?*
1957	5,480
1958	1,973
Total Prod.	**7,453**

*Serial numbers are listed for 1956, but production schedule shows none built that year. Models were built, but the production sheet simply records it a bit differently.

Farmall 240

1958	1,232
1959	1,481
1960	861
1961	136
Total Prod.	**3,710**

International 240

1958	3,960
1959	3,949
1960	1,663
1961	671
1962	86
Total Prod.	**10,329**

Source: McCormick/IHC Archives, "Tractor Production Schedule"

Like the 350, the 450 received subtle improvements over the 400. Traction control was added to the Fast Hitch system in order to provide steady draft control. Power steering was adding, and the rear tread width was power adjusted. This 450 was photographed June 19, 1957. The standard tread version bore the same equipment, and was named the W-450.

The fourth generation of the Hundred Series was the 40 Series machines (the third generation was the 30 Series, which were followed, and were quite similar to, the 50 Series). To add to confusion, the 240 and 340 were introduced at about the same time as the new 460, 560, and 660. The 40 and 60 Series styling was new, with a much more square profile that International would use through the 1970s. The 240 was the grandson of the Model C, and came in row crop, wide front, and high-clearance versions.

Right
The 560 was available with diesel, gasoline/kerosene/distillate, and LPG engines. The 560 had a weak transmission when first introduced, and would burn it up quickly. International instituted a warranty program to retrofit the machines with upgraded parts, and had people working around the clock to repair the tractors.

Farmall and International 300, 350, 330, and 340 Production

Farmall 300

Year	Production
1954	?*
1955	19,466
1956	10,528
Total Prod.	**29,994**

*A limited number of serial numbers are listed for 1954, but production schedule shows none built that year. Models were built, but the production sheet simply records it a bit differently.

International 300

1955	14,312
1956	18,864
Total Prod.	**33,176**

Farmall 350

1956	?*
1957	11,855
1958	4,950
Total Prod.	**16,805**

*About 500 serial numbers are listed for 1954, but production schedule shows none built that year. Models were built, but the production sheet simply records it a bit differently.

International 350

1956	?*
1957	13,575
1958	4,425
Total Prod.	**18,000**

*About 300 serial numbers are listed for 1956, but production schedule shows none built that year. Models were built, but the production sheet simply records it a bit differently.

International 330

1957	?*
1958	4,261

*About 950 serial numbers are listed for 1957, but production schedule shows none built that year. Models were built, but the production sheet simply records it a bit differently.

Farmall 340

1958	2,000
1959	2,574
1960	1,433
1961	1,221
1962	182
1963	77
Total Prod.	**7,487**

International 340

1958	1,927
1959	2,852
1960	2,889
1961	2,963
1962	988
1963	435
Total Prod.	**12,054**

Source: McCormick/IHC Archives, "Tractor Production Schedule"

TD-340 crawler, increasing the odds of the engine being an IHC-built unit.

Cooling was the standard thermostatically controlled water pump system, and the engine was lubricated by an oil pump. The tractor weighed in between 4,000 and 5,000 pounds, depending on optional equipment.

Torque Amplifier

The transmission on the 300 could be ordered as the standard five-speed, or with Torque Amplification (TA), which provided ten effective forward speeds. A gear reduction system was used, and the farmer could shift on the fly between two slightly different gear ratios, giving two ranges to each gear. This worked great for plowing in soil or varied consistency, or for any other situation that required a quick, subtle change in speed.

The new TA was a part of a new concept to tractor technology; matching load to speed. Research had shown that tractors work most effectively when power exerted is matched exactly to what is required. Anyone who has plowed with an older tractor where third gear is too high and second is too low understands this need. More gear choices make it more likely that load can be perfectly matched and the result is less time in the field and better fuel efficiency.

Standard equipment was similar to the previous 100s and 200s, with electric starting and lights and so on installed. The independent power take-off (IPTO) was another important feature for the 300s.

The 300s sold well for IHC, selling about 35,000 in 1955 alone with more than 100,000 sold from the introduction in 1954 to the close of production in 1963. Like the Farmall H that preceded it, the 300 Series were ven-

The new Farmall 460 and 560 were the high-profile machines in the new line for 1958. Both were designed with the horsepower-hungry times in mind, and used new six-cylinder engines.

erable, useful machines that were used on a wide range of farms and applications.

400 Series

The successor to the Farmall M and Six Series was the 400 Series. These tractors used the same engine as the Super M and its siblings, and featured the IPTO and TA that debuted on the Super M. The 400s had the new sheet metal and more power as well. They also featured an option of burning liquefied petroleum gas (LPG).

The 400 Series four-cylinder engine was the C-264 from the Super M, although it had more snort, with the standard gasoline burner putting out 45 belt and 36 drawbar horsepower. The engine could be equipped to burn kerosene, distillate, or LPG, and diesel version was optional.

Model 600 and 650

Produced for only a few years in the late 1950s, the big 600 and its successor, the 650, were IHC's largest, most powerful wheel tractor. They were also simply a rebadged Super Nine with a bit of new equipment. According to IHC records, the 600 and 650 were produced only as standard tread Internationals, with no Farmall models. The 600 and 650 used the big 350-cubic-inch engine from the Super Nines, and were rated

Farmall and International 400 and 450 Production

Farmall 400

Year	Production
1954	?*
1955	24,440
1956	16,517

*About 2,000 serial numbers are listed for 1954, but production schedule shows none built that year. Models were built, but the production sheet simply records it a bit differently.

International W-400

1955	1,336
1956	1,932
Total Prod.	**3,268**

Farmall 450

1956	?*
1957	17,852
1958	7,737
Total Prod.	**25,589**

*About 1,200 serial numbers are listed for 1956, but production schedule shows none built that year. Models were built, but the production sheet simply records it a bit differently.

International W-450

1956	?*
1957	1,091
1958	718
Total Prod.	**1,809**

*About 60 serial numbers are listed for 1956, but production schedule shows none built that year. Models were built, but the production sheet simply records it a bit differently.

Source: McCormick/IHC Archives, "Tractor Production Schedule"

for 60 belt horsepower. Weighing in at over four tons, the 600 also boasted all of IHC's latest innovations—IPTO, power steering, even an optional cigar lighter.

The 350-cubic-inch four-cylinder engine had coffee can-sized pistons, with a 4 1/2-inch bore and 5 1/2-inch stroke. The standard engine burned gasoline, but it could be equipped to burn kerosene or distillate. Diesel and LPG versions were available as well. The pistons were aluminum, and the cylinder sleeves were replaceable. The diesel engine used fuel injection and had a compres-

The 560, despite its shortcomings, was a successful model for International. The six-cylinder engine produced a broad torque curve and ran smoothly and efficiently. The combination of high horsepower (59 drawbar) and relatively light weight at just under 6,000 pounds made the 560 the tractor popular with farmers of the late 1950s.

sion ratio of 15.6:1. Battery ignition was standard, as were lights and an electric starter.

An International 650 was tested at Nebraska in 1957, and it recorded 55 belt and 43 drawbar horsepower. The horsepower figures are respectable, but the number that best describes the power of the 600 and 650 is the 530 foot-pounds of torque.

The tractor tested burned gasoline, and weighed well over 10,000 pounds with wheel weights. In the low-gear maximum pull test, the 650 snorted over 8,500 pounds of force—more than 80 percent of its weight.

The engine was cooled with a thermostatically controlled radiator and fan system. The transmission was a five-speed unit that ran through a 12-inch single-plate clutch. Top gear was for road use, and ran the 600 up to over 15 miles per hour. Disc brakes and 14x34-inch rear tires were standard.

Optional equipment included the IPTO, Hydra-Touch hydraulic system, belt pulley, foot-operated throttle, rice field tires, magneto ignition, high-altitude pistons, radiator shutters, tachometer, hour meter, wheel weights, heavy duty rear axles, and, yes, you read it right, a cigar lighter (real farmers who used tractors with over 530 foot-pounds of torque apparently smoked cigars rather than cigarettes).

Production Figures

Several IHC production sheets clearly indicate that about 2,000 machines were sold each year (see chart for

International 600 and 650 Production

International 600

1956	1,484
1957	32
Total Prod.	**1,516**

International 650

1957	2,561
1958	2,372
Total Prod.	**4,933**

Source: McCormick/IHC Archives, "Tractor Production Schedule"

specifics). Note that the 600 and 650 were both produced in 1957, although only a few 600s were built that year.

Considering the fact that the 600 and 650 were essentially Super Nines, the figure becomes even more plausible. The Super Nine sold a few thousand per year consistently, as did the International 660 that replaced the 650. The serial number references are quite confusing, but the production figures in IHC records are quite clear.

The International 560 was the standard tread version. The Farmall was much more popular, as most preferred the row crop version. The difference was mainly a front axle.

With less than 7,000 units produced, the 600 and 650 are among the rare birds of the line. The lack of information and the odd serial numbers—especially on the 600— lend a veil of mystery to these powerful tractors.

New Forty and Sixty Series

The next step for International was the first major departure from the basic styling of the Letter Series since 1939, nearly 20 years prior. It was 1958, and the new IHC tractors featured a square front end with a stacked-bar grill. The look was strikingly different. It would also be the styling that defined IHC tractors almost until the end. The tractors' appearance would become sleeker as time passed, but the tractor of 1980s didn't really look that much different from the tractors of 1958. Option choices were up, especially comfort options, and hydraulic systems were increasing in capacity.

The big 660 was an interesting anomaly introduced in 1959. The tractor's six-cylinder engine was good for more than 70 drawbar horsepower, but the unique feature of the 660 was the planetary drive on the outer axle.

Forty Series

The Forty Series tractors were the latest editions of the Hundred Series introduced in the mid-1950s, although they sported the new look and some new bells and whistles, including the new three-point Fast Hitch. A 140, 240, and 340 were offered as Farmall cultivating and International standard tread tractors.

Sixty Series

The Sixty Series tractors—the 460, 560, and enigmatic 660—were the real news in the new lineup. While the 460 and 560 were introduced in 1958 and the 660 in 1959, they shared a common design. All three used new IHC six-cylinder power plants, and bore the new square styling. More importantly, all three put up respectable numbers of horsepower. The horsepower race was heating up, and the Sixty Series was IHC's entry.

The standard engines burned gasoline, and the usual kerosene and distillate equipment was optional, with diesel and LPG versions available as well. The engines boast a host of new features, as well. A wedge-shaped combustion chamber and angled valves improved flow for more horsepower and better fuel economy. A 12-volt electrical system was used, and diesels had a new injection pump and glow plugs in each pre-combustion chamber. All of the machines had the Torque Amplifier coupled to a five-speed transmission, yielding 10 forward and 2 reverse speeds. The tractors were equipped with an independent 540-rpm power take-off.

New Hydraulics

The hydraulic system was upgraded, with the option of a one-, two-, or three-valve Hydra-Touch. The hydraulic system was housed in the rear end, with several different pumps available. The hydraulic system was fitted with a replaceable filter to keep the fluid clean, and the hydraulics were "live," meaning power was supplied whenever the engine was running.

The 460 and 560 were available as Farmall cultivating and International standard tread machines, while the big 660 came only as an International standard tread.

Farmall and International 460

The 460 used a 221-cubic-inch six-cylinder gasoline engine that produced 44 belt and 36 drawbar horsepower at 1,800 rpm. The 460's six-cylinder diesel engine displaced 236 cubic inches and produced the same amount of horsepower in both tests, also at 1,800 rpm. The tractor weighed about 6,000 pounds and sported a five-speed transmission that could be equipped with Torque Amplifier (TA).

Farmall and International 560

The standard gasoline engine in the 560 displaced 263 cubic inches and was good for 61 belt and 45 drawbar horsepower at 1,800 rpm. The same engine equipped for propane made about the same horsepower on the drawbar, but slipped to 53 belt horsepower. The 282-cubic-inch six-cylinder diesel put out 59 belt and 44 drawbar horsepower at 1,800 rpm. All versions weighed over 6,500 pounds.

Problems with the 560

Unfortunately, the high horsepower of the 560 over-powered its transmission. The fix was discovered when it was too late, and the company had to scramble to recall the machines out in the field and to fix the unsold machines that were off the production line.

To fix the problems with the 560, they applied a warranty program of a scope unrivaled in company history. Engineer Robert Oliver recalls the stories about the 560 warranty effort. "They had a crew of people work around the clock to repair tractors. They had the complete field at Hinsdale filled with those tractors off the production line. They worked around the clock, unlimited overtime. I heard stories of people who bought houses with the money they made from overtime." The problem was cured with later models and earlier ones were retrofitted, but the damage was done to IHC's nearly spotless reputation.

Farmall and International 460

The big 660 appeared a year later in 1959, and was quite a horse. It was the replacement for the Model 650, and used the new six-cylinder engine and Planetary Power hubs in an evolution of the W-9 chassis. It weighed nearly 10,000 pounds, and soared to over 15,000 pounds with front and rear ballast. The gasoline engine was the same 263-cubic-inch unit from the 560, but it ran at 2,400 rpm. The result was 81 PTO and 70 drawbar horsepower when tested at Nebraska in 1959.

The diesel engine was the 281-cubic-inch model with an 18:1 compression ratio. Power output was similar to the gasoline version, with 79 PTO and 65 drawbar horsepower. An LPG engine was also available, and it posted numbers identical to the gasoline version, at 81 PTO and 70 drawbar horsepower.

Sadly, the Sixty Series' biggest impact was the problems with the 560. Like the transmission problems suffered on the TD-24, the problems with the 560 sullied the reputation of an otherwise great tractor. In both cases, International had hurried the machine to the showroom, and suffered because of it. As the 1960s dawned, International's 30-year juggernaut was on rocky ground. It remained one of the powers of the industry, but the errors had tainted the integrity of the IHC label just a bit.

Sixty Series Production

Farmall 460

1958	3,851
1959	10,574
1960	7,444
1961	5,097
1962	3,637
1963	2,048
Total Prod.	**32,651**

International 460

1958	2,072
1959	3,823
1960	2,988
1961	2,152
1962	537
1963	19
Total Prod.	**11,591**

Farmall 560

1958	6,161
1959	18,063
1960	10,622
1961	11,296
1962	11,650
1963	7,794
Total Prod.	**65,586**

International 560

1958	671
1959	1,653
1960	1,077
1961	1,034
1962	585
1963	613
Total Prod.	**5,633**

International 660

1959	2,666
1960	1,100
1961	1,529
1962	1,030
1963	676
Total Prod.	**7,001**

Source: McCormick/IHC Archives, "Tractor Production Schedule"

208

Chapter Twelve

The 1960s and Beyond

"Let me make it quite clear that my associates and I are not interested in being custodians of a business museum, however fine."
—Harry O. Bercher, IHC Company President, 1963

The 1960s were an exciting time for International. John Deere, Case, Oliver, and IHC all introduced new tractor lines early in the decade, and the competition was fierce. The International Harvester Company (IHC) was looking to take back it's position as an innovator, and set teams of engineers to work on new technology and improvements for the line.

For full-size models, the news for the 1960s was again power and add-ons. Hydraulics began to play a huge role in tractor technology, and International's new 706 and 806 tractors boasted no less than three hydraulic pumps. Everything from steering to brakes became hydraulic, and horsepower requirements continued to spiral.

The increased demand for power made turbocharging a common practice for tractor manufacturers, and four-wheel-drive became a more significant factor. It was an exciting time for IHC, with the first new-from-the-ground-up tractors appearing since the introduction of the Letter Series in 1939. The industry in general was on the move, and International was poised to remain one of the leaders.

Beginning in about 1970, the tractor makers went through a raft of consolidations, sales, and failures that continues today. Where once there were hundreds of tractor manufacturers, only a handful remain. Through the 1970s and early 1980s, IHC struggled through a series of economic fluctuations. In 1985, the struggle ended when the agricultural division was sold to Tenneco and merged with the Case tractor division. The International name survived on the "Case-International" badges on the "new" tractor line, but it wasn't even close to the same.

404 and 504

The first new weapons for IHC were the 404 and 504, two mid-sized machines introduced in 1961 that had a number of improvements. The tractors were offered with an IHC-engineered draft control. The system was unique to IHC, and worked well, but would be outsold and pushed off the market by the three-point hitch. Other innovations of the 404 and 504 included an oil cooler and a dry-type air cleaner. The oil cooler was necessitated by the increasing horsepower of modern tractors, and became standard equipment for most tractors. The dry-type air cleaner simply made sense, just as the paper filters in automobiles do today. Another advance on these tractors was what IHC called Hydrostatic power steering. By using hydraulics to turn the front wheels, awkward, bulky mechanical linkages were eliminated. Both models were available in gasoline or LPG setups, and the 504 was available with a diesel engine as well.

Left
International brought out a number of significant tractors in the 1960s, but the 706 and 806 were the most successful. The high-horsepower tractors breathed new life into International and were billed as high-speed tractors. As the tractor improved, the farmer could cover more and more ground in less time with a single tractor.

Above
The International 4100 was a solution to the problem of putting a four-wheel-drive farm tractor into the line. The company brought the 4300 over from the construction division, but the machine was too big for row-crop work.

The 706 and 806 were designed to meet the horsepower needs of the times. The tractors featured 65 (706) and 85 (806) drawbar horsepower, three separate hydraulic systems, power steering and brakes, 540- and 1,000-rpm independent power take-offs, and a choice of two-point Fast Hitch or the newly standardized three-point hitch. This photograph was taken in September 1963, the year in which the new 706 and 806 were introduced.

The 706/806 was also available as high-clearance machines. The big 806 was billed as "The World's Most Powerful Row-Crop Tractor." The 361-cubic-inch six-cylinder diesel was good for 85 horsepower at the drawbar. The engines could pull hard from 900 to 2,400 rpm, giving the farmer a greater range of speed. The tractors put out one horsepower for every 100 pounds, compared to the one horsepower for every 500 pounds of the original International tractor, the Type A.

Both of these sold modestly, with total sales more than 10,000 when they were discontinued late in the 1960s. They were also one of the first IHC lines to sell greater numbers of the standard tread Internationals than the tricycle Farmalls, reflecting the change in demand on the farm.

Getting More Power To the Ground

The largest demand on the farm was still more power and, in the 1960s, two developing technologies brought that about: turbocharging and four-wheel drive. The two fed off each other, really. As the demand for more options and more power rose, the need for greater traction tagged along. It doesn't take a rocket scientist to see that turbocharging brought more power and four-wheel-drive put it to the ground more effectively.

The transmission for the 706 and 806 was all new. Considering the fiasco that occurred with the 560, International's last new high-horsepower model, the company was taking no chances with the 706 and 806. Note that the high-clearance model uses a dropped-rear drive mechanism like the high-clearance versions of the Model H and M.

Turbocharging is an effective way to increase power in tractor engines. Tractor engines run at low rpm with heavy loads, so traditional hot rodder's methods of increasing high-rpm horsepower are not effective on tractor engines. More efficient flow is a viable option, but increased complexity is undesirable for a machine that needs to run hour after hour without servicing.

Turbocharging pressurizes the intake with an impeller driven by exhaust gas. The drawback to turbocharging is poor throttle response. In a car or motorcycle, you can feel a bit of lag as the impeller gets to speed when you punch the accelerator. A tractor engine runs at constant speeds, so throttle response is really not an issue. Turbochargers provide engines with dramatic boosts in horsepower, and allow the machines to maintain reliability and decent fuel economy.

The rising power made traction more and more of an issue. Farmers were pulling larger implements, and doing more in less time. Dual rear tires helped, but they were somewhat unwieldy and clumsy to mount. Besides, the nearly 100-horsepower of the machines was at times more power than two driven wheels could get to the ground. Four-wheel-drive was a logical solution, but it presented a tricky engineering task.

One solution was Steiger, a company that formed in 1957 with the express purpose of building a high-horsepower tractor. Steiger found success building powerful, articulated, four-wheel-drive tractors, and some manufacturers bought machines from Steiger and rebadged them as their own. The situation was less than ideal from a profit standpoint, but allowed companies to put a big four-wheel-drive on the lot without the research and development costs.

4300

The big 4300 was just such a solution for IHC. The machine was an IHC product, but it was built for the construction division and was really too big for field work. It was brought over and sold as an agricultural tractor beginning in 1961. What it gave the company was bragging rights, as it was one of the most powerful machines on the market.

The mighty 300-horsepower six-cylinder engine was an 817-cubic-inch turbocharged IHC unit. The result was a monstrous tractor that was also the first IHC tractor to breath through a turbo. The drive was hydraulic, using a torque converter and six-range powershift transmission.

A 10-bottom plow was developed especially for the 4300, and with a total ballasted weight of more than 30,000 pounds, the 4300 was plenty capable of pulling the big plow.

The 4300 helped fill a hole in the IHC line, for the time being. The company had a couple of new models up its sleeve before finding a better solution for the big four-wheel-drive problem.

706 and 806

The 706 and 806 were a huge success for IHC, two new models designed from the engine housing back to handle high horsepower output. The tractors were introduced in 1963 and used hydraulics to power many of the systems, from brakes and steering to auxiliary equipment like front-end loaders. The hydraulics required large amounts of horsepower, and the 706 and 806 put out nearly double the amount of power produced by the big tractors of the late 1940s. These two backed up the big numbers with all the latest options, from power steering and brakes to both 540- and 1,000-rpm IPTO and a full bevy of gauges.

Farmall and International Models

As with previous IHC tractor lines, both International standard tread and Farmall tricycle-style tractors were available. The trend at the time was getting away from tricycle or cultivating tractors, but the sales of the 706 and 806 lines did not reflect that. This may have been because the standard Farmall included two auxiliary hydraulic valves and a three-point hitch, while the International had only one auxiliary valve and a swinging drawbar as standard equipment. The Farmalls were also longer and wider than the International models, with a greater range of rear tread width adjustment.

706 Engine

The 706 could be equipped with the D-232 diesel or the C-263 gasoline engine. The gas engine could be outfitted to burn LPG, and all were six-cylinders. Both the gas and diesel model were rated for 74 PTO and 65 drawbar horsepower.

In the mid-1960s, four-wheel-drive was becoming more desirable. Higher-horsepower tractors required all the traction they could get, and four-wheel-drive was a good solution. This drawing is of the 806 AWD Diesel model, a factory option package. A similar package was available for the 706.

806 Engine

The 806 could also be equipped with a gas, diesel, or LPG six-cylinder engine. The gas or LPG unit used the big C-301, and the diesel was the D-361. Horsepower for both was rated at 95 at the PTO and 84 at the drawbar.

New Transmission

The transmission for the 706 and 806 was a dual-range four-speed, giving eight forward speeds without the optional Torque Amplifier (TA). The addition of more gear selections and a wider effective engine rpm range (from 900 to 2,400 rpm on the 706 and 806), allowed the tractors to match power output to load as never before. With the optional TA, the 706/806 tractors had 16 effective forward speeds.

Evolution of the PTO

Power take-offs were also evolving. The independent power take-off (IPTO) was more or less standard by the mid-1960s. The latest development was adding the 1,000-rpm PTO to the standard 540-rpm PTO. The new tractors featured both speeds on the tractor, as the 1,000-rpm PTO was the newest addition, but many implements still required the 540-rpm PTO. Also, one of the problems with early IPTO, sudden engagement, was solved on the 706 and 806. When the PTO was engaged with the clutch, it was naturally engaged progressively as the clutch was let out. The new IPTO was engaged by a lever, and spun suddenly from zero to the rated rpm. The result was bent and broken implements. The solution IHC promoted on the 706 and 806 was to hydraulically activate the PTO, which gave a gradual engagement.

Hydraulics

Hydraulic power was used throughout the tractor, to power the brakes and steering as well, and the tractor bore no less than three hydraulic pumps. A 12-gallon-per-minute (gpm) pump in the main frame operated the hitch and mounted equipment. A 9-gpm pump in the clutch housing operated the power steering, power brakes, and TA system. A 3-gpm pump powered shifting and lubricated the IPTO. Draft control was done hydraulically as well.

Comfort and Convenience

The 706 and 806 were engineered to appease the operator, with more comfortable seats, shielded operator platforms, body panels that flipped up for easy servicing, and a full complement of gauges. Both could be ordered with factory front-wheel assist, making all four wheels driven.

The mid-1960s were an exciting time for IHC. The early embarrassment of the flawed 560 was put behind, and the new 706 and 806 erased any doubts about the company's ability to produce cutting-edge agricultural equipment. Although these tractors met the demand for more features and more horsepower, there was another challenge waiting for the company, one that it wouldn't solve to the staff's satisfaction until the introduction of the stunning 2+2 models in 1979.

4100

The 4300 was IHC's only big four-wheel-drive, and it wasn't filling the bill. Converted from the construction equipment line, it was not designed for the needs of the farmer. In 1963, with the new 706 and 806 at the dealerships, the company looked at building a big four-wheel-drive tractor designed specifically for farm use.

When John Deere came out with their snowmobile, IHC consider building one as well. Engineers traveled in Michigan and Wisconsin to see what the customer wanted, and drew up a basic design. Engineer Gordon Hershman was heavily involved in the snowmobile project, and he doesn't recall any prototypes being built. "We got the design all set, and had a picture made up, and made a presentation. I think that's when we decided it was too risky," Hershman said. *Courtesy of Gordon L. Hershamn*

The HT-340 Gas Turbine Tractor was one of the International's more interesting experiments. A jet turbine engine powered the machine through an experimental hydrostatic transmission. The tractor was donated to the Smithsonian Institute in 1967. The hydrostatic transmission showed up on a production tractor in 1967.

Rapid Development

With demand up for a big four-wheel-drive capable of working the fields, International pushed for the 4100 to get to market as rapidly as possible. The resultant development work was amazingly speedy, with design work beginning in August of 1963 and the first production tractor off the line in July of 1965.

Harold Schram, an IHC engineer, worked on the design team for the 4100. He explained how the company put the tractor into production so quickly. "I was asked to layout a four-wheel-drive tractor with approximately 150 horsepower. I started with the engine—of course, we always used IH engines. The ET429 was about that horsepower, so I started with that.

"We could not afford to design a new transmission, so we looked at various transmissions and we finally decided that we could stretch the transmission that was used on the 706 and 806. We did it by putting a reduction after it so there was less torque going into the transmission.

"The big thing at that time was independent drive axles that were used on wheel loaders. We picked up a couple of those. We looked at Clark and Rockwell Standard. We chose a steerable wheel system. We had a choice, because Steiger and Versatile had an articulated system and Case had a steerable system. We went with the steerable system, because we thought it was more compatible for use in row-crop situations.

"Basically, once you make those decisions, then you've got to have enough room to get an entrance up so you put your engine and transmission components in first and find out where you can set your axles and then you go up, building an operator's deck, fenders, making sure you've got enough space for both sets of wheels to turn and it just sorta' builds up. We went from there to building experimentals."

The time period from the drawing board to production was incredibly short. The original Farmall took more than five years of refinement to build, and modern tractors require a similar amount of time and testing. Schram went on, "We put that tractor into production in under twenty-three months, from the ground up. It was a brand new tractor in a brand new market that Harvester had never been in before, with ten people. We started August 15 of 1963 and the first production models rolled off in July of 1965."

Sorting Out the Bugs

There were a few initial problems, perhaps a natural result of the accelerated development. Schram said, "There were some problems, basically in the steering system. The major ongoing problem was with the rear-wheel steering. We had a linkage system in there and did not have a check valve in it originally and the wheels would tend to wander a little bit at road speed. Then we put a check valve into it, so we weren't just depending on the linkage. That held the rear wheels steady."

213

The industrial line was given a lot of attention in the mid-1960s, and produced an assortment of innovative products during that time. The 3600A backhoe/loader was significant as it was designed from the ground up as a backhoe, rather than just a backhoe and loader tacked onto an agricultural tractor.

Engineer Robert Oliver was working on the test group when Schram was working on design. He remembers testing prototype 4100s. "We had some real experiences in that. One of them was kind of the fun project. The clutch input shaft, or the transmission input shaft that the clutch hooks to. We could break that in like 10 feet. It took you all day to get it in or to get it out and get a new one put in it. It ended up being a resonance problem. We had to change the spring constant in the shaft to keep the resonance out of it. Once we got that out of it, it didn't break anymore," Oliver said.

Engine and Late Models

The engine was a 429-cubic-inch six-cylinder turbocharged diesel, and the cab boasted one of the first factory installations of a heater and air conditioner. The original 4100 was yellow and white, and the paint scheme went to red and white in 1972 with the 4166. The 4100 and various versions of it didn't set the world on fire with sales, but they remained in the line through 1978. Its replacement, the 3388 and 3588 "2+2" machines, would be the revolutionary four-wheel-drive tractor that IHC was searching for all along.

Other 1965 Models

Other new-for-1965 models included the 1206 and the 656. The 1206 was a larger two-wheel-drive tractor, the first Farmall to be rated for over 100 PTO horsepower. The engine was a turbocharged 361-cubic-inch six-cylinder diesel. The tractor had a 16-speed transmission. It was produced from 1965 to 1967, and was rebadged as the 1256.

These tractors could be equipped with a factory cab with heat and air conditioning. This was the first appearance of the cab on two-wheel-drive International tractors. The cab was built by Stolper-Allen of Menomonee Falls, Wisconsin.

The 656 was also introduced in 1965, and production ran until 1973. The tractor was powered by a six-cylinder turbocharged 281-cubic-inch diesel that produced 64 PTO horsepower. It was fit in the line just below the 706, and used a similar design. In 1967, the 656 was available with International's new hydrostatic transmission. The HT-340 Gas Turbine Tractor had been one of the first experimentals to carry the hydrostatic transmission, and the 656 was the first production tractor to use it. The hydrostatic transmission uses hydraulics to transfer power from the engine's flywheel to a standard final drive. Speed is controlled with an infinitely-variable single control known as the speed ratio (S/R) lever. The operator could choose from high and low range, and set the speed in each range with the S/R lever.

The advantage to hydrostatic was that speed could be fine-tuned to a greater degree than with standard transmissions. The disadvantage was that the hydraulic drive transferred power less efficiently and required more engine horsepower for equal drawbar pull.

The 656 was joined by several updated models that featured some new features and paint schemes. The 706 and 806 became the 756 and 856, while the 1206 was renamed the 1256. The optional cab for these tractors was changed to a model built by Excel Industries that had more operator room.

The Seven-Year Itch

By the 1970s, it took a peak year of tractor sales by the entire industry to top—just by a hair—IHC's total tractor production of over 170,000 tractors in 1951. The industry had changed, and tractor manufacturers simply could not sell the numbers possible in the past. The number of farms and farmers had declined, and the advantages of adding a new tractor to the farm had diminished.

Tractor sales seemed to cycle and peak about every seven years. With a peak in 1966, the next was appeared on schedule in 1973. A total of 196,994 tractors were sold that year, the peak for the decade as it would turn out. Sales would peak again in 1979, a year early for the seven-year cycle, at 188,267 units . As a side note, the Farmall name was dropped from the International line in 1973, ending a legacy that began nearly five decades earlier.

The tractors of the 1970s were going through the same changes as those of the 1960s, only on a larger scale. Horsepower was again climbing, and manufacturers turned to big-cubic-inch turbocharged and intercooled diesel engines for horsepower that went as high as 350. Front-wheel assist became a common option on most mid-sized to large tractors, and four-wheel-drive was the rule for the big machines over 150 horsepower or so. Even smaller models began using four-wheel-drive, and the small four-wheel-drive tractor would become one of the growing markets of the decade.

Foreign makers became increasingly competitive in the 1970s, especially with smaller tractors. In fact, it became more common for small tractors to be built overseas than domestically.

1969

In 1969, International had one new model and some new names for familiar faces, most of which were available with hydrostatic transmissions. The 856 became the 826, and was available in both gear-drive and hydrostatic transmissions. The hydrostatic version was rated for about 20 horsepower less than the gear-drive machine. Gasoline, LPG, or diesel models were available. The 1056 became the 1026, and was

also available with a hydrostatic transmission. The 4100 became the 4156, a tractor that used the chassis design from the 1056 and a larger, more powerful six-cylinder diesel engine. The turbocharged 407-cubic-inch powerplant put out 131 PTO horsepower through the gear-drive transmission. It was built until 1971, when it was rebadged the 1466.

66 Series (1971)

International's next big push for new models came in 1971, when the company introduced 11 new models. Most of the new tractors were in the 66 Series, with seven tractors ranging from 80 to 133 PTO horsepower. All used six-cylinder engines, and most were available with either hydrostatic or gear-drive transmissions. The biggest of the new models was the 1468, which was powered by a 550-cubic-inch V-8 diesel engine good for 145 PTO horsepower. Three smaller models, the 354, 454, and 574, were also introduced in 1971. These utility tractors ranged from 33 to 53 PTO horsepower.

1972

In 1972, the 4156 and 656 joined the 66 Series and became the 4166 and 666. The 4166 shed the yellow-and-white color scheme used since the original 4100 and was painted red and white like the rest of the line. Both of these models were built until 1976.

The Steiger-Built Internationals

One of the simplest ways to add a big four-wheel-drive to the lineup was to purchase it from another company and rebadge it. Steiger had been providing such tractors for many years, and International turned to them in 1973 with the 4366. At some point, International actually was a part-owner of Steiger, which made it more profitable for IHC to contract someone else to build tractors.

The big diesel in the 4366 was an International 466-cubic-inch six-cylinder engine that was rated for 225 PTO horsepower. It was an articulated four-wheel drive, and produced from 1973 to 1976.

In 1976, International put its 798-cubic-inch turbocharged V-8 diesel engine into a Steiger chassis and created the 4568. The big tractor weighed nearly 13 tons, was rated for 300 horsepower, and was produced only in 1976.

In 1977, the two models were renamed the 4386 and the 4586, but the tractors were essentially the same units. The 4386 had the 466-cubic-inch six-cylinder, while the 4586 had the big V-8 diesel.

The last addition to the Steiger line came in 1979, when a more powerful version of the IHC 798-cubic-inch V-8 was used in the same basic frame. The tractor was the 4786, and it was rated for 350 horsepower. All of the Steiger tractors disappeared from the line in 1982, when International sold off its share in Steiger in an effort to recoup some of the company's staggering losses.

The 66 Series machines were produced from 1971 to 1976. Turbocharging was fairly common by that time, as horsepower demands continued to rise. The narrow front end was rarely seen in large tractors by this time. This International 1066 Turbo Diesel used a 414-cubic-inch six-cylinder that produced about 110 drawbar horsepower. A sixteen-speed transmission was used.

86 Series

Late in 1976, Harvester introduced the 86 Series, a line of new tractors that included the Hydro 86, 686, 886, Hydro 186, 986, 1086, 1486, 1586, and 4186. Two Steiger-built four-wheel-drives, the 4386 and 4586, were also offered with the new "86" model designated. International also introduced a new 284, a compact tractor built by Kimco, a company formed by a joint venture between International and Komatsu.

Control Cab

The new two-wheel-drive 86 Series tractors featured the new Control Cab, which was moved a foot-and-a-half forward in the chassis. This reduced the amount of noise in the cab and improved the ride for the operator. The cab was part of Harvester's efforts to incorporate human factors in engineering, which applied principles similar to those of Raymond Loewy's influence on the Letter Series. The concept was to design the tractor to fit the operator. The new

The 1468 was the first IHC agricultural tractor to use a V-8 engine. The tractor weighed in at nearly seven tons, had 16 forward speeds, and about 140 horsepower (rating varied with years). Produced from 1971 to 1974, the 1468 used a 550-cubic-inch fuel-injected diesel engine. In the interest of better fuel economy, fuel was injected into only four cylinders under light loads. *Scott Satterland Collection*

control cab gave the operator better vision to the front and easier entry to and exit from the cab, as well as the improved ride and quieter environment.

The amount of noise inside the cab became an issue with the tractor industry, and the tests at Nebraska began measuring how much noise reached the operator. Engineer Robert Oliver said, "What they were doing was trying to relate hearing loss to how long the farmer had to sit on the tractor, exposed to loud noises."

According to Oliver, the result of quieter cabs was better instrumentation. The quieter cab isolated the farmer from the sounds of the machinery. It was harder to tell when something was going wrong, and the farmer had to be taught to watch gauges. "He couldn't tell if his chopper was plugging up, because he couldn't hear it. So, it was a whole learning experience getting the farmer to understand that he could run it with instruments. We had to start developing better tachometers and putting them in spots where they could see them better. It started the whole push on human factors engineering, so he could do all the things he needed to do inside that cab, and give the comfort that he still had control."

The Need for Synchromesh

International took the lead on noise levels inside the cab, and the 86 Series was a successful venture. But they lagged behind in transmission technology. The industry was turning to synchronized transmissions that allowed shifting on the fly. Harvester was well aware of the lag, but a new transmission would require millions of dollars of retooling costs. The company was unwilling to sink the capital into the new line, and the 86 Series carried capable but aging transmissions.

The powershift transmission would come to IH, but it would be too late when it arrived. In the meantime, the company had another innovative tractor up its sleeve.

The New-For-1979 Models

In 1979, the 30- to 60-horsepower machines were attended to, with some upgraded models and two new models. A more powerful Steiger-chassis machine was also added. The big news was the new 2+2 models, the four-wheel-drive 3388 and 3588. These two models were a whole new take on the four-wheel-drive tractor and were one of the company's most striking engineering advances of modern times.

The 2+2s gave the company another shot in the arm, and were a key part of a 1979 sales surge. A comparison of farm sales equipment found Deere & Company on top at $3.9 million of annual sales, with IHC not far behind with $3.1 million in sales. Massey-Ferguson was next with $2.5 million, with Ford and Sperry New Holland the only others (just) over a million dollars in 1979 sales. Bear in mind that these comparisons can be skewed significantly depending on how they are totaled (Do you include lawn tractors? Snow blowers?), so take the figures with a grain of salt.

The 2+2

Introduced as the International 3388 and 3588 in 1979, the 2+2 four-wheel-drive tractors were one of the company's last blasts. The big tractors were articulated, as most of the big four-wheel-drives were, but placed the engine well over the front wheels. By doing so, the big tractor had equal weight distribution over the front and rear wheels. The result was better traction without the addition of extra weights, and lightened ground pressure. Also, the tractors could turn in a 15-foot, 9-inch radius, which was impressive for such big machines. The original Farmall, hailed for its quick turning, needed about the same amount of space to turn around.

As a result, the big tractor was more maneuverable than typical big four-wheel-drives, which were great for plowing and such, but a bit clumsy for row crop work. A less-than-tremendous volume of the tractors were sold, but those that did sell received rave reviews.

Both models were assembled mainly from existing components. The articulated joint was all new, of course, but most of the rear end came from the 86 Series tractors. The result was more economical production, and lowered design and tooling costs.

The 3388 used a 130-horsepower six-cylinder turbocharged diesel engine, while the 3588 used a bored version of the same engine to crank out 150 horsepower. While these numbers were impressive, the two were only about halfway up the IHC horsepower chart. The Steiger-built 4786 was powered by a turbocharged V-8 rated for 350 horsepower.

The 2+2 was a breakthrough machine that combined the power and traction of a big four-wheel-drive tractor with the maneuverability of a row-crop unit. Two new-for-1979 models—the 3588 and 3388—were available, and rated for 150 and 130 horse-power. Both used six-cylinder turbocharged diesel engines and turning radiuses of 15 feet 9 inches. The 2+2s were revamped in 1982, and production ended in 1985. *Scott Satterland Collection*

The 50 Series was supposed to be the company savior, but it was introduced into a sagging market and didn't slow IH's massive 1980 losses. The engines were turbo-diesels similar to the units in the 2+2 tractors. The big news was the synchronized three-range six-speed transmissions which gave 18 forward and six reverse speeds. More importantly, they could be shifted on the fly. *Scott Satterland Collection*

The tractors were equipped with both 540- and 1,000-rpm IPTOs, and the Torque Amplifier allowed 16 forward and 8 reverse speeds. The cabs of the 2+2s were insulated, air conditioned, heated, and sound deadened, keeping the operator comfortable in any conditions.

84 Series

After the major revamp of the larger tractors for 1977, International looked to bolster its small and mid-sized tractors in 1979. Four models, the 363, 464, 574, and 674, were replaced with new 84 Series tractors and two new models, the Hydro 84 and 784, were added to the line.

384

The 384 was rated as a 36 PTO horsepower tractor and had a 154-cubic-inch diesel. The little tractor had eight forward speeds and served as a decent utility tractor, just slightly bigger than the larger garden tractors. The 384 was discontinued in 1982.

484

The new 484 used a 179-cubic-inch three-cylinder diesel engine that produced 42 PTO horsepower. The transmission had eight forward and four reverse speeds, and it was equipped with a 540-rpm IPTO and Category I three-point hitch. It was available in utility and row-crop models.

584–784

The 584 through 784 ranged from 53 to 67 horsepower and used four-cylinder diesel engines. Category II three-point hitches were standard, and the models were available in utility, row-crop, low-profile, and all-wheel-drive versions. The two larger models had an optional torque amplifier, and the 784 had both 540- and 1,000-rpm IPTOs. The Hydro 84 was a 59-horsepower model equipped with hydrostatic drive.

844

The line received a new addition in 1980, when the 844 came in. It was a 73-horsepower model that used a 268-cubic-inch four-cylinder diesel. The tractor was equipped with dual IPTOs and a Torque Amplifier was optional.

The new-for-1979 models performed well for International, and the year was a good one for the industry and for IHC. It seemed that the company would be able to overcome the debts and uncertainty that shrouded the tractor industry. Despite such optimism and IHC's strong sales, the company had only about five years left.

Into the 1980s

As the 1980s dawned, International's struggles became cataclysmic. The debt load that hung around the companies neck was enormous, and the times were difficult ones for tractor manufacturers. Most of the farmers were struggling under debt loads similar (relatively) to that of International, due to the flood of money and available financing in the seventies. In the early 1980s, farmers were refinancing or going belly up. The last thing on their minds was new tractors.

The early 1980s saw International introduce quite an assortment of new tractors. The 786 was added to the 86 line, and the 140 was replaced with the 274 Offset. The 140 was the long-lived descendant of the Model A, which was finally replaced. The 274 used a three-cylinder diesel engine, and was built by Kimco, a division that was a joint venture between IHC and Komatsu.

The line was revised in 1982, with the new 30, 50, and 70 Series tractors as the stars. The 2+2 tractors were revamped, and the Cub derivatives received a make-over and a new model as well. Despite the introduction of the new tractors, net losses for 1982 were $1.6 billion.

50 Series

Tragically, Harvester introduced its new 50 Series tractors in 1982, with farmers struggling just to stay off the auction block. The 50 Series tractors—the 5088, 5288, and 5488—featured the new synchronized transmission, but they were too late to avert the coming disaster. The new transmission consisted of a six-speed transmission coupled to a three-speed range transmission. The result was 18 forward and 6 reverse speeds. A differential lock could be engaged with a switch at the operator's heel, and the transmission could be power-shifted between first and second, third and fourth, or fifth and sixth.

The engine was a turbocharged six-cylinder diesel. The 5088 used a 436-cubic-inch powerplant rated for 136 PTO horsepower, while the 5288 and 5488 used a larger 466-cubic-inch engine that was rated for 163 and 187 PTO horsepower. A built-in ether injection system was supplied for cold-weather starting, and the engine and drivetrain warranty was for three years or 2,500 hours of use.

Modern tractors were becoming much more powerful for their size. The 5488 weighed about 15,000 pounds in two-wheel-drive form, and produced 187 PTO horsepower. Those figures compare quite favorably to the 65 horsepower of the 10,000-pound Super WD-9 back in 1954.

The 50 Series tractors used three hydraulic pumps, like earlier models, but the pumps were more powerful and mounted outside the transmission housing for easy servicing. All-wheel-drive was an option on all three models.

One of the features of the 50 Series was the reverse-flow radiator, a simple idea that had been around since the optional reverse fan on the Letter Series tractors. By drawing air from above the hood and pushing it out through the radiator, dust and chaff were blown off the radiator rather than sucked in. Also, the hot air was blowing away from the cab, giving the air conditioner a bit of a break.

The cab had become an amazing place by the 1980s, and the 50 Series was no exception. Heating and air conditioning were standard, and the seat and steering wheel were adjustable. The seat was suspended with an air and hydraulic fluid system, and featured arm rests and lumbar support. The International cab was one of the quietest in the industry, and had doors on both side for easy access. A computer display gave digital readouts of engine rpm, ground speed, exhaust gas temperature, and PTO speed. The cab had integral roll-over protection (ROPS).

30 Series

In addition to the mid-sized 50 Series machines, the slightly lower-powered 30 Series tractors were introduced and the 2+2s were upgraded. Two of the new 30 Series tractors were introduced in 1982, and

two more appeared in 1983. The 90-horsepower 3288 and 110-horsepower 3688 were introduced in 1982 along with the new 50 Series machines. These two tractors had a bit less power and fewer features than the 50 Series. The 3688 used a normally aspirated version of the 436-cubic-inch engine in the 5088, while the 3288 used a smaller 358-cubic-inch normally aspirated diesel powerplant.

The 1983 additions to the line were the 112-horsepower 3488 Hydro and the 80-horsepower 3088. All but the hydrostatic model used the same synchromesh transmission found in the 50 Series machines, with 16 forward and 8 reverse speeds. The forward-flow radiator was standard, as was the 540/1,000-rpm IPTOs, differential lock, and the heated and air-conditioned cab. The 30 Series had fewer bells and whistles as standard equipment, with the data center and plush interior optional on most of the line.

60 Series

The 60 Series was an upgrade of the 2+2 models and became the 6388 and 6588 that appeared in 1982, with a new 6788 added to the line in 1983. The two larger models received a somewhat larger engine, with 30 additional cubic inches bringing displacement to 466. They also received the new synchromesh transmission, allowing power-shifting at speed. The 6388 and 6588 had 16 forward and 8 reverse speeds, while the 6788 had 12 forward and 6 reverse speeds. These were the final and finest versions of the 2+2, as these tractors were dropped from the line after the merger, making 1984 the last year 2+2 tractors were built.

70 Series

A new 70 series of big four-wheel-drive tractors was supposed to be introduced in 1985, but never made it beyond the farm shows in September 1984. The tractors were in the 200-PTO-horsepower class, probably as replacements for the Steiger-built machines that were dropped in 1982. The sale of the International agricultural division was announced in November of 1984, and very few 70 Series machines were produced.

Synchromesh!

The 84 Series tractors received synchromesh transmissions by 1983, and were produced through 1984 when the imminent merger of the International agricultural division and Case was announced. In addition, the 484, 584, and 684 were produced as Case-Internationals after the sale.

Fall From Grace

Several factors contributed to fall. The first was the aforementioned debt load. Even during the boom of the seventies, the company could not escape this burden.

International Tractor Production 1961–85

Model Name	PTO Hp	Years
404	37	1961–68
504	46/53	1961–68
606	54	1962–67
706	76	1963–67
806	95	1963–67
424	37	1964–67
F-656	64/62	1965–72
I-656	66	1965–73
1206	113	1965–67
4100	110	1965–68
385	35	1967–71
444	38	1967–71
756	76	1967–71
856	93/100	1967–71
1256	116	1967–69
4300	203	1967–70
544	53	1968–73
826	92	1969–71
1456	132	1969–71
4156	140	1969–70
454	41	1970–73
574	53	1970–78
1026	112	1970–71
2400	53	1970–77
2500	68	1970–77
766	76/85	1971–76
966	101	1971–76
1066	126	1971–76
1175	123	1971–78
1466	146	1971–76
1468	145 (V-8)	1971–74
354	35	1972–75
664	62	1972–74
666	66/70	1972–76
4166	151	1972–76
Hydro 70	70	1973–76
Hydro 100	104	1973–76
464	45	1973–78
674	59/62	1973–78
4366	163	1973–76
1566	161	1974–76
1568	151 (V-8)	1974–76
4568	230 (V-8)	1975–76
Hydro 86	69	1976–81
Hydro 186	105	1976–81
284	26 (4-cyl.)	1976–81
364	35	1976–77
686	66	1976–81
886	91	1976–81
986	106	1976–81
1086	131	1976–81
1486	146	1976–81
1586	162	1976–81
4186	151	1976–78
4386	175	1976–81
4586	235 (V-8)	1976–81
Hydro 84	59	1978–85
384	27	1978–82
484	42	1978–84
584	53	1978–84
684	63	1978–84
784	65	1978–84
3388 (2+2)	130	1978–81
3588 (2+2)	150	1978–81
4786	265 (V-8)	1978–81
274	27	1979–84
884	72	1979–84
284	23 (3-cyl.)	1980–84
786	80	1980–81
3788 (2+2)	171	1980–81
3088	81	1981–85
3288	90	1981–85
3488 Hydro	112	1981–85
5088	136	1981–85
5288	163	1981–84
5488	187	1981–84
6388	130	1981–85
6588	150	1981–85
6788	170	1981–85
234	15	1982–85
244	18	1982–84
254	21	1982–84
383	37	1982–84
483	42	1982–84
3688	114	1982–85
7588	265	1982–85
7788	265	1982–85
7288	175	1985
7388	181	1985

Source: *Hot Line Farm Equipment Guide*, 1996

Note: Some dates conflict with introductions; the 2+2 tractors, for example, were launched in 1979, although a few bear 1978 serial numbers.

Management is blamed for making several key mistakes that led to the company's downfall, but it may be that the debt load was such that the company simply could not survive the times.

The second of International's problems was troubles with organized labor. Although the company had a long history of treating employees well, it had an equally lengthy record of struggles with unions. The McCormicks refused to bargain with organized labor, and that tone continued to the bitter end. Although International's employees were treated relatively well, management never seemed to master the art of dealing with organized labor.

In 1979, after the company showed record-breaking profits, management badly misjudged organized labor. Management pushed to bring wages and benefits down, and labor struck. International leaders refused to give and fought a losing battle for nearly six months. In the same time span, the economy swung toward recession, and the company lost reams of money that it could not afford to throw away. When the workers returned, International leaders misjudged the level of market demand built up during the strike, and overproduced tractors for a sagging market. By the time the 50 Series was introduced—the tractor that was supposed to save the farm equipment division—demand was almost nil and the company was incredibly overstocked with suddenly outdated machines.

The company's administration had been investigating the possibility of filing a chapter eleven—bankruptcy—since 1981. The move would have been unprecedented; no company of International's size had ever filed for chapter eleven. The banks were hounding the company, and the company was finding it difficult to obtain loans while losing millions each year. International began slashing costs wherever possible and, by the mid-eighties, rumors of a sale were circulating in the agricultural division. Harold Schram recalls these days as the only unpleasant time during his more than 25 years with the company.

"There were constant rumors about who was coming through to look at the Ag equipment division. We were told in mid-November of 1984 that there wasn't any substance to the rumors about the sale to anybody and, of course, it was rumored to be Tenneco. The papers here were even carrying articles that said the president of our division had been seen coming out of the Tenneco corporate office in Houston, Texas. About two weeks after we were told there was no substance to the rumors, the sale was announced."

In 1984, the farm equipment division was sold to Tenneco, the owners of J. I. Case. Case and International's tractor division were merged, and the tractors that ensued were known as Case-Internationals. Veterans of IHC and those close to the company say that the merger was not good for the International Harvester agri-cultural division. Plants were closed and workers from all venues were sent home with a pink slip. Most of the IHC models were discontinued, and almost all were replaced in the first few years of production. The Hinsdale Farm, the site of endless hours of testing of all kinds of IHC products, from tractor to implements to milking machines, was divided up and slowly sold off for development.

The 30 Series was quite similar to the 50 Series, with a bit less power and fewer accessories. Horsepower ranged from 90 to 110, the new synchronized transmission was used, and the forward-flow cooling which blew air out of the front of the radiator (keeping it cleaner) was standard, as on the 50 Series. *Scott Satterland Collection*

Farmall is long gone, only a memory, and International is but a fragment of its former glory. The employees of the company speak fondly of the company as a place where your co-workers were like family, the management was team-oriented, and your future was assured.

Long-time IHC engineer Gordon Hershman's comments are typical of those who spent a portion of lives with the company. "I love Harvester. They were a tremendous company. I always feel bad that we lost it the way that we did."

Harold Schram, another long-time engineer recalls his days with the company as some of the best of his life. "If you worked for Harvester, you were part of the family and you felt that way. There was a lot of loyalty both ways—employees to the company and company to the employees...It was more than just a job to us—it was a way of life."

Appendix

Recommended Sources

Gray, R.B. *The Agricultural Tractor: 1855-1950*. U.S. Department of Agriculture, 1954.
> A treasure trove of facts about how tractor technology changed and what effects it had on the farm.

Larsen, Lester. *Farm Tractors 1950–1975*. American Society of Agricultural Engineers, 1981.
> Information on how the tractor progressed from 1950 to 1975.

Gay, Larry. *Farm Tractors 1975–1995*. American Society of Agricultural Engineers, 1995.
> The only source of its kind on modern tractors.

Marsh, Barbara. *A Corporate Tragedy*, Doubleday & Company, 1985.
> If you want to know how the International Harvester Company management evolved and why the agricultural division was sold to Tenneco, this is the one to have. Out of print.

McCormick, Cyrus. *The Century of the Reaper*, Houghton Mifflin Company, 1931.
> The early history of the company is told with an colorful but slanted voice. Out of print.

Wendel, C. H. *150 Years of International Harvester*. Crestline, 1981.
> Where else can you find a book with listings for everything from disk harrows to cream separators? A must.

Williams, Robert C. *Fordson, Farmall, and Poppin' Johnny*, University of Illinois Press, 1987.
> A graduate thesis that examines how and why the tractor changed the farm.

Hot Line Farm Equipment Guide, Two-Volume Set, Heartland Ag-Business Group, Annual.
> Specifications, serial numbers, and prices for nearly every farm tractor.

Welsch, Roger. *Old Tractors and the Men Who Love Them*, Motorbooks International, 1995.
> Seriously entertaining stuff.

Leffingwell, Randy. *Farm Tractors: A Living History*, Motorbooks International, 1995.
> Stunning photographs of farm tractors and interesting text on farm technology.

Clubs and Magazines

International-Harvester Collectors Association
648 N. Northwest Hwy.
Box 250
Park Ridge, IL 60068

Red Power Magazine
Box 277
Battle Creek, IA 51006
712/365-4669

Antique Power Magazine
P.O. Box 1000
Westerville, OH 43081-7000
614/848-5038

Belt Pulley Magazine
P.O. Box 83
Nokomis, IL 62075
217/563-2612

Engineers and Engines
2240 Oak Leaf St.
P.O. Box 2757
Joliet, IL 60434-2757

Farm Antique News
P.O. Box 812
Tarkio, MO 64491
816/736-4528

Gas Engine Magazine
P.O. Box 328
Lancaster, PA 17608
717/392-0733

The Hook (Pullers' Magazine)
P.O. Box 937
Powell, OH 43065-0937
614/848-5038

Tractors on the Internet

There are dozens of ways to pursue your hobby on the Internet from photographs and stories to a whole community of fellow tractor enthusiasts with whom to commune. Listed below are only a few of the resources, but they will get you everywhere you want to go.

The Antique Tractor Mailing List
A discussion list for people who love antique tractors. Highly recommended. Send e-mail to Spencer Yost at yostsw@co.forsyth.nc.us or drop a line to him at 3160 MacBrandon Lane, Pfafftown, NC 27040 for guidelines about signing on.

Web Sites
Ageless Iron
http://www.agriculture.com/contents/sf/ageless/agiindex.html

Antique Tractor
http://freenet.co.forsyth.nc.us/TRACTOR/atis.html

Early Day Eng & Trac Ass'n
http://transport.com/~edgeta/edgeta.html

UC-Davis Tractors
http://www.ece.ucdavis.edu/~hulse/index.html

Index

Adams grader, 72
Air starter, on Titan and Mogul, 23
Akron Works, 21
Anti-Trust Suit, 26
Asphalt mixer, 18
Austin Motor Grader, 60
Auto Mower, 75
Auto Wagon, 20

B.F. Goodrich, 111
Baker, Elmer, 53
Baumgardner, LeRoy, 20
Benjamin, Bert R., 75, 76, 79, 81, 82, 85, 117, 132
Bermuda Clipper, 103
Bucyrus-Erie angle dozer, 178

Caldwell weed chopper, 169
Channel frame, 18, 51
Chassis, 155
Continental Engine in Model 350, 201
Control Cab, 216
Convertible intake, Farmall, 82
Cooling, spray or open tank, 18
Cooling, thermosyphon, 37
Corn harvesting, 13
Cub built on a production line, 188
Cub Scouts, 185
Culti-Vision, 131
Cutaway view, Farmall Regular engine, 81
Cutaway view, Farmall, 113

Date IHC tractors were first painted red, 123
Dealerships, consolidation, 27
Deering Harvester Company, 9, 26
Deerings, 86
Dropped-rear drive, 86, 107, 115, 166, 135, 136

Electrall, 200
Electrics, 123

F-12, cutaway view, 117
F-12, new engine, 120
F-20, wide front axle attachment, 113
F-20, controls, 105
F-30, engine, 108
Farmall, cutaway view, 113
Farmall Regular engine, cutaway drawing, 81
Farmall convertible intake, 82
Farmall on the showroom floor, 85
Farmall orchard fenders, 90
Farmall Works, 128
Fast Hitch, 147, 198
Field demonstrations, 54
Field trials, 9
First Farmall Cub off the line at the Louisville Works, 188
Ford vs. International, 55
Ford, Henry, 49, 54
Fordson, 54
Four-wheel-drive, 212
French & Hecht track, 96

Gear final drive, 46, 51, 82
Gear-drive machine, 51
Golf courses, 90
Gray, C.W., 77, 92

Hershman, Gordon L., 194, 199, 212, 221
Hiawatha train, 126
Hinsdale Experimental Farm, 184, 199
Horsepower ratings, comparison to truck, 160
Hussey, Obed, 7
Hydra-Creeper, 200
Hydraulics, 206
Hydrostatic drive, 195
Hydrostatic power steering, 209

IHC Red Diamond truck engine, 70

Implements
    Chopper, 152
    Combines, 96, 114
    Corn binder, 51
    Corn harvester, 13, 49
    Corn pickers, 10, 30, 82, 105, 147, 155, 160, 161, 196, 199
    Cotton picker, 158
    Cotton stripper, 197
    Culti-packer, 106
    Cultivators, 47, 80, 116, 118, 132, 133, 136, 140, 141, 149, 186, 189
    Cutter, side, 190
    Disk harrow, 18, 71, 124, 135, 177
    Disk plow, 171
    Disk, 94, 106, 118, 138, 139, 146, 150, 151, 167, 198
    Drill, 102, 121
    Golf course implements, 88–93, 128, 129
    Grader, 34, 60, 61
    Grain binders, 8–12, 20, 32
    Grain box, 199
    Hammer mill, 137
    Harrow plow, 163
    Harrow, 106
    Harrow, peg tooth, 156
    Harvester, 48
    Harvester, beet, 157
    Harvester-thresher, 45, 46
    Lift-All, Pneumatic, 134
    Loader, front, 57
    Manure spreaders, 67, 79, 81, 86, 106, 110, 112, 190
    Medium arch, 181
    Middlebuster, 143, 145
    Mower, 183, 187
    Packer, 124
    Planters, 78, 108, 187
    Plows, 14, 23, 30, 32, 56, 66, 69, 70, 108, 109, 113, 143, 144, 168
    Potato diggers, 134, 158
    Power sprayer, orchard, 165
    Snow plow, behind Mogul 10-20, 31
    Snow plows, 31, 58, 71, 192
    Sprayer, orchard, 97, 98
    Squadron hitch, 169
    Sweeper, front-mounted, 124
    Thresher, PTO-driven, behind IH 8-16, 42
    Tiller, Seaman, 152
    Water tank, 59
    Winch hoist, 181
    Winch, 63
Independent power take-off, 149
Industrial models, development, 61
Integral frame, 18, 53, 57, 97
International all-steel wagon, 126

Johnston, E.A., 20, 75, 76

KA80 medium arch, 181
Kimco, 194

Legge, Alexander, 45, 47, 49, 75, 81-84, 117
Letter Series decals, 143
Lift-all Retrofit for Farmall Regular, F-20, and F-30 tractors, 91
Lift-All, 111
Lighting system, 98
Lighting, 108
Loewy, Raymond, 72, 131, 132
Logging, 73

M-220-L cotton picker, 158
Madison-Kipp adjustable oiler, 36
Mass Production, 47
McCormick Harvesting Company, 26
McCormick I, Cyrus, 7
McCormick III, Cyrus, 7, 10, 49, 52, 54
McCormick, 8, 24, 47, 53
McCormick, Fowler, 156

McCormick, Nettie Fowler, 11, 12
McCormick-Deering combine, 114
Merger, 12, 27
Milkers, 88
Milwaukee Harvester Company, 26
Milwaukee Works, 21
Model A and B, new engine, 140
Models
    30 Series, 219
    40 Series, 202, 206
    50 Series, 218, 219
    60 Series, 219
    66 Series, 215
    70 Series, 219
    84 Series, 218
    86 Series, 216
    200 Series, 200
    300 Series, 201
    400 Series, 204
    Cub Cadet, 193
    Cub Lo-Boy, 191-193
    Cub, 183, 185-191
    Cub, 184
    Cub, first at Louisville Works, 188
    F-12 wide-tread version, 120
    F-12, 117–119
    F-12, converted to rural mail carrier, 117
    F-14, 120-123, 125
    F-20 Narrow Tread, 111
    F-20, 110, 112, 114
    F-30, 105, 106, 108
    F-30, high-clearance, 108
    F-30, narrow tread version, 107
    F-30, with high cane-type wheels, 111
    Fairway 12, 125, 128, 129
    Fairway Regular, 89
    Farmall Fairway, 90, 92
    Farmall Regular, 77-92
    Friction-Drive tractor, 16-18
    HT-340 Gas Turbine Tractor, 213
    Hundred Series, 197-199
    I-12, 124-128
    I-30, 68
    I-4, 164
    I-40 and ID-40 Production, 72
    I-40, 71
    IA-40, 72
    ID-40, 73
    ID-9, 172
    International 8-16, 41-43, 45, 51
    International A (Super), 145
    International A, 138, 142
    McCormick-Deering 10-20, 50, 52, 56, 60
    McCormick-Deering 15-30, 46-49, 52, 56, 59
    Model 10-20 Industrial, 57, 58
    Model 12s, 127
    Model 15 TracTracTor, 100
    Model 15-30 Industrial, 64
    Model 20 grader, 61
    Model 20, 58-60, 62, 63
    Model 30, 64
    Model 100, 198
    Model 200, 199
    Model 234, 191
    Model 244, 193
    Model 254, 193
    Model 274 Offset, 194
    Model 300, 198
    Model 350 Utility High-Clear, 197
    Model 384, 218
    Model 400 (LPG), 197
    Model 400, 197, 199
    Model 404 and 504, 209
    Model 450, 202
    Model 460, 204
    Model 460, 206, 207
    Model 484, 218
    Model 560, 202–205
    Model 560, 206

Models (cont.)

Model 584-784, 218
Model 600 and 650, 204
Model 600, 200
Model 656, 214
Model 660, 206
Model 706 and 806, 209–211
Model 806 AWD Diesel, 212
Model 844, 218
Model 1066, 216
Model 1206, 214
Model 3388, 3588, 2+2, 217, 218
Model 3600A backhoe/loader, 214
Model 4100, 209, 212
Model 4300, 211
Model A, 131, 132, 135, 136
Model A, 134, 137
Model AV, 138, 139, 142
Model B, 135
Model B, 140, 141
Model BN, 140, 141
Model C, 142, 143, 145, 147
Model C, 144
Model H, 149, 154
Model H, 150-152
Model HV, 153, 154
Model I-30, 67
Model M wide-front, 156
Model M, 155-157, 159
Model MD, 158
Model MDV, 159
Model MV, 149, 150
Model MV, 159
Mogul 8-16, 15, 29, 30
Mogul 8-16, 29, 30, 33
Mogul 10-20, 31-33
Mogul 15-30, 23
Mogul 30-60, 24
Mogul 45, 23, 24
Mogul Jr., 24, 29
MRS Special, 172
Nine Series, 169
O-12, 125, 127
O-4, 164, 165, 167
O-6, 163, 168
Rice Field Special, 171
Shop Mule, 139
Six series, 166
Snowmobile, 212
Super A, 142
Super A-1, 136. 145
Super C, 146, 147
Super H, 154, 155
Super M, 159, 160
Super M-TA, 149, 161
Super Nines, 173
T-20 TracTracTor, 101
T-20, 96, 98, 99
T-20, orchard-type, 95
T-340 and TD-340, 179
T-35 and TD-35, 103
T-35, 100
T-4, T-5, and TD-5, 180
T-40, 100
T-6 and TD-6, 175
T-6, 176
T-9 and TD-9, 176
TA-40, 103
TA-40, TK-40, and TD-40, 101
TD-14, 176, 178
TD-15, 176
TD-18, 175, 176, 180, 181
TD-24, 177, 178, 180
TD-25, 179
TD-30, 179
TD-35, 102, 103
TD-40, 99, 100
TD-6, 176
TD-9, 177
Titan 10-20, 32-37
Titan 12-25, 24, 28, 29
Titan 15-30, 24, 26, 28, 29, 31

Models (cont.)

Titan 18-35, 24, 29
Titan 30-60, 23
Titan Type D Road Roller, 21
Titan, 45-horsepower, 22
TK-40, 103
TracTracTor, 10-20, 96, 98
TracTracTor, 15-30, 100
Type A tractor, 18, 19
Type B two-speed tractor, 18, 19
Type B, 19
Type C, 20, 21
Type D Titan, 20, 21
Type D, 22
W-12, 120, 123-125, 127
W-30, 65-68, 71, 72
W-4, 164
W-40, 70
W-9, 169, 170
WD-40, 70, 73
WD-6, 167, 168
WD-9, 163, 170
WD-9, WR-9, and WDR-9, 171
WDR-9, 171
White Letter Series tractors, 146
WR-9, 171
Modular construction, 53
Moline Universal, 80
Morgan, J.P., 26
Morton tractor, 15, 16
Morton, S.S., 17
Motor Cultivator, 76, 77
Mott, Carl, 76

Newark Airport, 127

Ohio Manufacturing Company, 16, 18
Oil bath test stations, 100
Oliver, Robert, 199, 207, 217
Orchard fenders, 52
Orchard fenders, Farmall, 90
Orchard tractors, 52, 90, 95, 165, 166
Osborne & Company, 26

Painting tractors, on the production line, 188
Pan-Am, 103
Paris Exposition, 1915, 24
Perkins, George W., 26
Planetary Power Steering, 178
Plano Harvester Company, 26
Pneumatic (air-filled rubber) tires, 108
Pneumatic Lift-All, 134
Pneumatic tires, Farmall retrofit, 91
Pneumatic tires, 91, 110
Power lifts, 139, 153
Power take-off (PTO), development, 48–50
President Roosevelt, 26
Production line, 43, 44, 101, 188
Production figures
Cub Cadet Production 1961–67, 193
Cub Production, 194
Early International Tractor Production, 25
F-12 and F-14 Production, 119
F-20 Production, 111
F-30 Production, 111
Farmall Regular and Fairway Production, 89
I-9, ID-9, W-9, WD-9 WR-9, WDR-9 and Super Nine Production, 173
International 8-16 Production, 50
International 600 and 650 Production, 205
International Tractor Production 1961-85, 220
McCormick-Deering 10-20 Production, 62
McCormick-Deering 15-30 Production, 59
Model 20 Production, 63
Model 30 Production, 66
Model 100, 130, and 140 Production, 201
Model 200, 230, 240 Production, 202
Model 300, 350, 330, and 340 Produc

Production figures
tion, 203
Model A and B Production, 144
Model C and Super C Production, 147
Model H Production, 154
Model M Production, 161
Model O-4, OS-4, W-4, I-4, and Supers Production, 166
Model O-6, OS-6, ODS-6, W-6, WD-6, I-6 and ID-6 Production, 170
Mogul 8-16 and 10-20 Production, 34
Sixty Series Production, 207
Titan 10-20 Production, 39
Titan and International 12-25/15-30 Tractor Production, 33
TracTracTor 10-20 Production, 98
TracTracTor T-35 and TD-35 Production, 103
TracTracTor TA-40, TK-40, and TD-40 Production, 102
W-12, O-12, I-12, and Fairway 12 Production, 125
W-30 Production, 68
WA-40, WK-40, W-40, and WD-40 Production, 71
PTO-driven corn binder, 51
PTO-driven thresher, 42

Refrigeration equipment, 88
Reliance, 21, 22
Rice Field Special, 171
Ronning patent, 81, 91
Rubber tires, 48
Rural mail carrier, F-12, 117

Salt crusher, 99
Schram, Harold, 194, 213, 221
Seaman tiller, 152
Shop Mule, 139
Snowmobile, 212
Spray or open tank cooling, 18
Squadron hitch, 169
Standard Tread 12s, 125
Steam engines, 7
Steele's Tavern, 8
Steering clutches, 96, 97
Steiger, 211
Steiger-Built Internationals, 215
Steward, John F., 10, 11, 75
Synchromesh, 217, 219
Synchronized gear transmission, 179

TD-35 cutaway, 102
TD-35, engine being installed at factory, 101
Tenneco, 221
Texas, 79
Tractor Wars, 48, 54, 55
Thermosyphon, 37
Tobacco farmers, 184
Torque amplifier, 203
Total-loss oiling, 17
Touch control, 143
Tractor demonstration, 36
Tractor wars, round two, 160
Tractor Works, 47
Tractorettes, 140, 153
Trial, anti-trust suit, 27
Turbocharging, 211
Two-piece spark plug, on Titan 10-20, 39

Universal Mounting System, 145
Universal, Moline, 80

Warder, Bushnell, & Glessner Company, 26
Waukesha engine, in F-12, 119
World War II, 142, 153, 179